The

Mountain of

Silence

a search

for

orthodox

spirituality

image

new york   london   toronto   sydney   auckland

The

Mountain

of Silence

☩

KYRIACOS C. MARKIDES

An Image Book
PUBLISHED BY DOUBLEDAY
a division of Random House, Inc.
1540 Broadway, New York, New York 10036

IMAGE, DOUBLEDAY, and the portrayal of a deer drinking from a stream
are trademarks of Doubleday, a division of Random House, Inc.

The Library of Congress has cataloged the Doubleday hardcover edition as follows:
Markides, Kyriacos C.
The mountain of silence: a search for Orthodox spirituality /
Kyriacos C. Markides. —1st ed.
p. cm.
Includes bibliographical references.
1. Spirituality—Orthodox Eastern Church. I. Title.

BX382.M375 2001
248.4'819—dc21   2001028411

ISBN 0-385-50092-0

December 2002

First Image Books Edition

12 14 16 18 20 19 17 15 13 11

For Nikos and Dora

author's note

I am immensely indebted to Father Maximos, the central figure of this book, for his love, friendship, and spiritual guidance. Without his readiness to share with me his knowledge and experience of the Eastern Orthodox spiritual tradition, this book would not have been written. It goes without saying that whatever shortcomings one may find in the presentation of this wisdom tradition are exclusively mine. I would also like to thank the monks of the Panagia monastery in Cyprus and the elders, monks, and hermits that I met of Mount Athos, Greece, for their generous hospitality.

I extend my appreciation to my colleagues in the sociology department of the University of Maine for a sabbatical leave in the spring of 1997 and for their continuous support of my research endeavors. My thanks also go to the following individuals for their direct or indirect role in the making of this book: all those that I wrote about in these pages; Marlene Gabriel, my literary agent, and Eric Major, my editor and publisher, for their exemplary professional expertise and sustained faith in the value of this work; Bishop Kallistos Ware, Oxford professor of religion, for reading most of the first draft and offering me invaluable feedback; anthropologist

Eleni Stamiris for her insightful suggestions; Akis Lordos for introducing me to Mount Athos, thus exposing me to the extraordinary richness of Eastern Orthodox mystical spirituality; and Lambros Karris, friend and colleague, for exposing me to the uplifting joys of Byzantine chanting.

Special thanks to my friend Mike Lewis, professor of art at the University of Maine, for sharpening my sensitivity to the beauty of nature and helping me appreciate the important role that art can play in the spiritual awakening of humanity. I cherish his sustained interest in my work, his critical reading of the first draft of each chapter, and for designing the art piece on the cover of this book.

Many friends and relatives in Cyprus played an important role in keeping my wife Emily and myself emotionally connected to the country and its people. I would like to salute all these friends, particularly my boyhood friend Petros Yiassemides and his wife Ritsa for making us feel so much part of their lives.

My deepest gratitude goes to my sister Maroulla and my brother-in-law Vasos Christou and their family for their heartfelt generosity and genuine affection. Their presence in Cyprus, more than anything else, kept the embers of our love for our birthplace alive.

When I published my first book in 1977, our son Constantine was only a toddler and Vasia was yet to be born. By the time this book was in its first draft they were both providing me with their critical and valuable comments and assessments. Constantine read every page, offering suggestions for improvement through the critical eye of an aspiring author.

To my wife Emily I could only reiterate what I have said in my previous works. Her extraordinary energy, zest for life, and love for adventure provided me with the context that allowed me to enter into realms of experience that without her nurturing support I may not have ventured into. She has not only been my lifelong companion and the bedrock of my emotional stability and well-being, but my best friend, confidante, intellectual partner, and editor of everything I write. This book is a far superior book because of her painstaking and meticulous editorial assistance, in spite of her own pressing work in setting up in Cyprus, together with other peace practitioners, an "International Eco-peace Village" for women and youth.

A final note: I have employed the Greek conjugation when directly addressing Greek males in the dialogues. For example, Father Maximos is addressed as "Father Maxime," Kyriacos is addressed as "Kyriaco," and so on. Female Greek names do not pose such idiomatic problems. Most of the names in this work are pseudonyms in order to protect the subjects' privacy. For this reason I have occasionally interjected minor alterations in describing the actual location where some episodes took place. However, everything in this book is based on true dialogues, actual encounters, and real experiences.

Contents

✝

the

Mountain of

Silence

1

PROLEGOMENA

When I arrived in America in the early sixties for my higher education, I brought with me a naive faith in the Christian religion, the Church, and the God of my forefathers and grandmothers. It was a taken-for-granted faith based on an upbringing within the insulated and homogeneous confines of Eastern Orthodoxy, the dominant religion of Cyprus. The cosmopolitanism and multiculturalism of America, where religion is a preference rather than a fate, shattered that simple security of belief. After ten years of training as a sociologist I was turned from a believer into an agnostic. I had concluded, like most of my peers, that religion was a creation of society, after all. I came to consider it axiomatic that society gave birth to the gods, not the other way around; society created the religion it needed for its own survival. At worst, religion preserved class inequities by shifting people's focus from the real world of injustice and oppression to the fantasized beyond of "pie in the sky" salvation. At best, it helped people cope with their personal tragedies, a useful collective illusion for the maintenance of social stability and order. Therefore, when believers of all faiths kneel down to pay homage to their deities, in reality they unwittingly worship their society in disguise. It was a powerful, irresistible insight coming from the pens of the mightiest intellects of modern social philosophy and sociology.

By the time I completed my studies I had internalized this dominant yet unspoken worldview within the modern academic culture: religion, particularly traditional religion, which meant belief in a personal God, was a thing of the past, a residue of medievalism destined to an eventual oblivion.

I was not a cheerful agnostic. In fact, initially pondering the nihilistic implications of the death of God theology was extremely painful to me — "If there is no God then anything goes." But the intellectual universe I found myself in offered hardly any other alternative. A serious scholar could not be a believer in unprovable notions about the beyond, spirit beings, angels and devils, and the like. Those were the beliefs of preliterate peoples and of the loving and humble aunts that I had left behind in Cyprus. For a worldly man of letters, a social scientist, the only real world was the world of hard facts, of the concrete physical universe, and of ordinary consciousness. Any notions about the beyond were fantasies, delusions, or "mere beliefs."

Whatever ties I kept with the religion of my youth remained exclusively cultural. They were the result of my aesthetic appreciation of its chants and liturgical services, encoded in my mind since infancy. Religion became for me nothing more than a matter of personal identity. I continued to think of myself as a Greek Orthodox but a secular Greek Orthodox, in the same way that a secular Jew is still a Jew and a secular Arab is still an Arab. Therefore, during my agnostic phase, a relationship with Christian monks and hermits, the subject matter of this book, would have been virtually impossible. My mind was not open to the possibility that there may be value and wisdom outside the parameters of rational academic culture. At best, my tendency during my agnostic phase, was to consider such people nothing more than living museums of a world long gone. At worst, I would have explained the lifestyle of monks and hermits in psychopathological terms, dismissing the entire phenomenon of monasticism as a form of escapism which has no relevance to a postmodern age. That there were elders who, precisely because of their eremitic, silent existence of arduous personal struggles and spiritual practices, become possessors of genuine spiritual wisdom, was a totally unfathomable idea for me at the time.

But Providence works in mysterious ways. With my wife Emily, I arrived at the University of Maine in 1972 to begin my career as an assistant professor of sociology, and this was the beginning of my liberation from scientific materialism and agnosticism. My "liberation" began through the influence of a colleague who exposed me to the thought of the East and the yogi tradition of India. In addition to the controversial books of Carlos Castaneda and the writings of Alan Watts, Helena Blavatsky, Rudolf Steiner, and Georges Gurdjieff, the works of Indian sages like Paramahansa Yogananda and Jiddu Krishnamurti also became part of my regular spiritual diet for a number of years. The same colleague introduced me to transcendental meditation, imported to America by Maharishi Mahesh Yogi during the turbulent sixties, and I piously practiced TM for over seven years as I sought "cosmic consciousness" and deep relaxation.

Meditation, the reading of books on oriental religions, and scientific works like those of Fritjof Capra and others on the interface between modern science and mysticism led me gradually to shift away from my state of unbelief. It increasingly became clear to me that the secular assumptions about reality, dominant during my university training, were in fact a grand illusion, a materialist superstition that had kept Western thought stranded and imprisoned for the last three hundred years. It was a destructive superstition that led sensitive Western intellectuals by the droves into existential despair, and in some cases even to suicide and madness. The realization of the phoniness of scientific materialism had a tremendously liberating effect on my mind.

A most decisive episode in my life that freed me from the last fetters of agnosticism was my encounter with a formidable healer and mystic known as "Daskalos." He was a sixty-six-year-old clairvoyant and teacher of esotericism I met during a field trip to Cyprus in 1979. So radically was my academic worldview challenged by this flamboyant Western "shaman" that I set aside a sociological project I was working on at the time in order to study him and his circles of disciples. For the following ten years I carried out field research and wrote about the extraordinary world of these healers. It was a world of wonders, out-of-body travel, psychic phenomena of all sorts, exorcisms, and outlandish healing feats that I could not possibly explain through conventional logic.[1] How could I rationally explain the healing of a paralyzed woman that specialists both in Cyprus and in Israel had considered incurable? The cure took place in front of my eyes and was accomplished by Daskalos, who simply stroked her back for half an hour. New X-rays, taken immediately after his intervention, showed a perfectly normal spine as compared to X-rays taken a week earlier that showed a dislocated and damaged spine. Or how could I explain how this healer accurately diagnosed the medical condition of a woman living in New York City by simply touching her photograph with closed eyes, while her physicians were unable to find out what was wrong? Such phenomena were routine matters during my ten-year field observation of these psychic healers and mystics. I then found out that researchers in other parts of the world reported analogous experiences and observations. Meeting anthropologists like Michael Harner of the New School of Social Research, who studied shamans and witnessed similar phenomena, reinforced my self confidence that my own field observations were not personal delusions.[2]

Based on my research with Daskalos and his then close associate Kostas, I reached the conclusion that human beings have dormant abilities within themselves that extend beyond the five senses and that mind is not confined within the brain. Furthermore, I was led to understand that there may also be stages of consciousness that extend beyond the rational stage. I realized that there are trans-rational stages of consciousness that mystics of all traditions have talked about throughout history and that what we call death is nothing more than another beginning, a transition to a different plane of life and existence. The Cypriot mystics taught a well-integrated "Christocentric" system of mystical philosophy that appealed to my rationalistic predisposition and training but which also opened my mind to the possibility of other worlds, far beyond the world of gross matter and ordinary rational consciousness. It was gratifying to discover such a spiritual cosmology within my own cultural tradition.

The interest generated by my books on the Cypriot mystics offered additional support to my new understanding of reality. Since the trilogy of my ten-year adventure came out, scores of individuals from all over the world have contacted me to confide that they too lived in the extraordinary world of the Cypriot healers and mystics as described in my books. In this way I gradually realized that large numbers of people, both in the United States and elsewhere, live double lives. They live their ordinary everyday life while undergoing mystical experiences which they dare not reveal out of fear of being labeled as mentally ill. Such people, I should hasten to add, are found in all walks of life, including members of the academic community such as behavioral psychologists, sociologists, physicists, and biologists. I discovered to my amazement that there is a para-culture out there that scholars, because of deeply entrenched materialist prejudices, have failed to notice.

The Cypriot mystics may have helped me overcome my agnosticism and scientific materialism, but they played hardly any role in helping me overcome my negative attitude toward organized religion. On the contrary, I took it for granted that authentic spirituality could only be found and flourish beyond the boundaries of established religion. I considered self-evident the notion that organized religion unavoidably implied the corruption of religion. In the history of religion I could find abundant ammunition to maintain such beliefs.

Like most Western academics, I associated the representatives of institutionalized religion, if not with narrow-mindedness, intolerance, and corruption, then at least with irrelevance. Until my recent encounter with a

few extraordinary Christian monks and hermits, I had met no living "man
of the cloth" who had inspired me spiritually or intellectually. In my view
the clerical hierarchy seemed, with a few exceptions, boring and intellectually inadequate. Organized religion, I believed, had little to offer today
to the restless yet serious and intelligent seeker of inner knowledge. At that
time I couldn't have agreed more with a leading biblical scholar who
lamented that "Christianity as we have known it in the West is anemic and
wasting away."[3]

Once I freed my mind from the shackles of agnosticism and scientific
materialism, I assumed that in order to seriously engage in a spiritual, con-
templative practice for personal transformation and inner experience, one
had to take up methods of meditation such as those practiced by the lay
mystics that I had studied or the yogis of India, preferably under the guidance of a master. More romantically, one perhaps had to journey to the ex-
otic East and sit at the feet of self-realized gurus who dispensed their
wisdom from Himalayan mountaintops.

My change of heart about organized religion came with an invitation
to go on a pilgrimage. My friend Antonis, a Cypriot businessman interested in Christian spirituality, challenged me to join him in the spring of
1991 on a journey to Mount Athos, the Holy Mountain, a thirty-mile-long
by ten-mile-wide inaccessible peninsula in northern Greece, to meet "living saints that radiate the love of Christ." Their prayers, he claimed, cause
miracles to happen and their auras are like shining suns. Intrigued, I took
up his invitation, and my life and work turned around once again when
on that very first visit I met Father Maximos. During the years to come, this
extraordinary and charismatic Athonite monk became my mentor,
teacher, and key informant of Christian spirituality as it was preserved on
the "Mountain of Silence."

After agnosticism, after transcendental meditation, and after the philosophical breakthroughs from my long association with the lay mystics and
healers of Cyprus, I was ready for an adventure within the mystical, experiential tradition of organized Christianity that survived in a few ancient
monasteries unknown to the West and to mainstream Christianity. There
on Mount Athos, reserved since the ninth century as a refuge for hermits
and monks, I came in contact with a different Christianity.[4] As Antonis
promised me, and with the mentoring and help of Father Maximos, I was
able to meet with hermits considered to be saints who lived in remote parts
of the peninsula inaccessible and unknown to the casual visitor. They
seemed to me indeed like Christian yogis, the type that Westerners seek in
the ashrams of India. I realized then that the spirituality I encountered on
Mount Athos with its millennial history had all the hallmarks, and perhaps
more, of what we were searching for in the Vedas and Upanishads of In-

dia. "Mount Athos," I mused to Antonis as we sailed away from that first visit, "is like a Christian equivalent of Tibet."

Starting with *Riding with the Lion*,[5] I began to broaden my focus of exploration from the formidable world of Daskalos and Kostas to the mystical, established tradition of Christianity. To my amazement I discovered that the spiritual practices and psycho-technologies we seek in India and Tibet are also present at the very heart of the Christian tradition, preserved in the cliff-hanging monasteries and hermitages on Mount Athos since the early centuries of the common era. Yet churches of all denominations as well as biblical scholars of the West are oblivious to the mystical wisdom that still flourishes in some of these monastic communities.

Upon my return to Maine, when I mentioned to friends and colleagues that I planned to include in my studies the life and world of Christian monks and hermits, I realized that I had to explain myself. Monks and hermits have a dubious reputation in Western culture, both among academic circles as well as among the general public. In our post-Freudian, pleasure-oriented age the eremitic lifestyle is repugnant to the modern mind. Such a lifestyle is often equated with bodily mortification, sexual repression, even sadomasochism, not to mention misogynism and the unholy Inquisition. It is a heavy cultural baggage. Curiously, there is no such prejudice directed at monks arriving on American shores from the Orient. At a recent conference in Montreal where I spoke of my experiences on Mount Athos, an African-American writer, Luisa Teish, asked me whether the monks had done any cleansing around their heritage of having killed millions of women as witches. Dr. John Rossner, an Anglican bishop and professor of comparative religions who hosted the event, preempted my response as he jumped to his feet and declared to the audience that there was no Inquisition in Eastern Christianity. Dr. Teish was puzzled and pleased to hear that. "To blame the monks of Mount Athos for the Inquisition," I added, "would be equally as absurd as to also blame the Dalai Lama and other Buddhist and Hindu monks for that ghastly episode in Western history."

As I began to explore the mystical spirituality of Mount Athos, two persons played a crucial role in helping me clarify my thoughts and sharpen my focus: Emily and my artist friend and colleague Mike Lewis. Like Emily and myself, Mike has been deeply interested in spirituality but suspicious of organized religion, particularly the overly zealous variety. Furthermore, being a nonpractitioner of any formal religion, he was most helpful in sensitizing me to those elements of the mystical spirituality of Eastern Orthodoxy which would be relevant to the lives of not only Christians but to anyone interested in the deeper dimensions of human existence. Likewise, Emily, with her eco-feminist sensitivities, never tired of reminding me of the imperative for inclusiveness as I delved into the spiritual landscape of Christian monks and hermits.

The Athonite tradition that I came in contact with, in spite of its archaic cultural context, filled a gap in my quest. It was not just the abundant feeling of *agape*, the unselfish, altruistic love permeating the entire cosmos of the Holy Mountain that was so disarming to the pilgrim, but also the power of its artistic expression that touches the visitor on a profound level, at the heart. The chanting of spiritual poetry in Byzantine Greek during long services was an ongoing emotional high which led me to realize the power of art and music in the human adventure to find God. The chanting was a form of prayer meditation which catapulted me into deep moods of peace and tranquillity that I had not felt with any other form of meditation.

Mount Athos, however, was not just an emotional and spiritual high. It was also an intellectual challenge. Emily's and Mike's engaging conversations and input helped me clarify in my mind this aspect of my work and raise questions that would occupy my mind for the months and years to come. What are the basic characteristics of Athonite spirituality as it was preserved and shaped over the centuries in those ancient monasteries and hermitages? Why have Western scholars virtually ignored this experiential form of mystical Christianity at a time when numerous Westerners have turned their gaze toward Hinduism and Buddhism? What does Mount Athos have to offer to the Western world today that is not available within the mainstream churches?

My intention was to return at some point to faraway Athos in order, with the help of Father Maximos, to find answers to these questions. In the meantime I read, talked things over with Emily, and continued my peripatetic conversations with Mike. It was during those walks through the university trails that I began to see clearly what Mount Athos, the monastic autonomous republic of about two thousand monks and hermits, could offer to contemporary civilization.

One day as we walked, while the sun was setting behind the woods, I explained to Mike some of my theoretical ideas and speculations on what I considered to be the possible significance of Mount Athos for the modern world. The late Harvard sociologist Pitirim Sorokin and contemporary transpersonal thinkers like Ken Wilber claim that we can know reality in three ways: through the "eye of the senses" (empirical science), through the "eye of reason" (philosophy, logic, mathematics), and through the "eye of contemplation" (systematic and disciplined spiritual practice to open up the intuitive and spiritual faculties of the self).[6] These are three different and unique orders of reality with their own legitimate and distinct domains, laws, and characteristics that cannot be reduced into one another.

They are cognitive orders sui generis, realities unto themselves. An "integralist" approach to Truth, as the late Pitirim Sorokin always reminded us, presupposes honoring and cultivating all three "eyes" on an equal basis. What had transpired historically in the West was that one approach often became dominant, displacing and intruding into the other two domains. As the West developed in ways that the "eye of contemplation" was driven out as a legitimate path to knowledge, those who gave their lives to cultivating it were marginalized or even vilified, sometimes even persecuted All knowledge was thus reduced to the "eye of the senses." In Oriental civilizations, on the other hand, such as that of Tibet, the "eye of contemplation" remained alive and has been discovered by disenchanted poets and writers since the nineteenth century and by contemporary "new agers" in search of authentic spirituality.[7]

Mount Athos has, in its quiet way, also preserved the "eye of contemplation" while it was being displaced everywhere else within Western civilization. If, therefore, classical Greece primarily offered to the world a method for cultivating and developing of the "eye of the mind" (philosophy, logic, rationality), and if, likewise, Western Europe primarily contributed to developing of the "eye of the senses" (empirical science), then Mount Athos, a cultural preserve of the fallen Eastern Roman Empire known as Byzantium, could still make a contribution toward developing the "eye of contemplation" and restore the inner tradition of Western civilization. It could contribute to the development of an "integralist" approach to Truth. As I discussed these ideas with Emily and Mike, I came to the realization that Mount Athos might have the answer to the question of "why Christianity as we have known it in the West is anemic and wasting away." Therefore the Holy Mountain may have the potential to inject Christianity with the new vitality it so desperately needs.

2

eLDeRs anD saints

ather Maximos loved to tell stories about his spiritual master elder Paisios, the legendary hermit and contemporary saint of Mount Athos. I remember during my first visit to the Holy Mountain in the spring of 1991, as we walked for hours through rugged mountains to reach elder Paisios's hermitage, he shared some extraordinary tales. "Not long ago," Father Maximos said to us that day, "I was there with him when a large number of pilgrims began to arrive. It was a very tiring day for old Paisios. At some point during the afternoon, he informed the last group of visitors, 'Fellows, it is time for you to leave. The nearest monastery is a very long walk away. If you don't hurry you will find the gates closed.' But someone in the group urgently wished to speak to him about a personal problem. 'Father,' he said, 'I would like to see you privately for a few minutes.' Old Paisios waved at him and said, 'Go on my son. Go with the others. It is late and I am very tired.' 'But Father, please!' the man implored him. 'I have something very serious to tell you.' 'Go my son, go. There is nothing to worry about.' The man insisted and old Paisios seemed impatient. 'For God's sake, go before the monastery closes its doors.' 'But Father, my wife is very ill. She is dying from cancer.' Father Paisios paused, placed his arm around the man, and gently reassured him, 'Go, my dear and have no fears. Your wife is fine.'

"That fellow looked very despondent," Father Maximos went on to say while we walked towards old Paisios's hermitage. "With a heavy heart he walked back to the monastery with the others, feeling that he had accomplished nothing. That his journey, coming all the way from Athens to remote Mount Athos, hundreds of miles away, was a waste of time. He had heard that elder Paisios was a holy man whose prayers and intercessions often cured people from serious illnesses. Now his last hope had evaporated.

"You can imagine his amazement and great delight when upon entering his home he found his wife walking about and looking surprisingly well," Father Maximos continued as we approached the hermitage. "His wife claimed that while she was bedridden, a cold sweat took over her body and, after perspiring profusely, she felt completely healed. Her doctor later confirmed that her cancer had mysteriously and literally gotten washed away. Her husband asked about the time the perspiration and the changes in her condition began to happen and she replied that it was on Friday at about four in the afternoon. When her husband heard that he felt a chill. That was the time when elder Paisios had reassured him that his wife was fine."

Father Maximos took a deep breath and stood for a few seconds, gazing at the sea below. He then mentioned that on Mount Athos such phenomena, instead of being surprising, are part of the everyday experience of the monks and hermits who choose to live there in a continuous state of prayer and contemplation.

"When human beings completely obliterate their own egotism and reach the state of *Theosis,* or union with God," Father Maximos explained as we reached elder Paisios's gate, "then whatever they wish is what God wishes, and it is given. There is little separation between the individual ego and God, between the will of the perfected, Christified individual and the will of God. Such is the state of sainthood, the state that elder Paisios reached after his lifelong ascetical struggles. He freed himself of egotistical passions to such a degree," Father Maximos explained, "that he became a purified vessel through which the blessings and energies of the Holy Spirit were channeled." Before elder Paisios opened the door for us, Father Maximos hastened to clarify that a "Christified" human being continues to maintain a personal identity within that state of unity with God. In the Christian mystical tradition, the ultimate state of *Theosis* (see Glossary on page 250 for a complete list of terms) does not imply the obliteration of one's individuality.

I remember very vividly the first day I met Father Maximos in the spring of 1991 on that fateful pilgrimage to the *Agion Oros,* the Holy Mountain. Dressed in his cassock, with a broad, friendly smile on his round face, he waited with three other monks for our arrival at the entrance of Vatopedhi, that inaccessible, ancient monastery on the eastern slope of Mount Athos. What I experienced upon meeting him was one of those uncanny feelings we often have when we meet a total stranger with whom we instantly become "bosom friends." But I could not suspect the profound impact which that seemingly accidental encounter would have on my subsequent spiritual and professional life.

Right from the very first encounter I realized that Father Maximos was unusual, that in spite of his young age (thirty-two at that time) he possessed uncommon spiritual wisdom. I soon learned that Father Maximos was regarded by other monks as an "elder" (*gerontas* in Greek, or *starets* in Russian), someone who, like elder Paisios, was reputed for being endowed with divine *charisma*. Such an elder or eldress, irrespective of age, can play the role of spiritual guide to others in their efforts to unite with God. It was a major discovery for me to learn that a system of discipleship, or "eldership," thrived not only in Eastern religions but also within Christianity.

I was psychologically and intellectually ready to learn from him, a habit I had developed during my long association with the mystics and healers of Cyprus. Most important, Father Maximos indicated a readiness to take me under his wing and, given my limitations, be my mentor and key "informant" for further explorations into the heart of the Christian mystical tradition.

I began making plans to return to Mount Athos for a prolonged stay during my upcoming sabbatical, scheduled for the spring of 1997. I was further encouraged to make such plans through a number of letters from Father Maximos who reaffirmed his commitment to help me with my research as well as indicating his concern for my spiritual well-being. In one of those letters, in 1992, he mentioned in passing that he was "alas" elected the *Protos* [or "First"] of the Holy Mountain, a one-year rotating leadership post. It was a sign of the high esteem that Father Maximos enjoyed among his fellow monks. The position of *Protos* was also an indication of the extraordinary status of Mount Athos as an autonomous Christian theocracy at the fringes of Europe, a preserve of the defunct Byzantine empire.

Preserving that autonomy was not always easy. Father Maximos must have felt particularly burdened with responsibility, even if that responsibility was to last for only a short time. As I thought about the additional burdens of his new position, I remembered a conversation we had had one day as he took us around the monastery to show us some priceless pieces of religious art. At that time he explained how necessary it was for Mount Athos to remain autonomous in order to continue preserving the true spirit of monasticism. "Shutting down the monasteries," he explained in regard to developments in the West after the Reformation, "was like snatching the heart out of Christianity." He meant that it was in monasteries that the religious experience was systematically cultivated, providing a living witness to the reality of God. By closing down monasteries, the West came to rely exclusively on the intellect in its quest for God. But the way to know God, Father Maximos would say repeatedly, is neither through philosophy nor through experimental science but through systematic methods of spiritual practice that could open us up to the Grace of the Holy Spirit. Only then can we have a taste of the Divine, a firsthand, experiential knowledge of the Creator. Otherwise, he continued, "we remain stuck on the level of mere beliefs and ideologies." According to Father Maximos, the preservation of the Athonite mystical tradition was of paramount importance for the survival of Christianity.

It required skillful diplomacy and cleverness on the part of the monks to preserve those monasteries, a key task for the *Protos* and his advisers. I shall never forget some of the anecdotes I heard on Mount Athos during my first visit there about the ongoing struggles of the monks to guard the isolation and independence of the Holy Mountain from external intruders. And Mount Athos has seen plenty of intruders over the centuries.

The Athonite peninsula was originally chosen as a monastic and eremitic retreat because of its inaccessibility. Protruding thirty miles into the northern Aegean Sea, southeast of Thessaloniki, the peninsula is cut off from the rest of Greece by impenetrable, rugged mountains and an inhospitable coastline. Unlike most parts of coastal Greece it has no natural harbors, rendering it an unattractive target for potential invaders and unwelcome visitors—I found out about that in the summer of 1998 when, on a sailing trip with friends and family around Mount Athos, we were almost shipwrecked during sudden strong winds and high seas. There were no coves in which to find refuge.

Nevertheless, in spite of its inaccessibility, many monasteries have been ransacked over the centuries by daring pirates, marauding crusaders, and invading armies. For this reason, as well as to maintain the autonomy and silence of the Holy Mountain, the monasteries were built like castles on top of mountains or precipitous cliffs. The monks of Mount Athos, while keeping their focus beyond this world, also developed a culture of diplomacy that enabled them to handle problems of this kind in the world. When Thessaloniki, the second most important city of the Byzantine empire, fell to the Ottoman Turks during the fifteenth century, the *Protos* of Mount Athos, accompanied by a delegation of monks representing all the monasteries, journeyed there to submit their official surrender and express their loyalty to the Turkish *Pasha*. The monks were well aware that it was only a matter of time before Constantinople would also fall and wished to protect the monasteries from invading Turkish troops. The *Pasha* appreciated their surrender, did not invade the Holy Mountain, and let the monks manage their own affairs. Consequently Athonite spirituality survived unscathed throughout the four hundred years of Ottoman rule.

Following the same logic and similar diplomatic maneuvers, the monks managed to navigate through the convulsions of the twentieth century. When the Germans invaded Greece during World War II there were fears about the fate of Mount Athos. At that time the *Protos* sent a letter directly to Hitler asking him to place Mount Athos under his personal protection. So much was the Fuehrer flattered by this gesture that he ordered his generals not to interfere with the life of the monks. Although a German garrison was stationed on Mount Athos, no harm was done to any of the monasteries during the entire brutal period of the Nazi occupation of Greece. It was during that time that a number of Greek Jewish women and their children found refuge on the Holy Mountain. The Athonite fathers hid them there for the entire duration of Nazi rule. In doing so they violated a morbid, eleventh-century taboo barring entrance to women. It is allegedly the only time an exception was made to that prohibition.

The integrity and autonomy of the Holy Mountain was threatened once again when Greece was under a military dictatorship from 1967 to 1974. Rumors circulated during the early seventies that the government was making plans to develop the Athonite peninsula for tourism. There was even talk of turning some semiabandoned monasteries into casinos. The fathers were horrified. Such a development would have destroyed Mount Athos together with all of its mystical treasures. Such an action would also be a blatant violation of the Byzantine charter which established Mount Athos during the ninth century as an autonomous multiethnic retreat exclusively reserved for monks and hermits. In response, the *Protos* of Mount Athos dispatched a message to Leonid Brezhnev, then secretary general of the Communist Party of the Soviet Union, urging him to intervene on behalf of the Holy Mountain. Russia, the father wrote, had a cultural stake by Mount Athos. Many Russian saints and great elders had come out of the Holy Mountain. Furthermore, a most famous and historic monastery there, that of Saint Panteleimon, was mostly Russian. Brezhnev obliged by sending a stern letter to the Greek colonels warning of dire repercussions in the event that the Greek state, which was only a custodian of Mount Athos, interfered with its internal integrity. Once again the autonomy of the Holy Mountain survived.

It was that kind of diplomatic legacy that Father Maximos inherited in his new position as the *Protos* of the Holy Mountain. I wondered how he was getting along and looked forward to meeting him there for my continuous exploration of Athonite spirituality. But it was not to be. In the fall of 1993 my plans turned upside down after I received a letter from Stephanos, my old friend and confidant with whom I had shared many an experience with the Cypriot healers in the 1980s. A veteran of Sufi and

Hindu esoteric groups during his many years in London, Stephanos turned his attention to Christianity after retiring early from business and returning to Cyprus. "You will be interested to know," he wrote, "that an extraordinary monk from Mount Athos has come to Cyprus. In my estimation he has all·the hallmarks of a true master, and as you know, I have known several of them in my life. He is accompanied by two other monks and he is setting up a monastery somewhere on the mountains. I meet with him frequently and I have become some sort of an informal adviser about the local social scene. Theano [Stephanos's wife] also thinks of him the way I do. In fact she, like myself, has adopted him as her spiritual guide and confessor. At last we have found a real master who also happens to be a Christian. Next time you are in Cyprus I will introduce him to you. I am sure you will like him. His name is Father Maximos."

For a moment I assumed that the name, Father Maximos, was coincidental. After all, it is a common name among Orthodox monks, as common as calling an American Mr. Smith. I was certain that the Father Maximos I knew had no intention of leaving Mount Athos. He was a happy monk who identified fully with the ways and culture of the Holy Mountain. He had left Cyprus at the age of eighteen and as far as I knew had no plans to return. After studying theology at the University of Thessaloniki he entered Mount Athos and remained there ever since. "My country," he had told me during my visit there, "is the Holy Mountain. This is where I belong and this is where I will die. I have no intention of going anywhere else." He had already spent ten years as a monk on Mount Athos.

When I called Stephanos on the phone for further details, I realized to my great surprise that the newly arrived monk was indeed *the* Father Maximos I knew. But why did he leave Mount Athos? Stephanos replied cryptically that it was a long story and that I would find out more about it during my next visit to Cyprus.

As soon as I placed the receiver down I began rethinking my plans. Father Maximos, who was to be my key mentor in my exploration of Christian spirituality, would not be on Mount Athos when my sabbatical came up. It would not make much sense, therefore, for me to travel there and search for another elder who could offer me the kind of mentoring that Father Maximos was ready and able to provide. Besides, I had established close ties with him and thoroughly enjoyed his company.

This new situation, however, did not pose major difficulties for me in any way. On the contrary, Cyprus, in addition to being home, was also more accessible than formidable Mount Athos, a place difficult to reach for frequent visits, and an Athonite monastery in Cyprus would be easier to travel to. Furthermore, the presence of an authentic spiritual institution on the island might be of great help and solace to the local people, disheartened as they were by a church plagued by economic and political scandal. "Who knows," I mused, "perhaps Father Maximos could make a difference." I was particularly pleased that Stephanos, whose judgment on the authenticity of masters I trusted, thought so highly of him. Stephanos's enthusiasm provided additional support to my own perceptions of the Athonite elder.

While pondering this new situation, another unexpected development knocked at my door. It brushed aside any possible reservations that may have lurked in the back of my mind as to whether I should join Father Maximos in Cyprus or return to Mount Athos without the benefit of his presence there. A colleague from the University of Minnesota and a fellow Cypriot invited me in the spring of 1994 to join an international committee of scholars to promote research related to Cyprus. Being a member of that committee would require attending meetings on the island twice a year.

I held my breath when I read his letter, as if it were a clear message, an omen on what I should do. From now on I could have regular access to Father Maximos beyond my sabbatical. I could meet twice a year with him, summer and Christmas, and spend a few days at the monastery every time I traveled to the island for the meetings. I felt as if an Invisible Hand had arranged everything in such a way as to facilitate my work. For some mysterious reason the investigation of Christian spirituality which I started in Cyprus years earlier with the lay mystics Daskalos and Kostas had to continue in the same location with Father Maximos, the Athonite elder and former *Protos* of the Holy Mountain. With these considerations swirling in my mind I shifted my energy from Mount Athos back to Cyprus.

Had I been a tourist, Cyprus, the birthplace of Aphrodite according to Homeric legend, would have been an ideal location to spend my holidays at any period of the year. In February, when I planned to start my work with Father Maximos, I could enjoy skiing in the morning and in the afternoon drive down from the mountains and go swimming at one of the sandy beaches. Cyprus, the third largest island in the Mediterranean, being close to the Middle East, is also the warmest. Had I been a tourist I could also look forward to good food, inexpensive local wine, and friendly Cypriots eager to please foreigners, particularly money-bearing tourists. Had I been an archaeologist, Cyprus, lying at the crossroads of civilizations, would have been a perfect spot to spend my life digging its ancient soil, a soil that had witnessed the comings and goings of all the great empires that ruled the Eastern Mediterranean. Had I been a pilgrim on my way to the nearby Holy Land I could have made a stopover in Cyprus. While on the island I could have walked the streets of Paphos, the coastal town where it is said Apostle Paul gave some of his earliest sermons in order to convert the pleasure-centered, Aphrodite-worshiping pagans into pious and God-fearing Christians.

But neither I nor Emily, sitting next to me on the four-hour Cyprus Airways flight from London to Larnaka airport on that February afternoon of 1997, were tourists, archaeologists, or pilgrims headed for Jerusalem. For us Cyprus had a different meaning; it was a homeland of intense emotions where dear friends and relatives awaited our arrival, and it was also a place of painful, traumatic memories. With all of its seeming external luster of sandy beaches, sun-worshiping tourists, and all the usual trappings of high consumerism, Cyprus is a deeply troubled, divided, and threatened society, a place most in need of the prayers of Athonite monks. I wondered whether those reasons had brought Father Maximos back to the island after serving as the *Protos* of the Holy Mountain.

The recent history of the island has been a series of tragedies and disasters. The most dramatic of these tragedies took place when Turkey, only forty miles away, invaded the island in July 1974. The invasion came as a reaction against a military coup which, during that hot summer month, toppled the government of Archbishop Makarios, the first president of Cyprus after its independence from England in 1960. The coup was engineered by the then military dictatorship ruling Greece which, mindlessly ignoring the threat posed by neighboring Turkey, plotted to unite the island with the Greek mainland. When the mighty neighbor invaded with the purported aim of "protecting the Turkish minority," it captured almost 40 percent of the island's territory, forcing about one-third of the Greek Cypriot population to become refugees in their own country.[1]

Neither Emily nor I can forget those terrible days of 1974. Every time I land on Cyprus the memories flash through my mind like uninvited guests. During that year I was on leave from the University of Maine, carrying out research at the Cyprus Social Research Centre in Nicosia, the capital, while Emily worked at the British Library. We made plans to remain in Cyprus and live in Famagusta, the major commercial port and Emily's home city where her parents lived. But we had not yet unwrapped our wedding gifts when Famagusta was overrun by the Turkish army, turning the once prosperous tourist city into a barbed-wire "ghost town." After surviving the invasion, and the loss of our home in Famagusta with everything in it, including unopened wedding gifts, books, and photos, we returned to Maine. Emily's refugee parents went to London to live with their son for a while before returning to resettle in Limassol, the southern city that replaced Famagusta as the major port and tourist center of the island.

Twenty-three years after the invasion the Cyprus problem remained unresolved. Turkey maintained its control over the north while the older refugees, like my in-laws, went on dying one after another without ever fulfilling their longing for a homecoming. In fact, hope for a lasting and peaceful resolution to the problem seemed to have almost vanished when we arrived on the island in February 1997.

Those were the pessimistic assessments of everybody we met in Nicosia, the capital where we stayed for a while before I headed for the mountains to meet Father Maximos with the intention of staying at his monastery until summer. Emily was to remain in Cyprus for three more weeks and pursue, in the midst of continuous political tensions, her goal of setting up an international "eco-peace village" for youth. Transmuting her pain for the loss of Famagusta into peace activism, she envisioned the creation of a "village" where international youth from ethnically divided societies would come and live in the village for a certain period of time, learn how to live in peace with each other, and get training in ecological sustainability.

It was depressing for us to realize that local politicians, journalists, foreign diplomats, and Cypriots from all walks of life shared a deep anxiety that terrible things were about to happen. Since the previous summer, when two Greek Cypriots were killed at the Green Line, the notorious "dead zone" separating the southern part of the island controlled by the Republic of Cyprus from the Turkish-controlled north, tensions on the island had reached the boiling point. Many Cypriots feared that another catastrophic war was imminent, a war that the island republic of six hundred thousand Greek Cypriots could not win against a heavily armed state of over sixty-five million Turks. What a time, I thought, for Father Maximos to be on the island, away from the serenity of his beloved Mount Athos.

Feelings of despair were further intensified by strange phenomena. A number of icons of the Holy Virgin began "weeping" in several churches and monasteries. These alleged miracles were shown on television. At the Kykko monastery, where an icon began shedding tears first, as many as fifty thousand pilgrims visited it in a matter of a few days. My friend Philip, an American anthropologist on a Fulbright scholarship to Cyprus, sent me an e-mail just before I left for the island, saying: "The last thing we need here with all this political tension and fueling of nationalist passions are weeping Madonnas!"

For skeptics, crying icons were natural phenomena that could be explained rationally, a matter of condensed humidity perhaps. For the Turks on the other hand it was nothing more than Greek Cypriot propaganda, pure and simple. To believers, the tears were a sign from Heaven that more tragedies awaited Cyprus. This phenomenon added to the feeling of widespread anxiety that already prevailed. A theologian tried to soothe local fears by declaring in a televised interview that crying icons are not necessarily signs of coming calamities. On the contrary, he argued, they may be a good omen. But Stephanos, when I saw him in Nicosia the day following our arrival, told me that Father Maximos questioned this optimistic interpretation. He confided to Stephanos that those were tears of sadness, not joy. They were a warning that people must atone, that they must reach *metanoia* [literally meaning to radically and fundamentally change their hearts and minds] in order to avoid coming calamities.

Stephanos also related to me the extraordinary alteration in many people's attitudes that had come as a result of Father Maximos's arrival on Cyprus. Monasticism, considered until then a disappearing and for all practical purposes arcane and irrelevant institution, was given a new lease on life. Stephanos explained that in the short time since his arrival on the island, Father Maximos had brought about a spiritual revolution. An increasing number of people were gathering around him, finding solace and relief from their personal troubles and from the tensions of the political situation. But for those unsympathetic to the cloistered way of life and for some relatives of the new recruits into monasticism, Father Maximos's presence on the island was nothing short of anathema.

I had a firsthand experience of this explosive issue the day before I headed for the Troodos Mountains to meet Father Maximos, who had been appointed as the new abbot of the Panagia monastery. It all happened when I paid a visit to Thomas, a retired high school principal and a neighbor of ours during a previous extended stay on Cyprus. When he learned of my plans to spend time at the Panagia monastery, he began in an agitated tone to raise questions about Father Maximos's role in Cyprus. Brushing aside the objections of his wife, a strong supporter of the abbot, my friend Thomas claimed that Father Maximos brainwashed young people, enticing them to become monks and nuns. He nervously pulled out from a drawer some newspaper articles written about Father Maximos that he had saved. With tense hands he passed them on to me. The most scathing attack was launched by a journalist writing in the communist paper. In large black headlines it read: "Through devious means priest pushes young people towards monasticism."

Thomas was a man of letters, an intellectual. I tried to reason with him by raising questions about the importance of monasteries in society. I pointed out the historical role monasteries had played both in the East and in the West in preserving the knowledge of the past.[2] I argued that historically they had acted as the institutions that specialized in the cultivation of the religious experience, which is at the core of all the great religions. I explained to Thomas that it was monks who spread Christianity both in the West and in the East. Monks brought Christianity to England and Ireland, and during the Dark Ages it was the monks who played the role of intellectuals, meticulously copying and preserving the texts of classical civilization. I reminded him further of the artistic production of monastic orders, of both East and West, ranging from magnificent chants to liturgies

THE Mountain of Silence 19

and icon paintings. In the East, I pointed out to Thomas, who listened to my monologue with marked impatience, it was two monks from Thessaloniki who spread Christianity to the Slavic peoples of the north. They set down the foundations of their civilization which included the Cyrillic alphabet, offering these people a written language which later made possible the works of Tolstoy and Dostoevsky. I also reminded Thomas about the key role that Saint Kosmas the Aitolos, a monk from Mount Athos, had played in rescuing Greek language and culture. During the darkest years of Ottoman rule in Greece, Saint Kosmas left the silence of Mount Athos and risked his life traveling from village to village in order to set up not churches but secret schools for the teaching and preservation of the Greek language. I even naively attempted to hint a bit about my thesis, that Athonite monasteries, like the Panagia monastery of Father Maximos, are in the business of nurturing the "eye of contemplation," a corrective antidote to the dominance of scientific materialism. But Thomas was in no mood to hear about such theorizing. "Monasteries," he scoffed, "are anachronistic institutions that have no role in the modern world."

For some reason that I could not comprehend, Thomas was very angry at Father Maximos and went on to pour it out with vigor. "He targets vulnerable young people and enchants them with the idea of monasticism," Thomas repeated. According to him, Father Maximos's sole aim in coming to Cyprus was to recruit monks and nuns in order to fill up deserted monasteries. He objected to monasticism with the customary critique that it implied abandonment of the world for selfish reasons, in order to attain one's own salvation rather than help other fellow human beings. "Jesus was not a monk," Thomas said with emotion. "He lived in the world and went about helping people. He did not lock himself up into a monastery."

My puzzlement was solved when Niki, sensing my incredulity at her husband's reaction, explained the origin of his frustration. Thomas, a dignified man and a passionate social activist, was very upset because a friend's daughter had decided, against the protests of her parents, to become a nun. Everybody blamed Father Maximos for her decision. "It was a great tragedy for that family," Thomas lamented as he shook his head disapprovingly. "I ask you, is that fair?"

"It was her own decision," Niki answered calmly but with a firm voice. "Her relatives must respect her decision and leave Father Maximos in peace."

We remained quiet a few seconds as Thomas pondered his wife's words. "Perhaps," I suggested to Thomas, "you should meet face to face with Father Maximos to discuss this particular case and raise your concerns about monasticism. I am sure he will welcome you there." Given Thomas's negative predisposition toward Father Maximos, I had little hope that he would consider my suggestion. But Thomas's eyes lit up and he welcomed the idea. I promised that I would bring up the issue with the abbot and try to arrange a meeting.

It was mid-February on an early Monday morning when I headed for the mountains while Emily, before returning to the States, carried on with the project of the "eco-peace village," a dream that was gradually becoming a concrete reality. We were to reconnect during the summer in Maine. I had already spoken with Father Maximos on the phone and he was expecting me. Driving towards the mountains was a relief from the tensions of the political situation, the congested city traffic, and from breathing the ubiquitous fumes of leaded gasoline. It was springtime, and in spite of chronic drought the Cypriot countryside was at its most festive. The valleys were covered with the green of wheat fields interspersed by a myriad of yellow and red wildflowers. In the distance the mountains rose majestically in dark green, the color of forests and thick vegetation.

Clouds covered most of the sky that Monday morning with patches of sunlight shooting down through narrow openings, illuminating portions of the land. But by the time I began my ascent up the mountain slopes the sky was darkening ominously. The sunlight disappeared completely and a torrent of rain began pouring down. I drove with extra caution over risky curves as the rain blocked a good part of my vision. I stopped at a coffee shop in Kakopetria, a village below the snow covered Mount Olympus, the highest summit of the Troodos Range named since antiquity after Mount Olympus in Greece. As I sat in the smoke-filled coffee shop waiting for the rain to subside I witnessed a scene that I had known too well growing up on the island. Men "killing time," some absorbed in backgammon, others sitting around playing cards, while others read the local papers on the latest efforts by the United Nations to solve the perennial "Cyprus problem."

When I finally reached my destination, the winds were howling and the relentless rain was accompanied by lightning and thunder, a magnificent pandemonium. I felt good. I thought it was a positive sign that my arrival at the Panagia monastery coincided with a desperately needed rainstorm bringing relief from the extended drought.

I parked my Honda as close to the external gate as possible and ran for cover holding a bundle of newspapers over my head. There were no signs of life inside the protected corridor around the yard so I assumed the monks were taking their afternoon rest. I walked next into the *archondariki*, the guest room where visitors were treated to tea and pastries, usually brought over by pilgrims. There it was comforting to meet Father Arsenios, a monk I knew from Mount Athos who was one of the two disciples who left the Holy Mountain to accompany Father Maximos to Cyprus. A thirty-year-old ascetic with a long, blond beard and a permanent, good-natured smile on his face, Father Arsenios was reading the Old

Testament. He was waiting for the last pilgrim to complete her confession with the abbot when I interrupted him. Father Arsenios's task that day was to maintain order by handing out numbers on a first-come-first-served basis. He told me that as Father Maximos's reputation grew, the influx of pilgrims in search of spiritual counseling was beginning to reach almost unmanageable proportions.

"The last one is in," Father Arsenios said after greeting me in his warm way. "She is the forty-fifth person today."

Father Maximos had been confessing people since early morning without any rest, without turning away anyone who wished to confess. I looked at my watch. It was four-thirty in the afternoon. When he finally walked out of the confessional I noticed some gray hair here and there on his long, black beard. He looked exhausted but pleased to see me.

"You will need five hours of prayer to recuperate," I said jokingly. "No, Kyriaco," he snapped with a laugh, "I need fifty hours of sleep."

It was easy to reconnect with Father Maximos. Far from looking austere and ascetic, he was easygoing, enjoyed good food when not fasting, and routinely directed his attention to the funny side of things. Being an ordained priest and therefore able to conduct the sacraments, Father Maximos had a forgiving personality. People felt unburdened by pouring out their sins and souls to him.

Stroking his beard, Father Maximos invited me to join him for some food as he hadn't eaten anything since lunch the previous day. As we walked up the steps to the kitchen he explained to me that as a rule he puts absolutely nothing in his stomach prior to confessionals. To be an effective confessor, he said, it is important to first prepare yourself through fasting and prayer. That's how the Holy Spirit gets energized within you so that you may be able to offer the right spiritual counseling. This is also a principle, he insisted, that works for laypeople who live in the world and carry on ordinary lives. If you wish to undertake a task to help others and be effective, he advised, spend some time beforehand in prayer and fasting. When you do that you actually invoke the Holy Spirit to march ahead of you towards your goal and pave the way, making your task easier and raising the probability for success. Imagine, I mused to myself, psychotherapists and psychiatrists following such a regimen prior to seeing their clients!

We sat face to face at the kitchen table eating bean soup, olives, and bread. It was actually more like dinner than lunch since my watch showed that it was already past five in the afternoon. "So what happened?" I asked. "Why are you here and not on Mount Athos?" I assumed that Father Maximos had left Mount Athos to offer his services to his native country at a time when tensions on the island reached explosive proportions. After all, there was the precedent of Saint Kosmas the Aitolos who left Mount Athos in order to help the Greeks save their language during the darkest period of their history. Being an elder and a Greek Cypriot himself, it would only be natural.

Father Maximos smiled and shook his head. He must have expected my question. "Do you think it was my choice to leave Mount Athos?" he said and paused with a quizzical look on his face as if waiting for an answer from me. "I was expelled, Kyriaco. Do you understand? Expelled!" he went on and laughed at his misfortune.

"Expelled by whom?" I muttered as my face dropped. That was not the answer I had expected.

"By elder Paisios," Father Maximos replied. At that a grimace of puzzlement appeared on my face.

"Yes, it was old Paisios's idea that I should return to Cyprus, not mine," Father Maximos repeated.

"I thought he loved you," I blurted half jokingly.

"Of course he loved me. There was no question in my mind about his love for me and for everyone else for that matter. But for some reason he wanted me back in Cyprus. He was adamant about it. I pleaded with him, but in vain. Being my elder, I had to obey," Father Maximos said as he swallowed his last mouthful. "You see, we monks cannot have personal desires and preferences. Otherwise we should take off this cassock and stop pretending to be monks."

After a few seconds' pause and with a crafty, almost mischievous look showing on his face, he continued. "At first I was tempted to disobey, so much was my anguish with the notion of leaving Mount Athos. I was hoping that old Paisios was not very serious when he asked me to return to Cyprus. Sooner or later, I reasoned, he would forget. After all, he was an old man. No way. He reminded me every time I saw him that I should immediately make plans to return to Cyprus.

"I was so despondent that I walked all over Mount Athos, from monastery to monastery, from hermitage to hermitage, pleading with other elders to intervene and rescue me from what I thought at the time to be my misfortune of having to give up my life on Mount Athos. Perhaps, I hoped, the other elders would order me to do otherwise, to stay on Athos. That way, I reasoned, I could cancel out what old Paisios requested of me. But all the other elders advised me that I must follow the instructions of my spiritual master, who knew what was the most appropriate action to take. So, I left Mount Athos and here I am," Father Maximos said with a grin.

"I am glad you did. You're needed here."

"I may have left Mount Athos in the flesh but I am there in spirit," Father Maximos added with nostalgia in his voice. "Of course," he hastened to add, "we brought Mount Athos right here to this monastery. It is as good as being on Mount Athos."

"It makes me happy that you feel that way," I responded.

Father Maximos went on to repeat that his real home was the Holy Mountain, not Cyprus where he was born and raised. Knowing the obsessive attachment that expatriate Cypriots have for their island, Father Maximos's statement was extraordinary. But Father Maximos was no ordinary Cypriot. Unlike most of us, Athos had cut him free from the ropes that kept him emotionally tied to his native soil.

"Elder Paisios must have sensed his impending death," I suggested. "Perhaps that's why he was so eager to see you off before he was gone."

"Perhaps," Father Maximos replied. "He died exactly one year after I left Mount Athos."

"He must have known that you had no intention of returning to Cyprus on your own. Perhaps elder Paisios, being a saint with the reputed gift of prophecy, must have seen into the future that you had important work to do here."

Father Maximos laughed and brushed aside my suggestion. "When I came to Cyprus I assumed that I would create such a mess that the elders would be eager to call me right back. That's what I hoped."

How interesting, I marveled, that regardless of Father Maximos's own reputation, and regardless of the fact that he had served as *Protos* of the Holy Mountain, he had no other choice but to obey his hermit elder, who had lived for decades in total isolation from the outside world. But from the perspective of the Athonite spiritual tradition, being a miracle worker and a living saint, elder Paisios spoke with the authority of Heaven just like the Old Testament prophets. It would have been unthinkable and contrary to Athonite spirituality for Father Maximos to disobey. His eviction from his monastic Eden was brought about by none other than God Himself.

As Father Maximos explained to me how he ended up in Cyprus against his will, I remembered something that Swami Swaroopananda had told me when I was on a visit as a guest speaker at the Sivananda Yoga Retreat on Paradise Island in Nassau. After having dinner with the other presenters and showing slides from Mount Athos, we discussed the importance of monastic centers and the potential role they could play in a modern civilization. The impressive and wise Israeli swami and abbot of the ashram, after hearing various views, shook his head and commented that "the Athonite monks will have to come out of Mount Athos and share their wisdom with the rest of the world. The planet is in an extremely critical, dangerous state and such wisdom can no longer be hidden in ancient monasteries. If they don't do it voluntarily then God will force them out of there. That's how things work, you know. That's exactly what happened to the Tibetans." And that's what happened to Father Maximos, I mused to myself. Then I went on to point out to the swami that it was not exactly so. Athonite monks had been active outside of Mount Athos in several periods of history.³ Athonite knowledge and wisdom, I·told the swami, was never really "hidden." The modern world had simply never paid much attention to the spiritual treasures preserved on Mount Athos.

When we finished eating with Father Maximos, I raised the question of my possible role at the Panagia monastery. I mentioned that, besides researching and writing my book, I would also like to be of some practical service to the monastery. I suggested that perhaps I could be his chauffeur during my stay and relieve someone else from driving him around to various parts of the island for his many errands. Father Maximos himself had never learned how to drive. He smiled and signaled his consent with a nod and an "Okay." I was happy. Being his chauffeur would serve a double purpose. I would make myself useful but at the same time I would have easy access to Father Maximos for private dialogues and casual conversations.

Before he retreated to his cell for a much needed rest, he asked Father Arsenios to set me up in one of the available cells. I was assigned a centrally heated spacious room with a private bathroom and a shower. It even had a couch and a wooden desk for my portable computer. By monastic standards my living quarters were luxurious. I later learned that my cell was in fact the suite reserved for special guests like the archbishop and other dignitaries. I felt embarrassed but pleased that Father Maximos took an interest in my physical well-being. Stephanos had informed me earlier that Father Maximos was concerned as to whether I would be able to withstand the rigors of monastic life for any length of time. He must have known that I was not meant to be a monk.

As he was about to let me settle into my new room, Father Arsenios explained that due to Lent, food was only offered once a day, at lunch. Noticing a trace of incredulity on my face, he reassured me that it would be perfectly all right if I helped myself to some tea in the morning and evening. "We also have some tea to help us last until the next lunch." Being a monk is not an easy life, I thought, and I wondered how the thirty or so mostly young monks who became Father Maximos's disciples managed on such a rigorous and austere program.

The next day after services I described to Father Maximos the encounter I had with my friend Thomas. He agreed to meet with him and I lost no time setting up a meeting for the following morning. I had a feeling that important ideas about the nature of monasticism were bound to come to the forefront from such an encounter. I trusted both Father Maximos's deep knowledge and experience of the subject and Thomas's sharp and critical modern mind. I made certain that my tape recorder was working and prepared myself psychologically to witness what I expected to be a vigorous exchange on the subject of monastic life.

3

transformations

We sat waiting in a room adjacent to Father Maximos's office. Thomas looked tense as he held and nervously fondled a string of worry beads, a customary pastime for older men in that part of the world. Breathing rather heavily, Thomas warned me in a barely audible voice that he intended to be very frank with Father Maximos about Rosa, the aspiring nun. He had already rehearsed in his mind how he would tell Father Maximos of his complete rejection of monasticism as a way of being in the world. I assured him that Father Maximos would appreciate a frank conversation. Thomas nodded with satisfaction and began to breathe normally. His wife Niki sat next to him quietly but with eagerness all over her face.

The atmosphere changed the moment Father Maximos entered the room and shook hands with both Thomas and Niki. "I expected to meet someone old," Thomas marveled. "Everybody refers to you as a *gerontas* [elder]. I assumed you must be at least sixty." Father Maximos smiled and made a humorous remark about his relatively young age. Then Thomas learned that Father Maximos had been a high school student at the Paphos gymnasium when he was the school principal there. At that the ice began to melt somewhat, and Thomas's militant intentions softened up. In spite of his negative feelings toward monastic life he seemed to take an immediate liking to Father Maximos. But, true to his promise, he raised the issues that had brought him to the Panagia monastery.

"There are lots of rumors circulating around about you, Father Maxime," Thomas said gravely. After hesitating for a second he came straight to the point. "I am speaking specifically about the case of Rosa. You see, I am a friend of the family. They feel hurt, particularly the father. Their complaint is that you did not prevent their daughter from becoming a nun and that you treated them harshly."

"Harshly?" Father Maximos reacted with surprise.

"That you accused her father of not being a good parent. Well, I came here to find out for myself what's going on. We are speaking openly and freely now, yes?"

"Of course, of course," Father Maximos reassured him.

"This is my question to you," Thomas continued with force in his voice as he fiddled with his worry beads. "This young woman, a university graduate and a trained architect, had made plans to go to America and continue her studies. But since the day she came in contact with you, she began to get oriented toward monasticism. Her parents and relatives feel that you have been a bad influence in her life. Were you in a position to prevent her from becoming a nun? Please forgive me for being so direct with you but I raise these concerns for the sake of clarity."

Father Maximos sighed and reassured Thomas that he appreciated his forthrightness. "Let's start from the beginning. How did I get to know Rosa? One of my tasks here at the monastery is to provide people the opportunity for confession. I have no idea who comes to see me. I don't know who they are, where they come from, what kind of a job they hold. Often I don't even ask for their names. As a monk I avoid public appearances as much as I can and stay away from social gatherings. I do not accept invitations to private homes. My life is clearly monastic. Anyway, I saw Rosa only a few times. In fact, the first time she came for confession she was with her father. He even thanked me for having an audience with his daughter. They came for confession during a Saturday, when I see people all day long. When there are so many waiting for confession, I can only see each person for no more than ten minutes. In their case, I discovered later that her grandfather, who was a priest, was my own spiritual guide and confessor while I was a teenager at the Paphos gymnasium."

"I knew the late Father Kyrillos very well," Thomas said excitedly, and his wife concurred. It was an interesting coincidence that Rosa's grandfather happened to be Father Maximos's confessor in his early youth as well as an acquaintance of Thomas. In a small island like Cyprus, no bigger than the state of Connecticut, such coincidences are fairly common.

"I remember," Father Maximos continued, "that Rosa had a lot of questions in her mind and wished to continue her studies in philosophy. At the same time a young man who came for confession told me that he wished to marry and that he was attracted to Rosa," Father Maximos continued. "The young man was too shy and I volunteered, with his permission, to mention it to Rosa so that they could go out and get to know each other. Now please do tell me Thomas, had I been interested in converting Rosa into a nun would I play the role of a matchmaker?" Father Maximos asked in earnest.

"Obviously not," Niki rushed to interject as Thomas nodded reluctantly.

"Well, the two of them did go out together but it didn't work. The next time Rosa came for confession, she told me categorically that she was not interested in marriage. Her deepest yearning was to become a nun. 'Look Rosa,' I said, 'it is a very serious decision to abandon the world. You have no experience living in a monastery to really know what such a life is all about.' She was working as an architect. I advised her to continue in her profession and wait for a year to see how she would feel by then. She agreed. But a few months later she came to announce that she had made up her mind to become a nun. Once again I advised her to wait a while longer in order to make sure that she truly wanted to spend the rest of her life in a monastery. She waited until Christmas. Then she came to me and said 'Look Father Maxime, either you don't want me to enter a monastery here in Cyprus, in which case I will go to one in Greece, or there is some problem about myself that you just don't want to share with me.' "

"What did you tell her then?" Thomas asked in a low, inquisitive voice.

"I told her that I had no right to order her not to become a nun just as I had no right to order her to become a nun. 'You are a grown-up woman of twenty-five,' I said to her, 'and just as you have the right to marry anybody you wish you also have the right to become a nun.' I urged her to discuss the matter with her parents."

Father Maximos paused and then continued. "She did. They all came here including some other relatives. That was the day they claimed I did not treat them well. They were all together and started accusing me of being the cause of their daughter's decision to become a nun. Everything was up to me, they insisted, and demanded that I should order Rosa to give up her plans to become a nun. I tried to explain to them in vain that it was impossible for me to do such a thing."

"Is monasticism the only road to God?" Thomas asked abruptly.

"Of course not," Father Maximos responded. "But it is one way."

"Excuse me for getting off the subject, but before we go any further can you please briefly tell me what monasticism is, according to you,"

Thomas asked. Father Maximos replied that it is not easy to explain to outsiders what monasticism is. It is a mystery, he said, that can only be experienced. To outsiders the phenomenon of monasticism is simply incomprehensible. Nevertheless, Father Maximos went on to say, the best source for a possible brief explanation of what monasticism is all about is the testimony of the great saints throughout the ages.

"According to Evagrius of Pontus, a desert father of the fourth century," Father Maximos continued, "monks are those people who have separated themselves geographically from everything and everybody and yet are invisibly connected with everything and everybody through prayer and the love of Christ. According to Saint Maximos the Confessor, monks are those people who have removed their minds from the world of material objects, and through continence, love, prayer, and chanting, they become totally focused on God. And another elder thought of monks as those who have nothing in this life except Christ. This is what we try to do here."[1]

Father Maximos resumed the conversation about Rosa. "I explained to them that what they requested of me went contrary to my conscience. Nevertheless, I reassured them that since they insisted, I would ask Rosa never to come here to the monastery, ever again. There are other confessors on the island. She could go to them and do whatever she wished. Incidentally, this is not allowed on the part of a spiritual guide. I was at fault and I regret it. I had no right to tell someone not to come to me for confession so that I may avoid possible trouble. But I did. I told her that I no longer wished to have any contact with her so that I wouldn't be accused of influencing her life. She agreed and I've had no contact with her ever since.

"Then one day," Father Maximos continued, "her father came here and demanded that I tell him what is going on with Rosa. How could I know, I replied, since I had no contact with her? He started shouting and threatening me that he was going to kill me like a dog and drink my blood!"

"I believe he is quite capable of doing something like that," Thomas muttered somberly. Rosa's father, Thomas revealed to us, was no stranger to shooting people since he had killed several so-called traitors during the guerrilla war against the British in the 1950s.

"He also threatened," Father Maximos continued, "that he would write to the newspapers accusing me of being immoral and that he would even blow up the monastery sky high."

"As I mentioned," Thomas said gravely, "these people are no strangers to violence."

"I then realized," Father Maximos continued, "that I had to do something. I warned him 'I will call the police at this very moment and then we will see whom you will shoot and whose blood you will drink. Have I ever called your daughter on the phone? Have I ever bothered her? Have I ever invited her to come to the monastery? Why didn't you take care of your daughter if you thought she was following the wrong path? Since you were with her day and night, why did you let her come alone to the monastery? For God's sake, I met with your daughter for ten minutes every two months. She was with you every day and yet you were unable to have any influence over her. How could you accuse me of being the cause of her decision to become a nun, when she is in fact a twenty-five-year-old woman and a university graduate?' He would not listen and continued to threaten to shoot me and drink my blood. 'Okay,' I told him, 'go ahead shoot me and drink my blood.' That was how we ended the conversation."

"Don't you think it is your duty when people come to you wishing to become monks or nuns to urge them not to do so?" Thomas asked with some trepidation.

"If they are not qualified for monasticism, of course I should. But I would do that only if they are not qualified. In such cases I would tell them 'My dear, you cannot become a monk or a nun for such and such reasons.' "

"Another accusation directed at you," Thomas went further, "is that you seduce psychologically vulnerable people into monasticism. For example, a young woman with a love disappointment may be susceptible to you as a charismatic personality. She can easily be persuaded to become a nun."

Father Maximos laughed. "Thomas, do you know what monastic life is all about?"

"I am not the one who is saying these things necessarily," Thomas reacted defensively. "I'm simply relating what some people say about you."

"It's okay even if you believed in these rumors yourself," Father Maximos reassured him.

"What I remember most vividly," Thomas said, "is the case of the mother who implored you publicly to intervene and persuade her only son not to abandon her and become a monk. Then Christ came to my mind who, before dying on the Cross, told His mother, 'This is your son, mother,' pointing at John. And then turning to John, He said, 'Please look after my mother because I am leaving.' That was a Christian act in my estimation. If Jesus was so concerned about the well-being of His mother, then why must the Church appear so harsh? Isn't the Church at fault for generating so many sentiments of anger and resentment? Was it right to cause so many bitter feelings in the heart of so many people? So much psychic turmoil for the sake of one person? Shouldn't an individual sacrifice their life for the good of the many instead of looking after personal interests such as saving one's own soul? Must I lead others to despair and destruction for the sake of my own spiritual salvation?"

Father Maximos listened thoughtfully to Thomas's passionate pleas. He then calmly went on to clarify that the young man who had left his mother and went to Mount Athos to become a monk did so before Father Maximos arrived on Cyprus. Regardless, as with Rosa, it was assumed that Father Maximos could have just as easily persuaded him to abandon monasticism and return to his mother.

"Don't you think," Thomas went on to say with a resurgence of intensity in his voice, "that the real fighter must remain within the world to deal with everyday mundane life rather than look after his own well-being in order to gain eternal bliss? Nowhere in the Holy Bible have I heard Christ speak about monasticism. He wanted human beings to struggle within the world, to look after each other, to love one another. Don't you find it egotistical to lock oneself up in a monastery with the sole aim of saving one's soul?"

"A classic question!" I interjected, appreciating Thomas's genuine passion.

"Please make a note that I do not mean to put you down," Father Maximos replied, implying that Thomas was misreading and misinterpreting the Gospel.

"Don't worry about that," Thomas reassured him. Both men were eager for an open discussion on these issues. It was fascinating to see them being so frank.

"First of all, the way you read and interpret the Gospel is not the way the holy elders interpreted it. The Gospel is very clear about this issue," Father Maximos went on to say. "Let me give you an example. Do you recall the incident when that young man went to Christ and asked Him, 'Lord, what must I do to save my soul?' And Jesus replied, 'Sell everything you have and join me.' In another part we hear Christ say, 'Nobody can be my disciple if he loves his mother or his father, or his daughter or his fields more than me.' And He gave the first injunction, 'Love the Lord Thy God with all thy soul and with all thy heart.' That is, love God with your entire being. Just think of the Twelve Apostles. They were ordinary people that He picked from ordinary life, but they gave up everything in order to follow and live with Him."

"Yes, but Christ lived in the world. He did not lock Himself into a monastery."

"Let me ask you something, Thomas," Father Maximos replied. "How many years did Christ live in the world? Thirty-three years, right? How many years did He preach?"

"Almost three."

"Right. Of the thirty-three years, He preached for only about two and a half. What was He doing the previous thirty or so years?"

"Well, there is the apocryphal life of Jesus that we don't know much about," Thomas replied.

"That means," Father Maximos went on to say, "that for thirty years Christ maintained a life of silence. He neither preached nor did He do anything noticeable. The Most Holy Mother of God, the *Panagia*, the holiest human being that has ever existed or that could ever exist on the face of the earth, never did anything that we can pinpoint. Did she ever preach? Did she ever create any welfare institutions? The only thing we know is that the *Panagia* was in the temple praying and worshiping God. Then she was given her special assignment. Why was she chosen to give birth to the Christ? Certainly not because she was a great missionary, but because she was perfectly holy.

"Do you remember what Christ said to the apostles just after His Resurrection? Go and sit in Jerusalem quietly doing nothing and wait until the Holy Spirit comes to you. It came on the Pentecost. It was only after their enlightenment through the descent of the Holy Spirit that they were instructed to go into the world as healers and teachers. Christ showed them the way. He shows us that we are not to get on the road and become self-appointed missionaries. His example indicates that we must wait in silence and obscurity and focus our hearts and minds exclusively on our personal relationship with God. It is in this way that if and when we are called by God to go out into the world for a particular task, then we will be ready for it.

"Also keep in mind, Thomas, that the apostles lived communally. They gave up everything that connected them to the material world because of their exclusive preoccupation with God. They owned nothing individually. They lived celibate lives and were totally obedient to their master and teacher. This is exactly what we do in the monastery. So really, the roots and foundations of monasticism began right from the inception of Christianity by Christ Himself through His life with the apostles."

"Yes, yes," Thomas nodded, as if hit by a flash of insight.

"This is what we monks try to do," Father Maximos continued. "We try to do what Christ suggested, leave everything behind to attain perfection and wait until we are visited by the power from on high. Only then can we know what we must do. Christ Himself spoke clearly about this. Remember the fellow who approached Him and asked, 'Master, what must I do to become perfect?' His reply was, 'Follow the Commandments.' The other asked, 'What else?' And Christ replied, 'If you wish to become perfect, sell everything you own and give the money away.' In another story we hear of the man who asked Christ to wait for him until he buries his father, a very honorable and natural request. And what was Christ's reply? 'Let the dead bury their own dead.' In other words, what is of supreme importance over and above all relationships is our relationship to God. Isn't this an invitation to monastic life? Isn't that the beginning of monasticism?"

"Monasticism," I volunteered to add, "based on what I have read, is traced to the third century after the end of the persecution of the Christians and the beginning of the Christianization of the Roman Empire. The monks replaced the martyrs as the spiritual exemplars of the new religion."

"Right," Father Maximos responded. "The organization of monasteries starts with the appearance of fathers like the Great Antonios and the Great Pachomios in the deserts of Egypt and later on with the Great Vasilios, who set up the *Cenobitic* [communal] form of monasticism. But the basic principles of monasticism were already set down by Jesus Himself and His apostles."

"Jesus told the apostles," Thomas said dryly, "go and teach the nations of the world. He did not tell them go stay in a monastery."

"He gave those instructions to the apostles. They were not meant to be for everybody."

"Why not?"

"I will explain. But first let me ask you something, Thomas. Why don't you as a Christian, like myself, walk to the nations preaching the Gospel?"

"Well, when Christ speaks about the 'nations' He does not necessarily imply other countries. He means that you should use those gifts that you were offered by God for the benefit of your fellow human beings."

"So you promote the word of God amongst your fellow human beings, right?" Father Maximos inquired.

"I try to do my best. I was the principal of a gymnasium and I believe I did my duty by advising the young to follow God's path. When someone becomes a monk. . . ."

Before Thomas could finish his sentence, Niki, his wife, cut him short. "But isn't it true that hundreds of people come every week to this monastery seeking spiritual counseling and assistance with their problems?"

"I am not talking about Father Maximos," Thomas rushed to qualify. "I am talking about monasticism in general."

"Look, Thomas," Father Maximos said. "I am not the one who started the monastic movement. As I said, it has been part of the Church from the very beginning. Let me ask you a question. I hear from Kyriacos that you regularly go to church and that, in fact, you are also a chanter. Tell me, do you honor the saints?"

"Of course!"

"But my dear Thomas, most of the saints came from the ranks of the monks. So, you honor the saints but you do not accept the method by which they became saints in the first place. Isn't this an obvious contradiction? Remember, the Church was not made up only of the apostles. Who was John the Baptist? A hermit, wasn't he? And Christ Himself, of course, spent many days in the desert."

"John the Baptist," Thomas said, "prepared the way for Christ. People flocked to the desert to hear him. He was courageous and he condemned the corruption of the powerful."

"You approve in other words of what the hermits and prophets were doing."

"Naturally."

"Then why do you have such a difficult time accepting the work that we monks do here?"

"I am not criticizing you personally. You are helping people to be sure and I honor you for that."

"But before I came to Cyprus, Thomas," Father Maximos responded, "I lived in a cell all by myself, completely cut off from the world, praying constantly. When I decided to go to Mount Athos and become a monk I didn't go there so that I could learn how to become a preacher or a missionary. My return to Cyprus went contrary to my own wishes and desires."

"God placed you here for a special assignment," Thomas said, signaling a turning point in his attitude towards Father Maximos.

"I don't know that. I do know, however, that I never intended to become a missionary and end up being a confessor to thousands of people. Had I remained in my cell on Mount Athos, which was my deepest longing, I wouldn't be having all these problems. I wouldn't have people after me thirsty for my blood!

"Let me ask you the following question, Thomas," Father Maximos continued after we remained silent for a few seconds. "Do we have the right to oppose the wishes of a person who decides to devote her life exclusively to the love of God?"

With some trepidation in his voice Thomas replied, "Well, I wouldn't necessarily say no. I am somewhat uncertain about this, however. Should a person be free to act in a way that causes psychic turmoil and inflicts wounds on members of their family?"

"Let me ask you something else. You are married to Niki," Father Maximos went on and pointed at Thomas's wife. "Suppose your mother comes and tells you, 'My dear son, either you divorce this woman or I will commit suicide.' By the way, I have encountered several cases like this during confessionals. So, 'either she leaves or I will drink poison.' What would you do?"

"I will tell my mother that she is wrong. What she asks of me is immoral."

"Very good. So wouldn't you say it is something analogous with the monks and nuns? Don't they have the right to choose how to live their lives and who to be in love with?"

"I don't necessarily disagree," Thomas admitted. "That's why I intervened with this particular family and tried to calm them down."

"But they have not," Niki snapped.

"I will do my best to help them understand," Thomas promised.

Then Niki, who was active in an organization against domestic violence, declared emotionally, "There is this notion in our country that children are the property of parents and that they do not have the right to make decisions for themselves, even after they attain adulthood. The parents demand that they determine their sons' and daughters' marriages, their education, their life in general. And they monitor their children's lives in an oppressive way until their old age. The new generation is yet to realize that they are free agents of their own lives. That they have certain inalienable human rights. This situation creates many problems within families."

Heads nodded in agreement and Father Maximos continued. "Earlier on you raised the question, my dear friend, that psychologically vulnerable people are good recruits to monasticism. But anyone familiar with monastic life knows that from the point of view of worldly understanding of things it is a harsh and austere life with very few physical pleasures and comforts. We wake up at three-thirty in the morning and have liturgy until eight. During this particular period of Lent we eat nothing until after a two-hour service, at one-thirty in the afternoon. Lunch, our only meal, consists of a very simple diet. At six in the afternoon we go to church again. We remain without any food until the following day. Tomorrow we will have an *agrypnia* [all-night prayer vigil]. The same will be repeated on Monday. We constantly pray and make hundreds of prostrations in front of the holy icons. We have no personal property, no money. So what can we offer here to a young person in order to seduce them into monasticism? Particularly today when young people are so used to physical comforts, traveling overseas, spending their time in cafés, discotheques, and other worldly pleasures?

"Do you think it is easy for a young man who comes here as a novice? A lad raised on hamburgers, pizzas, and Coke has a difficult time getting used to the boiled vegetables and legumes that we eat. Then it is asked of them to go to the gardens and plow the ground. After that they are asked to get a broom and sweep the yard. And all these tasks are done while wearing an old, worn-out apron when visitors and relatives may be watching them. Do you realize what a humbling experience that is? Do you think a young woman or a man, disappointed with life and in a state of psychic collapse, will have the necessary stamina and discipline to go through such an experience and training?"

"Definitely not," Niki responded, and her husband mumbled along in agreement.

"Such a person will run away from the monastery in a few days," Father Maximos added. "In the monastery he will be in a state of constant spiritual struggle. This is not a place to sit back in a corner passively enjoying the sun. He is obligated to keep up with the calendar of the monastery. Can he be on time for services starting at four o'clock in the morning? If not he will have to give up the life of a monk."

I recalled asking Father Maximos some time ago what some of the preconditions are for accepting someone as a novice in his monastery. The first and foremost requirement, he explained to me, is that the prospective novice not suffer from any psychological problems. Nothing is more troublesome in a monastic community than mentally disturbed monks. They would do damage to themselves and create havoc in the monastery. Such individuals should never become monks. A monastery is not a mental asylum. Only well-grounded, mature personalities must be accepted. Careful screening is extremely important, therefore, before one is allowed to become a novice. An equally important prerequisite for acceptance, he explained, is that the individual be overwhelmed by his love for God and the passion to get to know and unite with Him. Nothing else should matter in the life of a novice.

Thomas, who by now showed clear signs of a change of heart toward Father Maximos, asked thoughtfully whether it is worthwhile for someone to abandon worldly activities and join a monastery. "If yes, then a parent can say, 'Okay, it is worth the sacrifice on the part of our family to have our son or daughter living in a monastery. But if it is in vain, why should my child waste her life like that?'"

"This question is answered by the very life of nuns, monks, and hermits," Father Maximos replied. "If we monks could not find a realization of our expectations here, do you think it would be possible for us to stay and carry on with this austere and deprived existence? What would be the purpose of it? Take me for example. I was eighteen years old when I became a monk. Being a monk does not mean that you do not have the normal urges of a man. You also wish to live with a woman, to go out and enjoy life as it is commonly understood. You have all the sexual urges that everybody else has, and like everybody else you would like someday to get married and have a family. Becoming a monk does not mean you have automatically transcended your human desires and ambitions.

"Yet, another power pulls you in the opposite direction and that is the experience of the Christ. When we enter the monastery we wonder, 'Am

I going to find what I am looking for?' Or just forget it, get this black cassock off, find a woman, marry, have children and live like any other ordinary human being? A monk owns nothing, not a single penny. Yet, we stay. And not only that, we are attracted to this life. It fills us with enchantment and it revitalizes us even after twenty, thirty, or forty years have passed since the time we started on this path. I meet some old monks in their eighties who are still enthusiastic about the monastic life. I have been a monk for twenty years and I have never, not for a single day, felt tired of this lifestyle. I have never experienced boredom, never felt that my life was monotonous, never had any doubts about whether I made the right decision to become a monk. Never! I feel as if my life is a continuous motion in the direction of Christ. I found what I was looking for. Had it not been so then neither I nor the other monks would have remained in the monastery. It would have been absolutely foolish and meaningless. Why should we undergo all this deprivation? Wouldn't I be an idiot to do all these things without some concrete spiritual gain? Therefore, the answer to your question is our very life. Each one of us is the answer."

"I honor your earnestness," Thomas reacted with emotion in his voice. "What you have just presented is an elegy to the spiritual life."

"Please realize that I do not diminish in any way the importance of married life. I honor and respect your freedom to live an ordinary, married life. At the same time I expect that you will honor and respect my choices in life and allow monks and nuns the freedom to lead their lives as they choose."

"Let me ask you another question. Who is more useful to society, a doctor or a monk?" Thomas asked pensively.

Father Maximos grinned and sighed. "I have been asked this question before. What does monasticism offer to society? Well, this question is characteristic of a modern way of thinking. It is an activist orientation toward the world. Every act, every person, is judged on the basis of their utility and contribution to the whole. Parents urge their children to excel so that they may be useful to society. Based on our spiritual tradition I prefer to see human beings first and foremost in terms of who they are and only after that in terms of their contributions to society. Otherwise we run the risk of turning people into machines that produce useful things. So what if you do not produce useful things? Does that mean that you should be discarded as a useless object? I am afraid that with this orientation contemporary humanity has undermined the inherent value of the human person. Today we value ourselves in terms of how much we contribute rather than in terms of who we are. And that attitude toward ourselves often leads to all sorts of psychological problems. I see this all the time during confessions.

"People using such utilitarian criteria," Father Maximos continued, "look at monasticism and conclude that it is useless and therefore must be discarded. But when we are willing to employ different criteria, monasticism offers the supreme gift to humanity that modern individuals may not recognize."

Father Maximos's argument reminded me of the case of elder Sophrony, the celebrated Russian *starets* who left Mount Athos in 1947. Accompanied by a small group of monks, he requested permission to enter England and set up a monastery there. The request was at first denied on the principle that monks have nothing to offer to England. Minds were changed when one member of the responsible government agency stood up and raised the following question: "What would the government have done if Jesus had arrived in England with His twelve apostles, asking for a visa?" His argument won the day and Father Sophrony was given a visa to enter England. In 1959 the Athonite elder set up a thriving spiritual center where both nuns and monks from various nationalities carry on their work. I mentioned the case to Father Maximos, who visited the monastery and personally knew the late Father Sophrony who built the monastery in Essex after a mystical illumination revealed to him its exact location.[2]

"So here's my answer to your question, Thomas," Father Maximos went on to say after briefly expressing his admiration for elder Sophrony. "Each person is assigned by God a specific task, a specific duty. I am not a doctor. I am a *pneumatikos* [spiritual guide, confessor], somebody else is a medical doctor. Kyriacos is a university professor and you are a teacher of English and a former high school principal. Each person leads a life in accordance to his or her *diakonia* [providentially assigned life's task]. A leg cannot tell a hand 'I do not need you,' neither can an eye to an ear. When we raise the question 'who is contributing more?' the very nature of the question is problematic. Why? Because, as I mentioned before, we must not evaluate human beings on the basis of their contributions and utility to society, but on the basis of who they are individually. This is the essence of Christian spirituality."

"The metaphor of the leg assisting the hand implies that there is cooperation among the various parts," Thomas pointed out.

"Obviously."

"Does monasticism exist in such a way within the overall system of society? I mean what is its contribution and relationship to the whole?" Thomas asked again.

"Here you go again," Father Maximos said with a laugh. With forcefulness in his voice, he went on. "I will tell you. Monasticism keeps alive in an unadulterated way the experience of the Christ. It is the space within which a human being is liberated from all biological and worldly concerns to redirect their focus and energy toward an exclusive preoccupation with the reality of God. Suppose I were to be married. I would be obligated to go to work, look after my kids, accumulate property for their education, and so forth. In other words, I would have a lot of worldly concerns. I honor all that. These are blessed tasks. But what are my concerns now? A great deal certainly, but of what nature? I now have prayer, confessions of hundreds of people, and sermons and discussions about the nature of spiritual life. I can do all these things because I am not obligated nor bound by worldly concerns.

"Everybody, you see, contributes accordingly. Nobody can see the liver working inside the body. Yet its contribution is monumental. The heart works ceaselessly and quietly, yet without its function the body dies."

"A concrete testimony to what Father Maximos is saying," I interjected, "is the accumulated bibliography on the life and experiences of saints. This literature," I went on to say as Father Maximos nodded, "is helping a great number of people in their everyday lives.[3] The saints are witnesses to the reality of God, giving solace to people who cannot abandon the preoccupations of the world and join monasteries or become full-time hermits in pursuit of the direct experience of divinity. It seems to me that the experiential testament of the saints offers to many people, myself included, indirect verification of God's reality. God would have been nothing more than a philosophical abstraction without the prophets and saints who over many centuries have testified through their miracles and personal example of God's living presence."

I had hardly completed my sentence when a black-bearded novice, in his early thirties and wearing regular street clothes, shyly entered the room. He inquired whether we wished to have any refreshments. As a novice he was assigned to the *archondariki* to assist Father Arsenios. He was introduced to us by Father Maximos as Andreas, a trained physician who decided to give up his career and join the monastery. Thomas was greatly surprised and perplexed and lost no time in raising a poignant question.

"Andréa, had you remained a physician, and parallel to that practiced your religion, don't you think you would have accomplished a double mission, saving lives as a doctor and saving souls as a religious person? Why did you abandon one to focus exclusively on the other?"

The young doctor, with a noticeable reluctance in his voice, replied that a powerful force within him pulled him to the monastic life and that had he remained in the world it would have been a torment. He could not find there what he was looking for. He had been a novice for ten months. Father Maximos pointed out that Andreas was not a monk yet and that it would take much longer before it could be determined whether he would be able to put on the cassock.

"He can walk out of the monastery any time he wishes," Father Maximos added. "So please tell me Thomas, how is it possible that a man who has completed medical training for over six years, who has lived abroad among fellow students, men and women, is going to be seduced by me into becoming a monk?"

"I assume not," Thomas replied, obviously impressed. Then turning toward Andreas, who was about to leave the room, he added genuinely: "It has been a real pleasure meeting you."

After Andreas left, Thomas expressed his admiration for him. Father Maximos added that hundreds of people come every week to the monastery to find solace through confession and participation in the liturgies and services. This, he said, is the concrete contribution of the monastery to society.

"Father Maxime," Thomas said as he stood up. "We have taken a lot of your time. Thank you. Be assured that I will do everything on my part to bring reconciliation and peace between Rosa's parents and yourself. They respect me and I believe I can persuade them."

Father Maximos escorted Niki and Thomas to their car. Thomas shook hands with Father Maximos looking a completely transformed man. As they drove off I chatted for a while with Father Maximos. "Isn't it amazing," he said shaking his head, "that people become so upset because a few men and women decided to become monks and nuns? Yet they are hardly concerned about the thousands who get hooked on drugs."

That day in the afternoon I took a stroll around the mountains and reflected on the meaning of my accidental encounter with Thomas and my casual suggestion that he pay a visit to Father Maximos. There was a silence on the mountain. The only audible sounds were the soothing murmur of the pine trees and the leaves crackling under my feet. The setting was ideal for contemplation and reflection. More than a week had already passed since I entered the monastery as a temporary resident. I diligently followed the monks' schedule, waking up at three-thirty in the morning to attend services by four. It was not an easy task at first, but by the third day I began to get adjusted to my new routine and even looked forward to the early morning chants and prayer meditations. There is something awe-inspiring about rising when the stars are still shining, without any lights to distract the clarity of the night sky, and the only sounds heard are the fast paces of the monks as they head toward the church for the four-hour service. Curiously, similar to my experiences on Mount Athos, the rituals and endless chants in the darkness of the church injected me with a greater amount of vitality than I would have gained by the extra morning hours of sleep, which I could make up anyway during the afternoon rest. What was even more surprising was the fact that for some mysterious reason I was never bored during the long morning services. During them I participated in a form of collective prayer meditation that affected my "bodymind" and transformed my experience of time.

I returned to the monastery just before they were about to shut the outer gate. That night during vespers I kept my eyes fixed on the icon of the *Panagia,* the central sacred relic of the monastery, which is believed to have miraculous properties. In the darkness of the night, with only a few candles lit, the monks chanted hymns to the *Theodokos* [Mother of God] while continuously crossing themselves and making endless prostrations in front of Her icon. They then kissed the icon one at a time. I followed them.

4

KNOWLEDGE OF GOD

y role as chauffeur to Father Maximos paid rich dividends. Driving him around the island for his various errands was a unique opportunity to spend many hours alone with him exploring various aspects of Christian spirituality. Dionysios, a young theologian and a novice, complained to me half-jokingly that I had spent more time alone with Father Maximos in a few days than he had during an entire year. Being alone with the abbot outside the more formal context of spiritual counseling and confession was considered a great privilege. I was therefore fully ready and energized when he asked me whether I could drive him at four in the morning to Saint Anna, a women's monastery. It would take us two hours to get there through mountain roads and he wished to start his work with the sisters no later than six in the morning.

Once a week Father Maximos made the long trip to Saint Anna, spending the entire day with the nuns who had adopted him as their elder. During this time he saw each one of them individually, a process that usually took until nightfall.

We started our journey when the fathers, as Father Maximos referred to his monks, began reciting the Six Psalms (King David's Psalms) at exactly four in the morning, as was the custom. The air was cool and the stars were still bright in the dark, clear sky above. I kept my eyes on the winding mountain road as Father Maximos sat next to me in his customary casual and unassuming way. We would be together for two hours without any distractions, except for the occasional hare racing in front of us, confused and frightened by the car lights. I lost no time in starting up a conversation about spiritual issues and pushed the button on my minirecorder, which I routinely kept on the dashboard.

I began by reminding him of the talk he had given a few days before to a group of pilgrims from Greece, which I found quite informative. But several questions had lingered in my mind that I didn't get a chance to ask during that encounter. Father Maximos responded that this would be a good time to raise them. He warned me, however, that he had no idea what he had talked about. On a different occasion he had explained to me that he never prepared for talks. He surrendered to the discretion of the Holy Spirit after praying for the particular event.

"You mentioned in your talk that Christians are misguided to assume that Christ taught that we should be unquestioning believers; that it was a mistake to believe that we should exert no effort in searching for evidence of the reality of God. What did you mean exactly?"

"Oh yes, now I recall. That would be a gross misunderstanding. In fact, Christ urged us to investigate the scriptures, to investigate, that is, God," Father Maximos responded as he remembered to buckle up. "God loves, you see, to be investigated by us humans."

"So," I continued while keeping my eyes firmly on the road, "when Christians recite the Creed, that does not imply that we should accept God's existence blindly without testing whether in fact God is a reality or an illusion."

"That is absolutely true. It would be foolish to do so."

"For an academic like myself your words are very comforting. But the immediate question that comes to my mind," I continued, "is that if God indeed urges us to be inquisitive, how are we then supposed to conduct our research? Are we to turn to science, to philosophy, or to theology as our starting point?"

I went on to elaborate further what was on my mind. Do we begin our search for God by observing nature? This was Aristotle's approach. By observing nature and by using his mighty logic, he concluded that there must be a Creator, an "unmoved Mover," a primal cause that set everything into motion. His four proofs for the existence of God became the foundation of Western theology after Saint Thomas Aquinas incorporated Aristotelian philosophy into theology.

I noticed a smile on Father Maximos's face. Avoiding a direct answer, he proceeded instead to raise further questions. "Let's make things simple.

Let's assume that we wish to investigate a natural phenomenon. As you very well know, in order to do so we need to employ the appropriate scientific methods. If we wish, for example, to study the galaxies, we need powerful telescopes and other such instruments. If we wish to examine the physical health of our hearts, then we need a stethoscope. Everything must be explored through a method appropriate to the subject under investigation. If we, therefore, wish to explore and get to know God, it would be a gross error to do so through our senses or with telescopes, seeking Him out in outer space. That would be utterly naive, don't you think?"

"Yes, if you put it this way," I replied. "Can we then conclude that for modern, rational human beings, metaphysical philosophy like that of Plato and Aristotle or rational theology is the appropriate method?" As I raised the question I thought I knew what Father Maximos's answer would be.

"It would be equally foolish and naive to seek God with our logic and intellect. But we have talked about this before, have we not?"

I nodded as Father Maximos continued. "Consider it axiomatic that God cannot be investigated through such approaches."

"So, Platonic and Aristotelian metaphysics are not the way to know God."

"But of course not. That's the message given to us by all the elders and saints throughout history. Logic and reason cannot investigate and know that which is beyond logic and reason. You understand that, don't you?"

"Yes. That's what the mystics have been saying time and again. That God cannot be talked about but must be experienced. But what does that mean? Does it mean that God cannot be studied?"

"No. We can and must study God, and we can reach God and get to know Him."

"But how?" I persisted.

Father Maximos paused for a few seconds. "Christ Himself revealed to us the method. He told us that not only are we capable of exploring God but we can also live with Him, become one with Him. And the organ by which we can achieve that is neither our senses nor our logic but our hearts."

Father Maximos reminded me while I strained my eyes on the narrow road that according to the tradition of the holy elders, a person's existential foundation is the heart. In addition to being the indispensable physical organ that keeps the body alive, he claimed, the heart is also the center of our psychonoetic powers, the center of our beingness, of our personhood. It is therefore through the heart that God reveals Himself to humanity. This is what the holy elders have taught throughout the ages, that God speaks to human beings only through the heart, the optical organ through which one can experience the vision of God. Therefore, those who yearn to see God cannot possibly do so through other means such as by reading Plato and Aristotle or by doing science. Great as their philosophy might be, it is not the way to God. It is only the cleanliness and purity of the heart that can lead to the contemplation and vision of God. This is the meaning, Father Maximos argued, of Christ's Beatitude, "Blessed be the pure at heart for they shall see God."

"Do you understand what that means? Those who wish to investigate whether God exists must employ the appropriate methodology which is none other than the purification of the heart from egotistical passions and impurities. If people manage to cleanse their hearts and still fail to see God, then they are justified by concluding that indeed God is a lie, that He does not exist, that He is just a grand illusion. Such people can reject God in all sincerity by saying, 'I followed the method that the saints have given us and failed to find God. Therefore, God does not exist.'

"Don't you think we would be utterly misguided," Father Maximos continued, "if we believed in a God for whom there was no evidence of existence, a God that was utterly beyond our grasp, a God that remained silent, never communicating with us in any real and tangible way?"

"But that means," I concluded, "that most believers are in fact blind believers, or as you called them 'religious ideologists,' that is, they believe in the ideas about God that they themselves concocted that may have little to do with God. No wonder there are so many problems with religion, so much religious fanaticism."

"Can you imagine how foolish we would be," Father Maximos expanded, "and how foolish the hermits and saints would appear, to carry on with their spiritual struggles simply because they believed in an imaginary God, or an utterly unapproachable and distant God? That would not be serious. In fact, one could call it pathological."

"I have no doubt that most modern secular psychotherapists and psychiatrists would view the monastic, eremitic lifestyle as another form of psychopathology," I pointed out. Then in a more serious tone I asked: "Are we to assume that the philosophical quest for God, one of the central passions of the Western mind from Plato to Immanuel Kant and the great philosophers of the nineteenth and twentieth centuries, has in reality been off its mark?"

"Yes. Completely."

We remained quiet. Father Maximos gazed out the window as I became tense while driving over a narrow dirt road. I shifted to first gear and as the engine moaned we slowly began climbing a steep curve that was to link us with another road. The Troodos Mountains are crisscrossed by such dirt roads, created by the forest service. A prayer by a venerated holy man, I thought with some nervousness, would be most appropriate now.

Driving in the dark up an unpaved narrow passage at the edge of a precipice was definitely unlike cruising down Interstate 95 in Maine. But having Father Maximos sitting next to me gave me a feeling of reassurance. Heaven was watching.

"So, when during the liturgy we recite the prayer 'I believe in one God . . . ,'" Father Maximos went on after I shifted to second gear, "we try in reality to move from an intellectual faith in God to the actual vision of God. Faith becomes Love itself. The Creed actually means 'I live in a union of love with God.' This is the path of the saints. Only then can we say that we are true Christians. This is the kind of faith that the saints possess as direct experience. Consequently they are unafraid of death, of war, of illness, or anything else of this world. They are beyond all worldly ambition, of money, fame, power, safety, and the like. Such persons transcend the idea of God and enter into the experience of God."

"But how many people can really know God that way?" I complained.

"Well, as long as we do not know God experientially then we should at least realize that we are simply ideological believers," Father Maximos replied dryly. "The ideal and ultimate form of true faith means having direct experience of God as a living reality."

I went on to mention that experiencing God may be as "simple" as seeing God in the beauty and complexity of nature. Father Maximos agreed but pointed out, however, that the experience of God is something much more profound than that, impossible to pin down with words or poetical constructions.

"If this is true," I reasoned, "then the Creed within the Christian tradition does not mean what most people assume to be its message, that is, a blind faith in the idea of God."

"That's a popular fallacy with all its disastrous consequences. True faith means I live with God, I am one with God. I have come to know God and therefore I know that He truly Is. God lives inside me and is victorious over death and I move forward with God. The entire methodology of the authentic Christian mystical tradition as articulated by the saints is to reach that stage where we become conscious of the reality of God within ourselves. Until we reach that point we simply remain stranded within the domain of ideas and not within the essence of Christian spirituality which is the direct communion with God."

There was an aura of authority around Father Maximos as he spoke those words. I felt that he spoke with the implicit assumption that he himself had had a taste of God, and that what he was telling me was not just the result of book learning and the assimilation within his mind of the spiritual tradition in which he found himself.

The morning light was beginning to break through the pine trees as I noticed some snow on the ground, a leftover of winter. The monastery of Saint Anna's was on the western side of the Troodos Mountains toward Paphos and beyond the village of Prodromos. Therefore we first had to climb to a higher elevation, closer to the summit of Olympus where there is usually plenty of snow during the winter months, and then descend on the other side.

"My next question may be naive, but I need to ask it for the sake of clarity," I pointed out. "When you say 'we can see God,' you don't of course mean that we can see God as a person, with facial characteristics, as God is usually depicted in icons and religious paintings."

"Oh, that goes without saying. It is of course possible that under certain circumstances God may appear to us in the image of a human being. Of course, this has happened historically with the Incarnation. But God in His Essence is amorphous, beyond all images and anthropomorphic characterizations. He does not have a physiognomy. Yet at the same time God is a Person insofar as He has the possibility and power to commune with human beings on a personal basis. After all, that is why as the Christ Logos He came down to us in the flesh, fully God and fully Human.

"The spiritual methodology developed by the saints," Father Maximos explained, "aims at offering us the possibility of the direct vision of God. When that happens, as I have said many times, it is no longer a matter of belief in the existence of God but a direct recognition of the eternal and unbroken relationship that exists between God and humanity.

"And of course, the essence of that relationship," he added, "is Love, which first emanates from God to humans and then from humans to God. It may sound scandalous to some people, but the full flowering of that relationship is the attainment of a deeply erotic relationship with God that lies far beyond the most intense and the most passionate erotic rapture between human beings. That state of ecstasy is what Saint Maximos the Confessor called the *eros maniakos* [maniacal eros]. Do you know what I am speaking of?" Father Maximos asked and turned toward me with a quizzing look on his face

"I am afraid I don't," I said softly. Having been blessed only with the experience of human *eros*, I could not possibly fathom what the *eros maniakos* might feel like. I could only imagine such a state intellectually. I could accept, for example, that all erotic relationships at all levels of intensity from the grossest to the most sublime are different manifestations of the all-consuming love of the absolute God. It is like the sun emanating its rays. Human *eros* is the experience of the rays. *Eros maniakos* must be the entrance into the sun itself.

I remember that when I first encountered that idea, my reaction was one of bafflement. How could Christian saints who deny *eros* in their personal lives establish an *eros maniakos* with God? Father Maximos's answer was simple. It is a matter of shifting your energy exclusively in the direction of God. Then through continuous prayer and spiritual practices something begins to happen within the consciousness of the praying person. One of his elders from Mount Athos described such a state in an autobiographical essay as follows:

> When Grace is energized in the heart of the one who prays, then the love of God floods his entire being to such an extent that he may not be able to take more. Then this love is transferred to the love of the world and the human person. His love becomes so powerful that he asks to take upon himself all the suffering and unhappiness of the others so that they themselves may be relieved. He suffers with those who are in suffering even for the suffering of animals, so much so that he sheds bitter tears when he becomes aware of their pain. These are attributes of Love. But you must keep in mind that it is prayer that energizes them and causes them. That is why those who have advanced in the prayer never stop praying for the World.[1]

[When I returned to Maine, I discussed this notion with my artist friend Mike Lewis during one of our walks. He suggested that perhaps the experience of *eros maniakos* was best captured in stone by Bernini in his portrayal of the *Ecstasy of St. Teresa*, stabbed through the heart by an angel, symbolizing divine love. She surrendered in his arms in a state of ecstatic rapture.]

It was daylight by the time we reached Prodromos and began the descent on the western slope of the Troodos Mountains. The monastery of Saint Anna was now only a few miles away. As we continued our conversation on how to know God, Father Maximos claimed that whatever existential angst human beings may suffer from comes to an end once God manifests Himself in their hearts. Any doubts, questions, philosophical dilemmas, and puzzlement about God's existence that are "natural to the fallen state" simply evaporate with such direct contact. Fortunately, he said, the tradition of the saints survived through the centuries, showing us the method and the way to know God. The saints provided us with the tools to purify the heart from its illnesses so that it can experience the vision of God and attain its ultimate therapy.

After the split of humans from God, Father Maximos said, after the Fall, the heart was invaded by illnesses, the real meaning of original sin. We as human beings, by virtue of our humanity, carry as our inheritance these illnesses that are an integral part of our human condition. He then pointed out that the Christian Church, the *Ecclesia*, must function and be

seen as a spiritual hospital for curing the maladies of the heart that obstruct our vision of God. And the *Ecclesia* has as a proof of its therapeutic
efficacy the experience and the life of saints, those human beings who
have, through arduous efforts, purified their hearts and were therefore able
to heal the split between themselves and God. The Bible, Father Maximos
claimed, would be inadequate by itself to lead us toward God. Without the
experience and the testimony of the saints about the reality of God, the
Bible would be an "empty letter."

When Father Maximos made these comments about the Bible, I realized how radically different his position about its value was from both religious fundamentalists as well as secular Bible scholars. The former confuse
the letter for the truth, while the scholars focus exclusively on the Bible's
historical accuracy, never tiring of unearthing contradiction after contradiction between the four gospels. But for Father Maximos the Bible had to
be seen first and foremost as a tool, a guidebook on how to conduct our
lives so that we may be helped to reestablish our connection with God. He
once quoted John Romanides, his former American-born professor at the
University of Thessaloniki, a celebrated and controversial theologian and
an ordained priest, who gave the example that if you wish to evaluate the
importance of a medical text on surgery, you don't give it to a group of
butchers. You must send it to well-trained surgeons. They are the ones qualified to offer an expert's opinion. Likewise, the role of the Bible must be
seen as a therapeutic tool to heal our existential alienation from God. And
those who can offer an expert's opinion about its worth as a handbook for
union with God are neither the fundamentalists nor the Bible historians,
but the saints who have extensively put it to practice. Furthermore, Father
Maximos added, the Bible by itself is not adequate as a guide to reach God.
One must take into consideration the entire experience of the *Ecclesia*, the
entire corpus of the spiritual tradition as articulated in the lives, aphorisms,
homilies, spiritual methodologies, and written testimonies of the saints.
And this tradition is being tested and retested by the experiences of the
saints. The Russian Athonite elder Saint Silouan, one of Father Maximos's
spiritual heroes, went as far as to claim that even if all the sacred books and
written records of the Christian religion including the Bible were lost in a
massive earthquake or fire, they could be rewritten because they are stored
deep in the hearts of the saints and can be brought out anytime when conditions permit it.[2]

"I would like to know more about what you mean by the 'illnesses of
the heart,' " I asked as I turned the last curve in the road. The monastery
of Saint Anna appeared in front of us, surrounded by a thick forest of pine
trees.

"That will have to wait for some other day, perhaps tomorrow," Father
Maximos responded as I stopped the car outside the tall, weathered,

wooden gate. It was past six when I turned the engine off. A happy look-ing, black-dressed, elderly nun, the abbess, and two younger nuns who had been waiting for Father Maximos's arrival welcomed us with the usual warm hospitality as the rest of the nuns continued on with services that had begun at four in the morning.

As their elder, Father Maximos had set up a program of spiritual prac-tices for the nuns that was identical to the one followed at the Panagia monastery. Spiritual work, Father Maximos told me once, requires a pro-gram which must be based on one's personal situation and capacities. A spiritual program for monks and nuns is different from a program for laypeople who live in the world and have to face the vicissitudes of every-day life. Even among monks and nuns there are idiosyncratic differences that an experienced elder must take into account when setting up their in-dividual regimen of spiritual exercises. Too many exercises for too long a period at a time may lead, Father Maximos explained to me, to the com-plete abandonment of the struggle for union with and knowledge of God. In order to have results, what is important is that whatever the program might be, it should be followed diligently, never allowing any other activ-ities or negligence to interfere with it.

Father Maximos spent the entire day, with a brief lunch break, seeing each nun individually for confession, counseling, and to monitor their program. I spent the day mostly in the library browsing through the books and taking long walks through the woods. During the afternoon Sister Athanasia, a former social worker from Athens, showed me around the monastery and the vegetable gardens that provided a big portion of the nuns' daily sustenance. As at the Panagia monastery, their food consisted mostly of vegetables, fruits, bread, and, on special occasions, fish.

It was not until eight-thirty in the evening that Father Maximos com-pleted his work, a total of more than twelve hours of continuous counsel-ing. Just before we were about to depart, all the nuns, happiness radiating from their faces, surrounded Father Maximos in the yard for a farewell. I will never forget that scene of adoration. It was as if they had in their midst a living saint. All of them escorted him to the car carrying along packages of food and sweets that they made especially for their "brothers," the monks at the Panagia monastery. I was packing the food in the trunk when the abbess approached me and placed a book in my hand. She had heard that I was a professor studying Orthodox spirituality and wanted to offer me a small gift. "It will be useful for your work. You will like this book," she said. "It is about the extraordinary life of eldress Gabrielia."[3] I briefly perused the newly published book, thanked her profusely, and then placed it in the back seat of the car. I promised to read it.

After Father Maximos blessed each one of them individually, we set off. A young nun opened the outer gate of the monastery for us to pass. As

I waved at her, Father Maximos turned toward me and murmured: "That's Rosa." I was ready to step on the brakes for a better look but he dissuaded me and signaled that I should move on. "She is fine now," he said.

It was about nine in the evening as we headed off for the two-hour drive back to the Panagia monastery. We remained mostly silent as we enjoyed the shadows created by the rising moon glittering through the pine trees. Father Maximos had talked all day long and I did not wish to burden him with my unquenchable appetite for questions and conversation. He needed a rest and he showed it.

There was no traffic, no other car, no soul in sight as we headed back. After a few casual remarks Father Maximos pulled a tape out of his briefcase and pressed it into the cassette player. For the next hour we listened to chants recorded at Simonopetra, one of the better known Athonite monasteries, famous for its Byzantine choir. But a few minutes after the tape stopped my heart rate shot up and all the soothing effect of the chants instantly evaporated.

"What on earth is going on?" I gasped, slamming on the brakes as we came face to face with a roadblock of armed men. Their powerful searchlight blinded me. The era of mountain guerrillas was long gone, I said to myself, thinking of the height of the armed rebellion against the British in the 1950s. "Who are these men?" I muttered. Father Maximos grabbed my arm and tried to soothe my anxiety. "Don't be afraid. It's nothing. I should have warned you."

Before he had time to explain, a rough looking fellow with a long, twisted, black mustache, a protruding belly, and a fearsome shotgun in his right hand peeked into the car, trying to get a better glimpse at us. "Father, it's you!" he exclaimed with an expansive smile, revealing a glittering golden tooth. My heartbeat went down to its normal tempo. "What on earth are you doing out here at this hour?"

"Good evening Pavlo," Father Maximos replied calmly. "I forgot to warn Kyriacos here that you fellows sometimes set up checkpoints."

Pavlos signaled to his companions and the searchlight was mercifully turned off. The others walked toward our car. When they discovered who sat next to me they extended their hands with eagerness and joy in their faces. The mountain "guerrillas" were rural constables guarding against night poachers going after hares. Not surprisingly they were also regular patrons of the monastery, with Father Maximos as their confessor.

"You got scared, didn't you?" Father Maximos said teasingly as we drove off.

"For a moment I did," I admitted. "It brought to mind so many painful memories of the past. There were plenty of armed guerrillas roaming around these mountains then."

The episode with the roadblock and the armed constables ended our silence and got us talking about the ongoing, chronic problems with the Turks, problems triggered by the E.O.K.A. (National Organization of Cypriot Fighters) rebellion of the 1950s. It was interesting to me to notice that Father Maximos, unlike most of the people I met on the island and true to his Athonite training and tradition, showed no anxiety or worry whatsoever about Cyprus's unstable political impasse. To him, all troubles and difficulties that we confront, personal or social, must never lead us to bitterness and despair, but must be seen as opportunities for spiritual development. I on the other hand could see the political crisis only from my worldly vantage point and had difficulty refraining from indulging in bitter criticisms of political personalities and institutions that I considered responsible for the tragedy. And that nocturnal incident gave me the opportunity to bring out what was on my mind concerning the destructive political role of the local church and its higher clergy.

Unlike the island's clerical hierarchy, Father Maximos steered clear of local politics and focused exclusively on his spiritual mission. Politics are matters of this world, and Father Maximos, as an Athonite monk, was schooled and trained to direct his energies only on matters beyond this world and only on goals of everlasting value. Therefore, when I became animated as I reflected on the political situation during the last leg of our trip, I was the one who did most of the talking while he listened with admirable patience.

I lamented that Cyprus would have been different and perhaps more peaceful had the spirit of Athonite spirituality dominated the Cyprus church, particularly during those turbulent years of the 1950s. But, alas, there was none of that among the higher clergy. On the contrary, the then Archbishop Makarios ("the Blessed One"), ignoring Heaven completely, turned out to be more of a nationalist warrior than a man of God. For historical reasons that go back to the four centuries of Ottoman rule which preceded the British, the then archbishop was also the *Ethnarch*, the religious and national leader of the Greek Cypriots, an anachronistic and in retrospect destructive role reminiscent of the warrior popes of medieval Europe. As *Ethnarch* he led the *Enosis* movement with vigor but without any trace of the Gandhian spirit of nonviolent resistance. Worst of all, ignoring the essence of the Christian message, it was he who conspired to clandestinely bring to the island a Cypriot-born Greek colonel with a well-known violent past to set up E.O.K.A. and wage a guerrilla campaign against the British colonial government. It was a grim, corrupting legacy that opened a Pandora's box, poisoning the lives of generations of Cypriots.

I went on unleashing my critique about these matters not only because I was emotionally and academically entangled with the Cyprus problem, but also because I had a feeling that someday Father Maximos might be called upon to play an important role on the island, perhaps more than he himself could imagine at the time. I felt that given his rising popularity among spiritual seekers, he could potentially shift the energy of the local church from its catastrophic and corrupt focus on power politics and wealth toward its ancient mystical roots of spiritual regeneration and healing. Perhaps, I thought, that is the reason why elder Paisios insisted on pushing him out of Mount Athos and back to Cyprus.

Just before we reached the monastery I wrapped up my long and non-spiritual monologue while Father Maximos tried to calm me down. He reminded me of how important it was to differentiate the *Ecclesia*, the teachings, that is, of the saints and holy elders on how to know God from the personalities that compose the organizational structure of the worldly Church. Furthermore, he reminded me to take heart that nothing happens in the world outside of God's providential will, though it must forever remain a mystery to human reason.

It was past eleven when Father Maximos turned the six-inch-long, ancient iron key of the monastery's front door. The squeaky sound disrupted the total silence that prevailed at that hour. By three-thirty in the morning every member of the monastic community including visitors would wake up for the start of the *orthros*, the morning prayer service. Given our late arrival, Father Maximos urged me not to wake up so early and try to get my sleep.

Yet I could hardly fall asleep that night as the ideas we had discussed on how to know God kept dancing in my mind. So I decided to read the book that the abbess of Saint Anna had given me. Once I started, I could not put it down. It was about the life of an extraordinary Greek woman, a podiatrist, who practiced her profession in London during the Second World War. Following an inner calling, she traveled to India where for several years she took care of lepers. At the age of sixty she returned to Athens, became a nun, and soon developed a reputation as a charismatic eldress, similar to the reputation of contemporary elders like Paisios. Before falling asleep I jotted down one of eldress Gabrielia's aphorisms relevant to the day's discussion with Father Maximos: "There is only one form of Education: to know and love God."

iLLnesses of the HeaRt

The following morning, after services, I reminded Father Maximos that our conversation on illnesses of the heart remained unfinished. Father Maximos reassured me that he had not forgotten and invited me to sit next to him on a bench outside his cell for a chat. While enjoying the warm rays of the sun, he went on in his customary, casual way to answer my questions. As we talked, the other monks went about their assigned tasks. Some worked in the kitchen, others labored in the vegetable gardens, some cleaned the church, and others worked with computers in the accounting office.

"The most basic illness that the holy elders talk about," Father Maximos began, "is **ignorance**. In their language, however, ignorance does not mean lack of the right kind of information or the right kind of intellectual knowledge. What they really mean is the heart's ignorance of God. And this lack of direct experience of God renders human beings incapable of knowing what it means to live apart from God. Consequently, they are not conscious of how abysmal their deprivation and predicament is."

"What you don't know you don't miss," I added. "I suppose it is analogous to people who are content to live in polluted cities. They are perfectly happy because they have never experienced the clean, fresh air of the mountains and the countryside."

"That's a good analogy. Speaking for myself, every time I go down to Nicosia I have a problem with the water. I just can't drink it. It cannot be compared to the mountain water we have here. But for the people who live in the city, their water tastes just fine. So, it is similar to our relationship with God. There is a period in our lives when we have no experience of God whatsoever. Therefore, we do not miss Him. Then, either through sudden illumination or through a long process of practice we get glimpses of God's presence. My own feeble experience of God helped me understand what Christ really meant when He said 'I am the light that lightens the world.'

"I then became aware," Father Maximos continued, "of the darkness that I was living in up to that point. It was a darkness so thick that you could grasp it with your hands, even cut it with a knife. When we don't know, we are content with the darkness. Recognition emerges when we experience the light, not before. You see, while we are in the dark not only do we assume that it is the natural state of things but that it is also beautiful."

I told Father Maximos that what he just said reminded me of Plato's parable of the cave. Most human beings, Plato wrote, live in a dark cave. They are tied to a pole facing the wall. The light that comes from the opening of the cave creates shadows on the wall. These shadows are taken for reality by the people tied to the poles. A few brave souls manage to untie themselves and with great difficulty and effort crawl out and experience the sunlight. They become ecstatic with their discovery. These liberated few set as their life's mission to return to the cave and tell their friends of the good news, that there is life and light outside the cave, that they don't have to spend their lives in the dark. Yet, when they announce their discovery hardly anybody believes them. The overwhelming majority prefer to stay tied to their poles, taking the reflection of their shadows as the only real world.

"Plato's light outside the cave," Father Maximos pointed out, "is in reality Christ, and those who see the light are the saints who have been witnesses to the light through the aeons. The cave dwellers who do not respond to the message are those whose hearts are shut and who therefore are nonreceptive to the good news. That is why the holy elders advise that before you speak to someone about God, you must pray for that person so that Grace may proceed ahead of you and prepare the ground. But even so, people whose heart is shut cannot experience the light, no matter what."

Father Maximos went on to say that the ultimate therapy of the heart requires a tremendous amount of effort before it can have *gnosis Theou*, knowledge of God. "As we discussed yesterday, knowledge of God is not gained through books on theology and dogma. Knowledge of God can only be attained through long and arduous spiritual practices."

Father Maximos fiddled for a few seconds in silence with his *komboschini* (see Glossary) which he always carried with him. It was as if the *komboschini* gave him extra strength and energy.

"We lost the knowledge of God," he went on to say, "at the moment when we transformed the *Ecclesia* from experience into theology, from a living reality into moralistic principles, good values, and high ideals. When that happened," Father Maximos said humorously, "we became like tin cans with nothing inside."

There was passion in Father Maximos's words. I still recall an incident when he jokingly rebuked a group of young theologians who introduced themselves as "theologians." "To call yourselves theologians," he teased them, "means that you have become graced by the knowledge of God, like Saint John the Theologian or Saint Basil the Great. Have you? Can you truly call yourselves theologians because you just read some books and earned a degree in so-called 'theology'? Don't you think this is rather presumptuous on your part?" Father Maximos offered them a lesson that day on the difference between knowing God through theology courses and knowing God through the heart. He told them that a poor and humble peasant may become a saint as a result of arduous spiritual practices and ceaseless prayer, and therefore have knowledge of God, whereas a scholar who publishes volumes on theology but who is proud because of his worldly achievements may be completely ignorant of God.

"After ignorance as the primary illness of the heart," Father Maximos went on, "there is the related illness of **forgetfulness**. The heart does not remember God. It forgot how to be in a prayerful state."

"Not being in a prayerful state is considered an illness?" I wondered.

"But of course. The saints repeated this truth time and again over the centuries; that the natural state of a human being is the continuous contemplation and memory of God. I do not mean by that a cerebral memory of God but a memory that works from within the heart."

"How does that work? How can I remember God in the heart? It is easy for me to nod in agreement with what you just said but I am still not clear on how such a state is attained."

"Let me explain. The mind is a form of energy, right? It is natural that whatever we do such as reading, writing, washing the floor, cooking, and so on, we do it by employing our mind. It is at work. For those who engage in spiritual *askesis* [exercise], however, the most important center, the center of the heart, is also at work. So while their mind is focused on a certain activity, such as washing dishes, their heart is doing something else simultaneously. I am fully aware that it must be difficult to comprehend this. But believe me, it is possible. The heart is attached to God, lives with God, functions in God, and is joyous with the presence of God while the praying persons are absorbed in worldly activities. They may be even asleep but their heart functions within the Grace of the Holy Spirit."

"This, I suppose, takes place naturally when a person masters the art of prayer, how to pray ceaselessly. This is what you said before, right?" I interjected.

"Exactly. The method within the Athonite spiritual tradition for attaining that state is to learn how to say the *Efche*, the Jesus Prayer [Lord Jesus Christ, Son of God, have mercy upon me, a sinner], continuously. It is the practical way of mobilizing the mechanism of the heart to open up to Grace. You see, Kyriaco, embedded in the name of Jesus is the very power of God. By invoking, therefore, the sacred name repeatedly we invite the Grace of God to take possession of our hearts and minds, protecting us from harmful effects. As elder Sophrony put it, the Name of Jesus Christ for the believer is like a high fortress-wall that gives the soul the strength to resist harmful influences from outside."[1]

"It is not easy to do that, I mean to keep the mind focused on the Prayer. How can I read a book, or lecture in a class and be in a state of prayer at the same time? I am puzzled by this. In fact, I recall reading the work of an elder who suggested that inexperienced practitioners of the Prayer should not attempt to combine it with intense intellectual work, such as lecturing in a class or reading an academic book. If we try to do two things at once, we end up by doing both badly."

"That is certainly wise advice," Father Maximos responded. "It is easier at that early stage of the practice to recite the Prayer when you do some task that does not require concentration, such as washing dishes. But your inexperience should not discourage you. This is a challenge that you can overcome with time. Keep in mind that at the early stages of spiritual practice you must not be concerned with the quality of the Prayer, whether your mind is focused on the words or not. Whatever you do at that stage, your mind will be wandering. There is no way to avoid that. But the Prayer has its own power and energy. As you repeat it in your mind or aloud it will have a gradual impact within your psychospiritual world. Believe me," Father Maximos added, "it will work like a bulldozer which opens up the road, gradually demolishing rocks and pushing the dirt away. That is how the Prayer works. It opens the road for Grace to visit the heart. And when that happens, then the heart works by itself independently of whatever else you do. It enters into an ongoing relationship with God."

"I suppose that's how forgetfulness as an illness of the heart comes to an end."

"Precisely. The uninterrupted memory of God returns to the heart. That's how human beings become what they were prior to the Fall, exactly as created in the image of God. That is why you will see monks reciting the Prayer while going about doing all kinds of odd jobs."

When I visited Mount Athos this method of prayer, which was recited sometimes in the mind in silence and sometimes aloud, struck me as quite outlandish at first. During my stay at the Panagia monastery I sat with a group of monks in a circle, peeling potatoes in silence. I volunteered to help them and found myself having to take turns reciting the Prayer aloud over and over. By then, far from it appearing bizarre to me, this practice felt perfectly natural and I thought of it as a form of collective meditation, something I would never have felt comfortable doing back at the University of Maine. I was finally beginning to get acclimatized to the monastic culture.

"Is this practice fit only for monks and hermits?" I asked, having in mind the objections of lay critics about monasticism, that whatever the monks do is for themselves, applicable only to themselves, and irrelevant for ordinary mortals living in the world.

"No," Father Maximos replied emphatically. "Anyone can practice the Prayer and see results over time. People are just unwilling to make the effort or they don't believe that anything is going to happen. But based on the testament and cumulative experience of the saints and great elders, continuous prayer is the key to the purification of the heart and its opening to the gifts of the Holy Spirit, to Grace."

Father Maximos advised that people recite the Prayer every chance they get in their daily lives, while filling in idle time or doing some monotonous work that does not require concentration. Furthermore, laypeople can devote a few minutes in the morning and a few minutes at night to concentrate exclusively on the Prayer. With prolonged and systematic practice the Prayer will eventually become self-activating so that regardless of what the person is doing it will work on its own. He insisted that the Prayer may have been invented by monks and hermits as a method of spiritual practice but that it is in reality applicable for everybody.

Just then I had to interrupt my conversation with Father Maximos. A black-clad woman in her middle thirties had come to the monastery for confession. It was not the day set aside for confessions, but as I noticed time and again, Father Maximos made frequent exceptions to the rule for emergency cases. The woman had just lost her husband in an accident and was in great emotional turmoil.

While waiting for Father Maximos to return I reflected on the Jesus Prayer. I had just read several days earlier Timothy (now Bishop Kallistos) Ware's work on *The Orthodox Church*, where he elaborates on the power of this particular Prayer to affect peoples lives. "The Jesus Prayer," he wrote,

> is a prayer of marvellous versatility. It is a prayer for beginners, but equally a prayer that leads to the deepest mysteries of the contemplative life. It can be used by anyone, at any time, in any place: standing in queues, walking, travelling on buses or trains; when at work; when unable to sleep at night, at times of special anxiety when it is impossible to concentrate upon other kinds of prayer.[2]

It was the nineteenth-century Russian classic *The Way of the Pilgrim* that made the Jesus Prayer known outside the culture of Eastern Orthodox monasticism. This anonymous work narrates the spiritual adventures of a Russian peasant who embarked on a walking pilgrimage to various sacred shrines and churches all over Russia while continuously reciting the Prayer taught to him by an elder. A particular passage that tells of the profound impact the Prayer had on this pilgrim's life remained vivid in my mind:

> And that is how I go about now, and ceaselessly repeat the Jesus Prayer, which is more precious and sweet to me than anything in the world. At times I do as much as forty-three or forty-four miles a day, and do not feel that I am walking at all. I am aware only of the fact that I am saying my Prayer. When the bitter cold pierces me, I begin to say my Prayer more earnestly, and I quickly become warm all over. When hunger begins to overcome me, I call more often on the Name of Jesus, and I forget my wish for food. When I fall ill and get rheumatism in my back and legs, I fix my thoughts on the Prayer, and do not notice the pain. If anyone harms me I have only to think, "How sweet is the Jesus Prayer!" and the injury and the anger alike pass away and I forget it all. . . . I thank God that I now understand the meaning of those words I heard in the Epistle—Pray without ceasing.[3]

When the troubled woman came out of the confessional wiping her tears, Father Maximos walked up the steps to where I was sitting. I mentioned to him about what I had been thinking in regard to the Jesus Prayer, and he promised that before I left for Maine we would discuss that most important topic further. We then resumed our discussion about illnesses of the heart.

"Father Maxime," I said, "so far you have identified two illnesses of the heart, ignorance and forgetfulness. Are there any others?"

"Yes. Another one is what the elders call **hardness** or toughness of the heart. A person may fervently desire to listen to the word of God, to desire union with God, to come in contact with wisdom that comes from God, but the heart is impenetrable. The Grace of God cannot enter the essence of that person. The heart does not allow the seed of God's grace to take root. Based on the experience of the saints, this is a given for all of us. If we consider ourselves as a parcel of land that we begin to dig and cultivate with the Prayer, we'll notice that at first the ground may be soft and relatively easy to plow. But as we continue digging we reach a level full of pebbles. Further down we reach solid rock. It is like sowing on granite. Nothing can penetrate it." Father Maximos looked thoughtful and serious, as if speaking from direct experience.

"So, what happens after that?"

"The hardness becomes even more impenetrable," he said with a somber tone and remained pensive for a few more seconds.

"Why so?"

"Because of three things," Father Maximos replied, bringing forward the three middle fingers of his right hand. "Over preoccupation with worldly affairs, focus on physical pleasures, and obsession with wealth. These are three fundamental passions that toughen the heart. They rob the power of the heart to channel its energy toward God. We consume this vital energy with worldly preoccupations and the allurement of all the things around us. Our attention becomes fragmented, scattered."

"But Father Maxime," I protested, "not everybody could or should become a monk."

"I am not suggesting that. I am explaining how the heart gets hardened through the concerns and seductions of the world. We just need to know that and become vigilant so that we keep the mind focused on God, regardless of whether we are monks, hermits, or ordinary people living in the world. For instance, upon waking up, anybody can begin the day with the Prayer. If you do that, whether you are a monk or not, you will notice the following. When you discipline the mind to start being preoccupied with God from the moment you wake up, your day will begin to unfold within the Prayer and will bring a certain inner peace."

"Is this the way to begin breaking the granite?" I asked.

"That's a first step. It requires great effort and patience to hammer against that rock and, through prayer, to ask for God's assistance to turn it into dust. But it is work that is certainly worth doing. That's what King David wrote in one of his psalms, 'Kardian syntetrimmenin kai teta-pinomenin O Theos ouk exoudenosi,' that is, 'God will never spurn a crushed and humbled heart.' It is the way the saints pray. They ask of God to crush their hearts."

Father Maximos laughed as he remembered an episode in the life of elder Paisios. "For a period of time," he said, "old Paisios lived as a hermit outside Mount Athos near his hometown in northern Greece. Every Sun-

day he would walk from his hermitage to the church and take communion. He would stay inside the sanctuary and assist the priest with the
liturgy. He himself could not conduct the liturgy because he was never ordained as a priest."

"Never? How come?"

"He just preferred to be a simple monk living the life of a hermit. He
refused ordination. Not all monks are ordained priests, you know. Anyway,
one Sunday while walking to church he prayed that God may humble
him and 'crush' his heart. Then he stepped inside the sanctuary to assist
the priest with the service and waited his turn to get holy communion. But
when the priest was about to offer him communion, for no reason whatsoever, he unleashed a virulent attack on poor old Paisios. He told him
that he was a nuisance and that he was fed up seeing him around in the
sanctuary Sunday after Sunday. Old Paisios was flabbergasted, not knowing what to make of it. Then he remembered what he had prayed for on
his way to church. After the liturgy, the priest approached him full of
apologies and remorse for his outburst. He bowed in front of elder Paisios,
kissed his hand, and asked for the elder's forgiveness. 'I just don't know
what came over me,' he complained."

"So," I asked, "does it mean that to have a crushed and humble heart
we must pray for it?"

"It is one way. But, of course, it happens through systematic *askesis*:
fasting, ceaseless prayer, all-night vigils, work, and the like. Beyond that,
and most important, it is when human beings learn how to have patience
with the many and unavoidable sorrows that they will encounter in life."

"This emphasis on patience is what critics of religion consider a di-
version from protesting against personal and social injustices. Some people would say that this is an ideology that serves the interests of the powers
that be, religion as 'the opiate of the people,' " I said provocatively.

"Nonsense," Father Maximos scoffed and waved his hand in a dismissive way. "Learn how to accept sorrows as divine gifts, including personal
failures. Through experiences of grief human beings have the opportunity
to place the stone of their heart into a grinder and turn it into dust. They
must go through these sorrows of the heart. Through grief they may come
out victorious. Life itself is a form of *askesis*. People just don't recognize it
and lose heart."

"What does not kill me gives me strength," I muttered, quoting the
well-known aphorism.

"Right," Father Maximos replied and nodded. I was almost certain
that he had never heard of Nietzsche.

"That's why in the Apocalypse," he went on, "the saints are referred to
as 'those who have passed through great sorrows.' Their life was not easy."

"This is not a message that would entice people used to a life focused on pleasure and comfort," I pointed out.

"Yes, I know. But sorrow is an unavoidable part of life regardless of when and where you live. It is an integral aspect of human existence."

"I understand what you are saying," I pointed out. "After all, the suicide statistics have gone up, not down in our modern age. Yet the message of sorrow and sacrifice is not an attractive message to the modern mind."

"Well, this is part of the problem of the modern mind. What the *Ecclesia* teaches about these matters is geared for those who have eyes to see and ears to hear. Anyway, when I say sorrow, it does not mean that we celebrate suffering as if it is something to cherish and pursue. Rather, to the extent that suffering is unavoidable, accept it as a gift from Heaven. Then it will have a therapeutic impact on your heart. Redefine it in your mind as an opportunity for spiritual growth. Because that's what it is in reality. Whether people realize it or not, we live in a world of ongoing *askesis*. Do you follow me?"

Father Maximos's words on suffering reminded me of a refugee aunt of Emily's and the Viennese psychiatrist Viktor Frankl. Emily's aunt was a wealthy woman in Famagusta, the thriving tourist city of Cyprus overrun by the Turkish army in 1974. As an uprooted and impoverished refugee, she discovered her spirituality and became a model of selflessness and altruism at a period when others became embittered and aggressively angry. Her case was a classic application of Frankl's celebrated work on "logotherapy."[4] A survivor of Auschwitz, Frankl taught that the primary motive of human beings is neither Freud's "will to pleasure" nor Adler's "will to power," but rather the "will to meaning." People commit suicide because of meaning deprivation, never from sex deprivation. Insofar as suffering is an unavoidable aspect of the human condition (death, illness, loss of loved ones), it can also be a source of meaning and purpose in life, assuming that the suffering is not self-inflicted. Logotherapy is the psychoanalytic method that enables people to heal themselves by discovering their own unique meaning to their existential situation. Frankl, an inmate in the death camp, discovered meaning during his ordeal through the memory of his wife (his longing to survive and reunite with her) and his wish to rewrite his book on logotherapy that the Nazis confiscated and destroyed upon his entrance into Auschwitz.

I briefly explained to Father Maximos the essentials of Frankl's work. He nodded in full agreement with the Viennese doctor's basic ideas. For Father Maximos, every calamity in one's life is an opportunity to discover God. He hastened to add, however, that every success and good fortune are also opportunities to discover God. Both negative and positive events in our lives, he claimed, are temptations sent to us by Providence to enhance our spiritual development. Whether we respond to them in a way that is spiritually beneficial is entirely up to us. [It was brought to my attention by another elder that the Greek word *peirasmos* (temptation) is broader in scope than the English term "temptation." In Greek it also means "trial" or "test." *Peirasmos* could be a trial or test sent to us by God in order to help us progress on our spiritual way or it could be a suggestion from the devil.]

Father Maximos was not an intellectual in the Western sense. His knowledge about existential matters derived exclusively from his own experience and from his study of the spiritual legacy left behind by the holy elders of Christianity. His language and the concepts he used to understand the world derived exclusively from the wealth of the patristic spiritual tradition. Therefore, I never engaged him directly in the kind of discussions about Western thinkers that had been my own intellectual nourishment for decades. I was interested first and foremost to learn about Father Maximos's spiritual wisdom, not in debating with him the comparative worth of the thought of Nietzsche, Freud, Frankl, or whomever. In my mind, however, I carried on a continuous but silent dialogue between the teachings of the holy elders of Christianity and the secular thinkers of the West as well as with the wisdom traditions coming out of Buddhism and Hinduism. When he talked about "purifying the heart," I could hardly avoid contrasting it with the Buddha's "eightfold path." I was fully aware, however, that devout Christians, the Athonite monks included, are averse to any comparisons between Christian revelation and spiritual practice and the mysticism and spiritual exercises of the East. In the eyes of such Christians, comparisons may undermine belief in the centrality and divine uniqueness of Christian revelation, a fear that as an academic I could not share. I therefore stayed clear, on the whole, of the *peirasmos* in comparative debates.

"Something very paradoxical happens within the heart of saints who experience, for one reason or another, deep grief and sorrow," Father Maximos went on to say. "It is the mystery of God's Grace. While everything goes wrong, at a certain point there is a sudden inner transformation and illumination. That which was experienced as intense grief now becomes the cause of a great amount of Grace, so much so that the bitterness of the grief is annihilated. Grief is transmuted into ineffable joy. I don't know if this makes any sense to you, but it is true."

"It does," I reassured Father Maximos, then we remained silent for a few seconds, reflecting on the issue he had just raised.

"I advise people," Father Maximos went on to say, "that when they learn how to make it a practice in their lives to be patient with small temptations of grief, they can gradually learn how to accept the greater temp-

THE (OUNTAIN Of SILENCE   63

tations of suffering that they will unavoidably experience in their lives. With practice they learn not to become lost under the weight of such temptations. Their heart may be shredded into pieces but they are not lost. It is a problem with people today that they are incapable of dealing with the slightest sorrow or temptation. They often disintegrate as human beings." Father Maximos then went on to elaborate on additional illnesses of the heart that afflict human existence. "The holy elders talk about **blindness** and **contamination** as two related illnesses of the heart. When the heart suffers from hardness it is incapable of distinguishing between good and evil and is consequently rendered unable to recognize the presence of God. It is blind.

"Sometimes unbelievers ask 'Where is God? Why can't I see Him? Why doesn't He manifest Himself so that I may believe?' or 'Prove to me that God exists.' But how can anybody do that for someone who lacks sight? Their case is similar to a blind man who does not believe that there are chandeliers. He just does not have the eyes to see them. But those with eyes to see know from experience that all of reality is permeated with God. And you know what a sweet feeling it is to have that experience? To be within creation and to feel everywhere God's presence? Then life becomes intensely joyous. Everything is blessed. When you don't have this experiential understanding of God's Grace, then with the slightest provocation you become critical, constantly blaming others, constantly finding fault with them. When you are in that state of mind, the holy elders teach that you should consider it axiomatic that the problem is actually you. Look at the saints," Father Maximos continued, "the people who have gotten to know God. You will never hear them complain against anybody. They are critical of no one, often not even of the devil himself, believe it or not."

"It's very difficult to think that way and still live in the world," I snapped.

"It is extremely difficult. But that's what it means to be God-realized. As a result of long and hard practice the sensibilities of the saints are radically altered. Unlike us, they perceive things around them differently. They see everything and everybody in their true state, permeated by God. Everybody is perceived as a being within Providence. Therefore, for a real saint nothing is apprehended as really hostile. That is the reason why saints have absolutely no fears.

"Have you ever wondered," Father Maximos continued, "why whenever we monks meet each other we bow and kiss each other's hands?"

"I must say that from the point of view of an outsider this form of greeting looks quite bizarre, to put it mildly," I mused.

"That's how I felt myself when I first visited Mount Athos," Father Maximos said. "I remember the first time I saw two monks make deep prostrations and kiss each other's hand as they passed one another on a path. At that time it appeared to me very funny. I barely controlled my laughter. Of course, I soon learned that this behavior is based on the belief that whenever you meet someone on your way, in reality you meet God. And as you honor God you must honor the other because you have in front of you the presence of God. You don't turn the other way to avoid someone you don't like." He hesitated for a second and then went on. "That's what I usually do myself." Then Father Maximos went on to narrate another episode from the life of elder Paisios as an example of the right attitude in such circumstances.

"One day old Paisios was visited in his remote hermitage by a group of five obnoxious young men, full of pride and arrogance. He patiently spent several hours showing them extra attention. But a theology teacher who was present became irritable and impatient. 'How could you tolerate them?' he asked him. And the elder replied, 'Have you ever wondered how God could tolerate you?' "

After reminiscing with a few more anecdotes from the life of his beloved elder, Father Maximos returned to the issue of the other illnesses of the heart. When the heart gets accustomed to putrid thoughts, or *logismoi*, he said, then it suffers from contamination.

"Are you suggesting," I asked, "that whenever negative thoughts enter the mind they unavoidably contaminate the heart like viruses?"

"Not necessarily. It is unavoidable to be assaulted by negative thoughts. The problem is when we allow these thoughts to enter the heart and stay there. When putrid thoughts get cultivated within the heart then the heart becomes accustomed to them. In fact it relishes them."

"So the heart becomes a hostage to these addictions," I noted.

"Yes. It becomes accustomed to extracting pleasure from putrid conditions. Such a heart cannot be without this ongoing contamination. Contrast that with the 'pure at heart' who are incapable of contemplating a putrid thought even if they tried. On the other hand, hearts that are contaminated are turned off by whatever is pure and clean. Do you see what is happening?"

I nodded and Father Maximos went on. "Another illness of the heart is **imprudence,** which means that the heart is not even aware what its true interests are. Take for example a very wealthy man in his late seventies. He cannot possibly use his wealth even if he tried. Yet he cannot stop being fully absorbed with making more money that he does not need."

"In such cases the problem may not be the desire to have more money but to maintain status or power. In any event, most of us who live in the world suffer from imprudence." The moment I said that, my academic world flashed through my mind. How imprudent most of us are, I thought, accumulating our publications and our honors, just like the business tycoon accumulating wealth in his eighties. We act and behave in our classes and our faculty meetings as if we are immortal, hardly ever pausing to reflect on the deeper reasons for our existence.

"Whatever the causes for such behavior," Father Maximos said, "the individual is not aware that he will die soon and all his wealth and social positions are useless. He does not have *mnemen thanatou,* memory of death. The heart is imprudent. It suffers from folly."

I remember how shocked I felt when, on Mount Athos, I witnessed a ritual that from the point of view of ordinary life would appear macabre. On a regular basis the monks, holding torches at night in procession, visit a place that looks like a catacomb where they have stored the bones of monks who have been dead for at least three years. There they pray and chant for their deceased brothers. This ritual, I was told, is to train the monks to have *mnemen thanatou* so that they may reach a state of complete fearlessness toward death. As one young monk told me, "At first I was horrified, but then not only did I get used to it but it helped me overcome whatever fears I had about death. Now I even know the exact location where my bones will be stored when I am gone." It was an attitude, I thought at the time, completely at odds with our modern, worldly tendency to deny death, hiding it in funeral homes.

"All illnesses of the heart," Father Maximos went on to say, "are interconnected. However, the primary illnesses out of which spring all the others are ignorance and forgetfulness of God. Whenever human beings make contact with the inner self and discover the divine reality within, they automatically get healed from all the heart's illnesses. This is the real healing of the self."

A hermit like elder Paisios, Father Maximos would often say, was someone who had overcome the ignorance and forgetfulness that afflict us all from the first day of our existence. Through the knowledge and memory of God he was healed of the hardness of the heart and all other illnesses, becoming a beacon of spirituality for all. One would expect such hermits, who spend their entire lives in the wilderness continuously praying and carrying on an ascetic life, to be nasty, brutish, and coarse. But no. "I have known hermits," Father Maximos claimed, "who lived the ascetic life for forty, even sixty years. Such persons, under ordinary circumstances, should look and behave like wild beasts. Yet there is refinement in their expression and a gentleness that is hard to describe. They radiate love to such a degree that visitors remain incredulous and unable to comprehend. They are literally baptized with the fire of holiness." Had I not met elder Paisios myself I would have thought that Father Maximos was either exaggerating or imagining things.

Our morning conversation ended when a busload of Germans, Britons, and Scandinavians led by their Cypriot guide entered the yard. From the open corridor of the second floor where we were sitting, we watched the commotion unfolding below us. Father Maximos stood and leaned on the railing as he waved to the uninvited guests. Trying to guard the silence of the monastery was not always easy. Unlike Mount Athos, the Panagia monastery was accessible by motor vehicles and, given its historic importance, an attraction for the growing tourist industry. Father Maximos, however, had set rules on when travel agents and the Cyprus Tourism Organization could bus their guests to the monastery and what areas they could visit once they arrived. Tourists and visitors were allowed to visit the church, light candles, walk about the monastery grounds, and visit the bookshop. They were not permitted to walk by the monks' quarters. Where we stood was off limits to visitors, local or international.

Gathering around their guide, the European tourists listened to a brief summary of the history of the Panagia monastery. "This monastery," she began in her accented English, "was founded during the last years of the twelfth century and today it is one of the most significant and active Orthodox monasteries in Cyprus. It is believed that the icon of the Holy Virgin, which you will soon see inside the church, was painted by the apostle and evangelist Luke. An unknown hermit brought it to Cyprus from Asia Minor in order to save it during the reign of the iconoclasts between the eighth and ninth centuries. This hermit sought refuge on these mountains and lived in a hidden hermitage. Following his death, the icon remained there until the arrival of two other hermits around the year 1145 who, guided by divine revelation, rediscovered it. This monastery was eventually built at the very spot where they found the icon, with money sent from Constantinople after the defeat of the iconoclasts. Since its founding in the twelfth century, the monastery has burnt to the ground and been rebuilt three times, the last time being at the end of the nineteenth century."

Father Maximos tried to listen, but knowing hardly any English he could not follow what the guide was saying. I just mentioned to him what the general topic was. As she began talking about the history of the monastery during the Frankish, Ottoman, and British periods, Father Maximos asked me to join him on an inspection of some construction work being done at an underground warehouse there. It was being turned into a repository for rare icons and other religious artifacts dating back to Byzantine times. Holding a flashlight, I followed him down the steps into the dark warehouse, used in past centuries as a hiding refuge from invading armies, robbers, and pirates.

6

ICONS aND IDOLS

It was Friday morning. I had just completed my note-taking and sat on a bench outside my room facing the sunny courtyard. I watched the monks dressed in their black cassocks carrying on with their various errands. Pilgrims walked in and out of the church at the center of the courtyard, lighting candles and paying homage to the miraculous icon of the Holy Virgin.

I closed my eyes for a few minutes, enjoying the rays of the sun as I contemplated life in my new surroundings. The Panagia monastery was a different kind of monastery than those I was familiar with while growing up in Cyprus. During that time the island's many monasteries were virtually abandoned. Only a few elderly monks still lived in them despite the fact that Cyprus had once been a hub of monastic activity, thanks primarily to its close proximity to the Holy Land and the deserts of Egypt, where monasticism emerged and flourished during the early centuries of Christianity. During those times, so many saints were produced by these monasteries that Cyprus was considered by the faithful as "the Island of Saints." Some of these saints, like Saint Spyridon and Saint Epiphanios, played an active role in the formulation of the early doctrine of Christianity. But af-

ter the Second World War the monasteries that were still in operation became places for recreational activities such as picnics and free overnight
accommodation. Spiritual renewal was not a preoccupation for most patrons. Ordinary people could take their families there for a few days of rest
and do nothing more spiritual than attend a morning service now and
then. Since monasteries were built in remote, wooded areas on the mountains or by the sea, they became ideal locations for free vacationers, the
equivalent of the national park system in America. When the available
rooms were filled on a first-come-first-served basis (it definitely helped if
you knew the abbot), people would then camp out on the surrounding
monastery grounds and enjoy the great outdoors.

Before the arrival of Father Maximos there were hardly any monks at
the Panagia monastery, and visitors would come and go for reasons that
had little to do with the salvation of their souls. At that time, in fact, the
monastery was a favorite place for die-hard nationalists who would yearly
visit its grounds to commemorate the sacrifice of a Cypriot guerrilla rebel
who died in the mid-fifties fighting British troops on a nearby mountain
slope. It was also a favorite resting spot for hunters who enjoyed a good,
hearty lunch at the restaurant next to the monastery after their excursions
into the surrounding mountains to shoot partridges and hares.

With the arrival of Father Maximos in 1993 everything changed. The
increasing number of young and educated monks that began joining the
Panagia monastery, thanks primarily to the abbot's charismatic appeal, injected a new vitality into the place at a time when most people, myself included, assumed that monasticism was a thing of the past. Pilgrims also
began to arrive in droves for spiritual guidance and to participate in the
monastery's demanding regimen of fasting, prayer, meditation, and all-
night vigils and rituals. I felt that I was a witness to a major revolution in
the history of monasticism on the island, and perhaps beyond the island.

Having achieved the revival of spirituality at the Panagia monastery,
Father Maximos took some radical steps to protect the silence needed for
serious spiritual work and concentration. The restaurant, rented out by the
monastery for the entertainment of visitors, was shut down in spite of vigorous protests from its operators and regular patrons. It was inconceivable,
Father Maximos explained to me, to try to engage in spiritual work when
just outside the gates rowdy vacationers would drink, dance to loud music,
and consume generous portions of meat roasted on open-air skewers, the
aromas reaching the nostrils of monks fasting in their cells.

With monetary contributions from pilgrims and wealthy patrons, Father Maximos demolished the restaurant and in its place constructed an
additional and spacious *archondariki* that could accommodate large numbers of people. There all visitors were offered free tea, coffee, and pastries

after services on Sundays and on special holy days. On top of the new *archondariki* he erected an impressive chapel in honor of Saint Gregory Palamas, the fourteenth-century bishop of Thessaloniki who successfully defended the lifestyle and spiritual practices of Athonite monks at a time when rationalist currents within the Eastern Church threatened to undermine such practices. With the erection of the chapel, Father Maximos sent a clear message about what he was trying to do at the Panagia monastery: to rescue and preserve the mystic practices of the *Ecclesia*.

Guests to the monastery were now welcome to stay for a few days, assuming that they were there for spiritual work and not for a free vacation. Baptisms and marriages were no longer performed at the monastery as these sacramental rituals generated worldly commotion, undermining the indispensable need for quietude.

"They are here, Kyriaco," I heard Stephanos calling me. He had stayed the night before in a cell next to mine and we had spent the evening talking about Athonite spirituality while the monks practiced ceaseless prayer in their cells. "They are waiting at the *archondariki*."

"Good," I replied, as I opened my eyes, stretched, and stood up. "I hope Father Maximos will have time for us this morning."

We walked down the steps where our friends Eleni and her husband Theodoros waited. I introduced them to Stephanos and to Father Nikodemos, a monk in his early thirties who happened to be present.

"Father Maximos will be with you shortly," Father Nikodemos said. "In the meantime you may wish to visit the church." Eleni got on her feet and led the way.

In her mid-forties, Eleni came from a well-to-do family of Limassol, the southern port city. She was successfully recovering from a ten-year struggle with cancer, an experience which, she claimed, had gradually turned her attention inward, toward more spiritual concerns. That was the gift of the cancer, she told me, to open up to the reality of God. It was not the first time I had heard someone pronounce in utter sincerity how a life-threatening disease had opened them up to spirituality. I remember that several years ago in Vermont, while conducting a workshop, a frail-looking man from New York approached me and with tears in his eyes confided in me that had it not been for AIDS, he would have gone through his entire life without the slightest interest in things that truly matter. By viewing the terminal disease as a gift from Heaven, he had found peace of mind.

There were no lights in the church and the few candles burning created the sense of mystery and awe so typical of old Byzantine churches. Eleni walked in first. After lighting a candle at the entrance of the church, she crossed herself and kissed the miraculous icon of the *Theotokos* [Mother of God], the patron of the monastery. She then proceeded to the *iconostasi*, the icon screen separating the sanctuary from the rest of the church. She was about to do the same in front of the large icon of Christ when she began shaking slightly, her eyes becoming moist. "It is the same icon," she whispered. "It's identical."

"Amazing!" her husband marveled. "What an amazing coincidence."

Barely controlling her emotions as tears ran down her face, Eleni remained glued in front of Christ's image. It was an unusual icon portraying Christ clad in imperial garments, but instead of thorns over His head He had a jeweled crown depicting not the crucified Christ, but the *Pantokrator*, Ruler of the Universe.

After leaving the church I helped Theodoros carry a large, heavy icon from the back of their car to the guest room. The sole purpose of their visit was in fact to bring the icon to the monastery. We carefully leaned it on the wall and Father Nikodemos removed the white sheet. At that moment I realized why Eleni had appeared so moved. The icon, which they were about to hand over to the custody of Father Maximos, was virtually identical to the icon at the monastery. Father Nikodemos, a trained archaeologist, pointed to a spot where the year 1860 was inscribed.

"Few icons like this were ever made," he said. "It will be safe here." Then he went on to inspect the *Pantokrator* more carefully. He hypothesized that the church to which the icon belonged must have had a fire in the past as the back side of the icon had some burned parts. Other than that the icon was in excellent condition. "I don't know if the two icons were painted by the same artist," Father Nikodemos explained as he went on inspecting it at close range. "Both the icon in the church and this one were definitely made during the same period. This form of art was introduced to the island for a brief period in the nineteenth century. It is a rare style combining Byzantine art with Western influences."

Father Maximos entered the room as we enjoyed an aromatic mountain tea made of herbs gathered by the monks. He apologized for the delay and then spent a few minutes gazing at and scrutinizing the icon. "We'll take good care of it," he reassured Eleni. When we sat down she explained how the icon had come into her possession and how she decided to turn it over for custody at the Panagia monastery.

About fifteen years ago a stranger knocked at their door one night and implored them to rescue a rare icon that was to be smuggled out of the island in the diplomatic sack of a foreign embassy. A diplomat who had access to the Turkish-occupied part of Cyprus was ready to buy the *Pantokrator* from a Turk for three hundred Cypriot pounds (at the time about $650). The icon had belonged to an unknown church that was ransacked and looted after the invasion of the island by Turkey in 1974. Eleni and Theodoros did not have that much cash in the house and had to rush from relative to relative to gather the money so the icon could be rescued. The smugglers would have otherwise delivered it to the foreign diplomat that very evening. Her intention was to eventually hand it over to the authorities, but she procrastinated and fifteen years passed by. During all that time she felt a heavy load weighing on her heart, as she put it, for not doing anything with the icon other than keeping it hidden in a closet. She knew that the icon did not belong to her. At the same time, given the lapse of time, Eleni was reluctant to turn it over because of possible legal entanglements. She needed to deliver it to an authority that would guarantee their anonymity. Furthermore, she did not wish to give the icon to the government, which would have most probably placed it in a museum. Eleni was emphatic that she wanted the icon to end up in a place of worship. "When I talked to Kyriacos the other day," Eleni told Father Maximos, "he suggested that I bring it here."

"Good," Father Maximos said reassuringly. "We will place it for public worship until we identify the church from which it was stolen and return it there when, God willing, the Turkish troops leave Cyprus."

Theodoros, who up to that point had remained silent, asked whether he could raise a few questions about the role of icons in religious worship. Eleni had warned me earlier that her husband, a successful, down-to-earth businessman, was resistant to spirituality and considered kissing icons downright silly. It required a considerable amount of diplomacy on her part to persuade Theodoros (his name literally meaning "Gift of God") to join her at the monastery. Here is another "Doubting Thomas," I mused to myself. When Father Maximos signaled a readiness to entertain his request, Theodoros felt free to speak his mind, to the chagrin of his wife.

"Why is there such an obsession with icons in the Orthodox Church? Isn't it a form of idolatry?" he asked provocatively.

Father Maximos smiled. I was certain he must have confronted such a question many times ever since he left the isolation and silence of Mount Athos to enter into the modern, noisy world of Cyprus. The issue that Theodoros raised was, of course, an ancient one.

"My dear friend," Father Maximos replied, "this is a standard criticism directed against the Church. But let me first ask you a question. Don't you think it would be quite foolish for the *Ecclesia* not to honor the second commandment? I mean not to honor the prohibition against the worship of idols? Do you think it possible that the holy elders, who throughout the ages have delved experientially more than anyone else into the mysteries of the Bible, would have been unaware of God's commandment and ignorantly insisted on using icons in worship?"

Theodoros listened without saying a word. Father Maximos then went on to explain the position of the saints and holy elders on the importance of icons. "First of all, let us clarify what is meant by the word 'idol.' " He looked at the icon of the Christ *Pantokrator* resting on the wall. Pointing his finger at it, he went on. "Idolatry means to mistake this icon for the Christ Himself. On the other hand, when I say that this icon represents the image of the Christ, then it is a different matter altogether. It is just an icon. We must be very clear about our motives and intentions when we kiss icons. Through this ritual we simply honor the icons. Nothing more. We must definitely not worship icons."

"I just don't see the difference," Theodoros reacted wryly. I gave a quick side-look at Eleni, who appeared less than happy with her husband's devil's advocate bravado. I signaled her not to be concerned.

"Okay. Let me ask you this," Father Maximos continued with determination. "You do have a camera, right? Do you take pictures of people?"

"Yes," Theodoros replied, somewhat puzzled.

"Do you take pictures of relatives you love, such as children, parents, grandparents, and have them in your house decorating the walls?" Father Maximos asked again.

"Sure."

"Suppose you kissed the picture of a loved one that was no longer in this life. Would this be idolatry?"

"Obviously not," Theodoros replied.

The exchange between Father Maximos and Theodoros jolted me a bit and brought back painful memories. When my mother died of breast cancer at the age of thirty-six, when I was not quite five yet, my father was inconsolable. He never remarried. Instead he had my mother's picture next to his bed and every night before going to sleep he would kiss it. He did that for the next forty-five years, until the day he died. I never assumed he worshiped the photograph.

"Suppose," Father Maximos went on, "Jesus was here today and you took a photograph of Him and you placed that photograph in your home and kissed it every day. Would that be idolatry?"

"I guess not," Theodoros agreed reluctantly.

"God Himself instructed Moses to create angels out of wood and place them on the Ark of the Covenant. Do you think God would violate His own commandment?" Father Maximos said with a quizzing look. Theodoros nodded, indicating an understanding of Father Maximos's point.

I sympathized with Theodoros's dilemma and difficulty with icons. During my agnostic phase the ritual of bowing in front of icons and then kissing them after crossing oneself appeared to me at that time, if not idolatrous or silly, certainly meaningless. In fact, an early "iconoclast" emperor of Byzantium passed a decree prohibiting the use of icons in worship, fearing that the ritual was a form of idolatry and a violation of God's second commandment. Believing that the military defeats his empire had suffered at the hands of Islam were God's punishment for engaging in idolatry, he unleashed his troops against churches to confiscate and burn icons, an act that destroyed a large number of precious pieces of art. But the vigorous opposition of monks in an alliance with influential women eventually forced the restoration of icons as central to worship. In the West on the other hand, the notion of idolatry in reference to icons remained, particularly in Protestantism.

The restoration of the importance of icons in my own mind took place during my visit to Mount Athos, where elders like Father Maximos explained to me the proper attitude to have toward icons: they were nothing more than an aid for spiritual focus and work. I then realized that all religions, including Buddhism and Hinduism, use objects of worship similar to icons for spiritual purposes in ways reminiscent of Athonite monasticism. But I could also see how easy it would be to forget the inner meaning of such practices and turn them from means to ends, make icons into idols. I wondered whether the Protestant reformers abolished icons from worship altogether in fear of such a prospect. I was intrigued when, during a visit to the Cathedral of Saint John the Divine in New York, I noticed several large Byzantine icons decorating the entrance of the church. That was quite a major innovation, I thought to myself. But the icons were placed high up to prevent anyone from touching or kissing them.

"Since we are discussing icons, can you tell us the difference between icons that are considered miraculous and those that are not?" I asked.

"Actually," Father Maximos replied, "all icons are miraculous insofar as they depict one Person. Miracles happen through the Grace of the Holy Spirit, the Grace of the Christ. Sometimes certain specific icons are considered miraculous because of a historical incident associated with that particular icon, such as a miraculous healing. But it is not the icon that generates the miracle. Neither is it the wood nor the paint. It is the Person represented in the icon who is considered to have caused the miracle through the Grace of Christ and because of the faith of the individual healed. As it is written in the acts of the apostles, the shadow of Peter caused miracles to happen. Was it really the physical phenomenon of the shadow of Peter that caused those phenomena? Obviously not. Was it Peter himself? Again the answer is no. It was rather the Grace of Christ that worked through Peter which caused those miracles. So, strictly speaking, we cannot distinguish between miraculous and nonmiraculous icons. It is Christ who manifests miracles. I know of miracles that took place around icons that were simply paper reproductions of the original." He then went on to tell us of an experience of a hermit who, while cleaning his hermitage, found an old paper reproduction of Archangel Michael. Since it was a worn-out piece of paper rather than an original icon, he thought of burning it with other papers he had no use for. But at the last moment, instead of throwing it into the fire, he changed his mind and pinned it instead outside his door. The next day, upon returning to his hermitage, he found a radiant stranger inside who introduced himself as Archangel Michael. He had materialized there to assist the hermit with spiritual matters.

Father Maximos stressed that such experiences of saints and angels materializing and dematerializing and making themselves visible to the naked eye have been common in the lives of hermits and monks throughout history. Therefore, he insisted, it would be unwise to automatically dismiss such reports as hallucinations.

"If there are no differences between icons, then why are there icons that shed tears and others that do not?" Eleni asked, referring to the strange phenomena that took place in Cyprus earlier.

"Because, my dear, we are weak and we need phenomena to strengthen our faith. But icons of the Holy Virgin or of the Christ are mere icons. It is only because of our own weaknesses and inadequacies that we offer greater honor to one particular icon rather than another. The Person of the Christ that all icons represent is one and the same, at all times.

"You must keep in mind," Father Maximos continued, "that an icon is not a photograph of the physical face. For example, the icon of Christ represents the Person in both his divine and human nature. And the icons of saints represent their humanness at the end stage of *Theosis*, union with God. That is why iconographers are interested in portraying not the physical characteristics of the particular saint but the spiritual essence of the *theosized* or the God-realized person."

"In other words, they paint the archetype," I commented.

"But we must be careful," Father Maximos responded. "The personal characteristics of the saint are still retained, although in a transfigured form."

"What do you mean by that?" Eleni asked.

"An icon of Saint Seraphim of Sarov is not the same as an icon of Saint Nektarios, the contemporary Greek saint. We know what both of them looked like. In Saint Seraphim's case, from a contemporary portrait; in Saint Nektarios's case, from photographs. Do you understand?

"In any event," Father Maximos continued, "what we must bear in mind is that the purpose and meaning of an icon is to help us reach Christ. To be fixated on the icon itself would indeed be a form of idolatry."

"Idolatry may be considered anything that we as human beings create and then worship, forgetting that we are the ones who created it to begin with," I suggested. "It is part of our alienation from our divine nature."

"That's exactly what it is," Father Maximos concurred.

"That means," I went on to say, "that the ideologies that animate vast numbers of human beings, be they nationalism, communism, patriotism, religious fundamentalism, capitalism, or any other 'ism' are in reality idols. We first construct them collectively. They then become objectified, external realities out there. We create these realities but soon forget that we did so. We then internalize these idols which literally take possession of our hearts and minds. Then we kneel in front of them and worship them as if they were real gods. A simple example is the worship of the flags of various nations that stir up so much nationalist fervor," I went on, speaking like a sociologist. "People are ready to kill and be killed for these idols in the same way that people have been killing each other over the ages for their religious idols."

"Anything that we worship other than God is a form of idolatry," Father Maximos stated. "Whenever we absolutize something, be it an ideology, money, or even scientific knowledge, we are into idolatry. The meaning of the second commandment was a warning against all that. Unfortunately, Christians often fall into this trap of idolatry. They create an idol of Christ which they worship but which has little relationship to the real Christ."

"Like the 'christ' of the Inquisitor," I added.

"That's obvious. There are other more subtle forms of Christian idolatry, you know. People may think of themselves as devout Christians but their notions of Christ may have no relevance to Christ. It is a form of illness, another of the illnesses of the heart that we talked about before. We clerics are particularly vulnerable in worshiping an idol of Christ that we create in our heads rather than Christ Himself. It is as if we create our own God, an idol which we call 'Christ' and then we bow down and worship it. For example, people may think of themselves as Christian until you ask them for something which goes contrary to their interests and desires."

"What is the root of this problem?" Eleni asked. "Why do clerics and ordinary people fall victim to this form of idolatry?"

"It usually happens," Father Maximos replied, "when we construct a form of spirituality without real guidance, without spiritual pedagogy by an experienced elder. We then fall victim to the myriads of *logismoi* [thought forms] that we incessantly create in our heads, get trapped within an idiosyncratic image of Christ, an idol that we create in our minds."

"I suppose it would be similar to someone trying to learn chemistry on her own without an experienced chemist as a tutor," I added. Father Maximos nodded. He repeated, once again, that the holy elders were experienced scientists in search of God and that the methods employed in some monasteries, such as those on Mount Athos, are in fact forms of a spiritual science.

Theodoros, who had not said a word during Father Maximos's explanation of the nonidolatrous stand of the holy elders vis-à-vis icons, raised another question. "Are icons necessary?"

Father Maximos smiled. "Within the context of a perfected faith there is obviously no need for icons or any other religious objects or relics for that matter. The holy elders instruct us in fact that when we pray we must not have any icons in our mind, such as the icon of Christ or the *Theodokos*. This is a principle related to what we call 'pure prayer.' Rather we are asked to pray by establishing a direct contact with the spirit of God."

"If this is so, then what is the use of icons? I think this is what he is wondering about," I said and pointed at Theodoros.[1]

Father Maximos remained thoughtful for a second. "You see," he replied, "there is a diversity of spiritual ages within the Church. Icons can be a useful aid for younger spiritual age groups in the ascent toward God."

"But why so?" Theodoros asked again.

"Because the senses can be of assistance in our efforts. Just as putrid images that assault our senses can stir up putrid passions, so icons can have the exact opposite effects. When we contemplate icons, good and wholesome holy meanings are created within us. A human being, you see, is not just soul and spirit but also mind, imagination, feelings, senses. An individual is a unified whole, a unified entity. The aim of the *Ecclesia* is to divinize the person in his or her totality. It is the whole person that strives to reach God. This is the reason why we offer exercises in the *Ecclesia* that relate to the body, such as fasting, prostrations, staying up during all-night vigils, all the rituals that the saints have been doing throughout the ages."

"These are somatic exercises," Theodoros pointed out. "Why punish and deny the body of ordinary comforts?" With an ironic tone he went on to ask, "I do not suppose it is for the sake of mere physical exercise in order to build muscles?"

"Of course not," Father Maximos reacted. "The struggle with the entire being—soul, mind, and body—aims at divinization. You see, dear friend, just as we have psychic passions, like egotism, jealousy, cunningness, and so forth, we also have bodily passions like gluttony, sexual avarice, addictions of all sorts such as alcohol, drugs, you name it. We need exercises to overcome these maladies. Icons can help us in the struggle against such destructive passions that keep us cut off from God.

"The perfected individual," Father Maximos went on, "needs neither icons nor chants, nor liturgies. But we are not perfect, and as long as we are not perfect we need aids like icons, psalms, chants, and the like. We find these aids in the Old as well as in the New Testament and they are always available to us as long as we have not reached our destination in unison with God."

The discussion on icons brought to mind a dear cousin of mine who discovered she had lupus, a life-threatening disease. She quit her job and directed her energies toward healing herself. One of the most beneficial effects she experienced was when she took up iconography (creating icons) by enrolling in classes offered by local artists. She was eventually capable of painting icons with such skill that they could even be used in local churches. She thought of her new hobby as a formidable medicine that helped her cope with her problem by offering a spiritual outlet not open to her before. "Every time I see the icon taking shape and form, I experience a tremendous feeling of calmness and blessing overtaking me," she once told me. "I just feel healing energy emanating from the icon, covering my entire body."

Satisfied with their encounter with Father Maximos and the happy resolution related to the icon of the *Pantokrator*, Eleni and Theodoros prepared to leave for Limassol. As she was about to walk out of the room, Eleni asked with some hesitation in her voice whether she could have a private audience with Father Maximos for a few minutes. While waiting for Eleni, I kept Theodoros company outside the gates as he lit a cigarette, a prohibited act within the grounds of the monastery.

Twenty minutes later Eleni emerged from the confessional, wiping her tears. "You can't imagine what a burden came off my chest," she said in a low voice. It was the first time Eleni had ever went through confession.[2]

"Remember," Father Maximos said as he escorted them to their car, "whatever good or bad things happen to us, they have only one single purpose, to awaken us to the reality of God and help us on the path toward union with Him. There is no other reason for being born on this planet, believe me. It is up to us whether or not we take advantage of these wake-up calls."

Eleni smiled and sighed with a sense of relief. Her ten-year struggle with cancer was her own wake-up call.

7

SIGNS AND WONDERS

Father Maximos asked Stephanos to join us for a journey to the port city of Limassol and then to Lania, a village at the southern slopes of the Troodos Mountains not far from Limassol. He wanted Stephanos to come along not only because of his good company but also because Stephanos served as his principal adviser on matters related to the secular world outside the monastery. The relationship of the sixty-year-old Stephanos with Father Maximos was a beautiful friendship from the start. Stephanos helped Father Maximos with the affairs of this world while Father Maximos coached Stephanos on the world beyond. I was the happy beneficiary of their relationship. Stephanos, being my own close friend and confidant, spent many hours with me exchanging notes and talking about the extraordinary world of Father Maximos and the other fathers of the Panagia monastery. In addition, as my key lay informant, Stephanos would brief me on major happenings at the monastery during my absences. I was therefore pleased that Father Maximos had invited him to join us. Good conversation between the three of us was bound to emerge during the journey.

The local authorities of Lania invited Father Maximos to a special town meeting to explore the prospects of setting up a monastery at a plateau overlooking their village. Two years earlier a twelfth-century icon of the Holy Virgin was discovered near there hidden in a cave. Presumably the exact location was revealed to a villager through a vision that indicated to him where to dig and find the icon. Based on that revelation and discovery the villagers concluded that it was an omen from God to build a monastery there in honor of the Holy Virgin. They summoned a native son who had spent time on Mount Athos as a monk to return to the village for that purpose. But they also wanted the input and advice of Father Maximos, the foremost monk on the island with connections to the Holy Mountain. Their request was another sign of the impact Father Maximos was having on the revival of monasticism in Cyprus.

We set off at eight in the morning right after the services were over and as the sun generously spread its brilliance over the mountains. We were to drive first to Limassol for a brief visit with Father Maximos's mother and stepfather, and then drive on to Lania to attend the town meeting.

Stephanos sat in the backseat and Father Maximos sat next to me, his temporary chauffeur. When we crossed the outer gate I pressed the button of my tape recorder and shot my first question as a way of getting the conversation started. A wide smile appeared on Father Maximos's face. By now he was used to my modus operandi.

"Father Maxime," I began, "what was the most extraordinary event you experienced as an apprentice to elder Paisios?"

During the last two years elder Paisios, who had died two years before, had become a legend among followers of Athonite spirituality. Already several books had appeared on the extraordinary life of that Christian hermit and contemporary saint. Father Maximos, being one of his closest disciples, had intimate knowledge of the elder's life. It was the type of knowledge he was always ready to share with his own followers, particularly now that the elder was no longer in this world. Routinely, Father Maximos urged his disciples that in addition to studying sacred texts and systematic practicing of the Prayer, reading about the lives of venerated saints is essential for the spiritual life. They serve as guiding lights for the soul aspiring toward perfection. Saints, he argued, are the exemplary models of what we may be. The presence of saints among us provides a living testimony to the efficacy of the Gospel in the same way that the presence of scientists and their works provides concrete evidence of the value and efficacy of scientific textbooks.

Responding to my question, Father Maximos took a deep breath that sounded more like a sigh and mentioned that he had witnessed so many extraordinary phenomena around elder Paisios that he didn't know where to begin.

"Perhaps you can tell Kyriacos the episode with the swinging candles. That's a good one," Stephanos suggested. I took a quick glance at the rearview mirror and signaled a thank you to my gray-haired friend. He was deeply interested in my project and I could always rely on him to be a catalyst for invigorating conversations.

"Oh that incident," Father Maximos responded. "That was one among many experiences that I will never forget. Haven't we talked about that?"

When he realized that I wished to hear more details about the story he had only briefly mentioned to me several years back, Father Maximos went on. "As I mentioned earlier, elder Paisios hardly ever slept. And that is not an exaggeration. I really don't think he slept for more than one or two hours a day. He spent all of his time praying. He followed to the letter the program of daily services and prayers as practiced by all other monks living in monasteries. In addition, he kept vigil every night from sunset to sunrise, praying continuously for others and the world. I became a witness to his ceaseless prayer every time I was in his company. He prayed an hour for each different category of people, such as orphans, widows, refugees, the sick, those who were about to have an accident, soldiers at war, and others in need."

"Frankly," I interjected as I kept my eyes on the road, "it's hard to imagine how anyone can spend an entire life on a remote mountain doing nothing but praying."

"Frankly," Father Maximos snapped with a wide smile on his round face, "old Paisios always wondered how people could live their lives without continuously praying.

"Just to give you an example of how important prayer was for him," Father Maximos went on, "during the Gulf War he shut himself in his cell, cutting off all contact with visitors. That went on during the entire duration of the war. In fact, he intensified his prayers so that the war, as he told me later, would not get out of control and become even more destructive."

"Did he really believe that his prayers made a difference? That they truly affected the war in the Gulf?" I asked, and gave Father Maximos a puzzled look. In spite of my many years of exposure to mystics, healers, and hermits, in spite of being a witness to spectacular healing phenomena, and in spite of recent scientific research on the possible efficacy of "intercessory prayer,"[1] the academic skeptic always lurked at the back of my mind, ever ready to jump to the front seat.

"But of course, Kyriaco!" Father Maximos replied in earnest, implying that I should have known by then the power of prayer. "That is why holy men, like elder Paisios, constantly pray. Do you think they are fools? Why does that surprise you? Whether people recognize this fact or not, the prayers of saints for the good of the world are extremely valuable and very, very effective."

"God listens to them," Stephanos volunteered from the backseat.

According to the Athonite spiritual tradition, when a human being eradicates personal desires completely and reaches the state of *apathia* [liberation from egotistical passions], they become a "vessel of the Holy Spirit." Then whatever that person wishes is given because it is what God actually wishes. The consciousness of the saint is fully attuned with the spirit of God.

We had just passed by Kalo Chorio (Good Village) surrounded by blooming cherry, apple, and almond trees. After marveling for a few moments at the sights and colors of spring, Father Maximos began narrating the story that I had interrupted with my skeptical question.

"I remember it was the summer of 1977 when I went to spend several days with old Paisios at his hermitage. That period also happened to be the celebration of the Holy Cross. He instructed me that on that night I should join him for the *agrypnia* [all-night vigil] that was to last until sunrise.

"At four o'clock in the afternoon," Father Maximos continued, "he asked me to do vespers with him and practice the Prayer. We first recited the Prayer jointly for a couple of hours, repeating ceaselessly the 'Lord Jesus Christ, Son of God, have mercy on me.' At six o'clock, just after sunset, we had a short break for tea and then returned to our cells, which were really small and narrow. He instructed me that we continue with the Prayer on our own, this time using the *komboschini*. He gave me special instructions on what posture I should maintain during the prayer, on how to breathe while reciting the Prayer, and so on. He was going to call me around one o'clock so that we could read together the liturgy of the Divine Ascension. We would then continue once again with the Prayer until sunrise."

"What a regimen!" I marveled.

"I tried to follow his instructions to the letter," Father Maximos continued, "and while doing that, I heard him pace up and down praying and sighing continuously. It was a frightful experience."

"Frightful?"

"Yes. I was young and afraid to be in the middle of that wilderness with nothing around except darkness, trees, and wild animals. But having elder Paisios pray near me was comforting. He was like a pillar of security for me.

"Every two hours," Father Maximos went on, "he tapped the wall that separated our cells to reassure me that he was there. He wanted to make certain that I stayed focused and awake. There was not much of a wall between the two cells. One could bring it down with a kick. At about one o'clock in the morning we entered his chapel. It was tiny and narrow with five icons at the *iconostasi* and a single *stasidi* [furniture found in Greek churches for standing, leaning for support, and occasionally sitting]. He asked me to remain at the *stasidi* as he positioned himself next to me. I then began reading the service of the Holy Communion. When I reached the verse that reads 'Mary Mother of God Thy Fragrance . . .' the elder responded with the *'Doxa si O Theos emon Doxa si'* [Glory to Thee O God, Glory to Thee] and then the *'Yperagia Theodoke soson emas'* [Most Holy Mother of God Save us]. Every time I recited a verse he made a prostration. So there I stood, holding with the left hand a candle, reading the verses. When the elder repeated the *'Yperagia Theodoke soson emas,'* in a deeply mournful tone, and while I was getting ready to recite *'Maria Meter Theou . . .'* [Mary Mother of God . . .] suddenly and inexplicably everything was transformed around us. Things changed so suddenly and dramatically that I could not figure out what was happening." Father Maximos remained pensive.

"Well?" I probed and gave him a quick side glance.

"Suddenly everything changed," Father Maximos repeated. He implied that extraordinary, wondrous phenomena took place that he could not fully reveal. He did, however, go on to say that "a very subtle wind rushed into the chapel even though the door as well as the window were both firmly shut. The lamp in front of the icon of the Holy Virgin began swinging back and forth by itself. There was a lamp in front of each of the five icons. Only the one hanging in front of the Holy Virgin went on moving back and forth, back and forth."

"Were you afraid?" I asked.

"To tell you the truth," Father Maximos replied, "I was neither afraid nor rejoiced. I simply witnessed those events like an outsider. I just turned with curiosity toward elder Paisios, trying to figure out what was happening. He signaled to me to remain quiet as he knelt down and touched the floor with his forehead, remaining in that posture for some time. I stood there perplexed, holding the candle in my hand while the strange phenomena went on around me. After about half an hour, and while the lamp in front of the icon of the Holy Virgin continued its back and forth motion, I resumed the reading of the service. When I reached the seventh prayer of the blessing of Saint Symeon the lamp gradually stopped swinging. The luminosity that had inexplicably filled the room up to that point vanished and everything went back to normal. Elder Paisios stood up and signaled me to follow him outside for some fresh air. 'What was that all about?' I asked him. 'What?' he replied, pretending not to have a clue of what I was talking about. 'That phenomenon in the chapel. What happened, really?' I asked. 'What did you see?' he asked me again. I told him that I saw the lamp in front of the icon of the Holy Virgin swing back and forth and described everything else that took place. He asked me whether I saw anything else. I said no. 'Oh . . . it was nothing, it was nothing,' he said and waved his hand. 'Don't you know that on the Holy Mountain the *Panagia* [The Most Holy One] goes from monastery to monastery, from cell to cell to find out what we monks are up to? She just passed by here also. She saw two idiots praying and moved the lamp to let us know that she was paying us a visit.' As he finished his sentence he burst out laughing."

"What impressed me about elder Paisios during the brief period that I met with him," I commented, "was his good humor."

"That's who he was. Even such intense experiences could be a cause of laughter for him. Saints, like all other human beings, have their own unique personality characteristics. Some are gregarious and lighthearted like Paisios. Others are somber and introverted. I've known both types. The attainment of sainthood, you see, does not make everybody share identical personalities."

"Human beings are unique and remain unique all the way to *Theosis*," Stephanos commented from the back.

"Always so," Father Maximos added and chuckled as he remembered his first encounter with elder Paisios in September 1976. "I went to see him with two of my classmates while I was still a student at the University of Thessaloniki. We had heard so many rumors about miracles attributed to him that we were very curious to meet him. We expected to find a frightful looking hermit, an extraterrestrial being. Instead, we met a humble and simple-looking old man who cracked one joke after another, making everybody roar with laughter. At one point he took off his shoes and started jumping up and down on his mattress like a clown. It was hilarious but at the same time quite disappointing. I started having doubts about whether he was, in fact, a saint. Most likely, I thought, he was a half-crazed old man."

"He tried to obliterate your preconceptions of him as a saint," Stephanos pointed out.

"Precisely," Father Maximos replied. "But I was not aware at that time of the ways of the saints. I thought he was really mad rather than pretending to be mad. Of course, it wasn't long before I soon realized that old Paisios had hidden within himself all the magnificence of the Grace of the Holy Spirit."

I later learned that there were reliable reports about the extraordinary lives of the early "desert fathers" of Christianity documenting both their miraculous feats as well as their good humor and exuberance. One such report read: "Many accounts of the desert fathers are derived from scholarly churchmen noted for good judgment and critical sense. . . . Reports of the desert monks by men such as these, through their internal consistency and accord with other records of the day, lend plausibility to stories about the holy fathers' transcendence of pain and discomfort, their small intake of food and sleepless vigils, their longevity, serenity, and healing powers, and their contagious exuberance."[2] Such characterizations fit well with the descriptions that Father Maximos painted of elder Paisios and with my own brief experience with this contemporary desert father. "Anyway," Father Maximos continued, "the episode with the swinging lamp was a turning point in our relationship. It cemented it. In reality elder Paisios was deeply moved by that particular episode and since then he confided in me, on many occasions, other extraordinary events from his life."

Father Maximos remained silent for several minutes as we climbed up to a higher elevation, driving through Palechory (Old Village) with its terraces of vineyards, its stone houses, the narrow streets, and the occasional donkey loaded with firewood. He then went on to tell us of another extraordinary experience that elder Paisios shared with him that very night as they sat outside his hermitage after the episode with the lamp. This incident took place after the elder returned from Thessaloniki, where he had some problems with a bishop there, a phenomenon not so uncommon between monks and the established clerical hierarchy.

On a certain night, according to the story, Saint Efymia, a martyr of early Christianity, knocked at the hermit's door. It took some time before elder Paisios was convinced that she was not the devil masquerading as Saint Efymia, but a real saint who materialized at his doorstep in the middle of the night.

"Saint Efymia was also accompanied by the Holy Virgin and John the Evangelist. He hardly had a chance to open the door when all three of them passed through and joined him inside."

"Was he in some kind of an ecstatic state?" I asked, giving Father Maximos an instant glance. I assumed that elder Paisios was experiencing a vision, what transpersonal psychologists would have probably called an "altered state of consciousness," an outcome of his ceaseless prayer and fasting. Father Maximos was emphatic that this was not the case. This was not a subjective experience that had taken place inside his elder's mind. Elder Paisios saw Saint Efymia, John the Evangelist, and the Holy Virgin with his earthly eyes. They materialized in their physical bodies in a manner similar to that in which Jesus had materialized in his physical body when He appeared to Maria Magdalene and the apostles after the Resurrection.

"First the Holy Virgin entered through the door," Father Maximos recounted. "Upon seeing her, the elder knelt down and kissed her hand while She stroked his head. Following the Holy Virgin was John the Evangelist. Elder Paisios knelt down once again and also kissed his hand. Without a word the two walked toward the small chapel while Saint Efymia stayed behind to have a conversation with the elder. For eight continuous hours they discussed all sorts of issues, some related to her personal life and to theology. Old Paisios explained to me that listening to her describe her life was like watching a movie. Every episode of Saint Efymia's life paraded in front of his eyes in every minute detail. After he witnessed the torments that she went through, the elder sighed and wondered how it was possible for a young woman to withstand so much suffering. Her response was: 'Father, for the kingdom of Heaven, that was nothing. Had I known at the time what awaited me in God I would have tolerated infinitely more.'

"That night Saint Efymia helped him resolve his problems with the bishop in Thessaloniki. After she departed, his cell emanated an exquisite fragrance for the next ten days. During that period the elder got no sleep, ate nothing, saw no one, and remained in a state of continuous prayer and contemplation. Elder Paisios was offered a great gift of Grace that night from this saint. From that day on he celebrated with visiting pilgrims yearly on the day designated by the Church for the commemoration of Saint Efymia."

Father Maximos paused for a few seconds as he reflected on the life of elder Paisios. "His entire life was an ongoing revelation of Divine realities. Even though he was in a material body he simultaneously lived among the saints in Heaven."

Had I heard of such stories before I began exploring the world of mystics and healers I would have brushed them aside as figments of a troubled imagination. At best, I would have assumed that elder Paisios's experiences with dead saints, the Holy Virgin, and the like were hallucinations resulting most probably from sleep deprivation and extreme ascetical practices. Thanks to my field research I have learned, however, during the last twenty years, to avoid reaching such rushed conclusions, products of my own rationalistic academic training and imagination. I have learned to maintain a phenomenological attitude and approach in confronting the miraculous. I no longer dismissed reports of extraordinary experiences of others a priori, as nothing more than mere fantasies. Such a negative attitude, I came to understand, could not serve us well in our endeavors to seek a fuller understanding of reality.

In fact, one of the basic forms of training in Athonite spirituality is to learn how to develop *diakrisis* [discernment], to be able to differentiate that which comes from God from that which comes from Satan, who tries to confuse and disorient the soul aspiring for perfection. Elder Paisios's experiences with revered spiritual beings, similar to other stories that I had read or heard about on the life of saints and great prophets, would not fall under the category of hallucinations. Hallucinations are not from God. Individuals who experience hallucinations later come to recognize them as hallucinations. Elder Paisios's visitations were real and concrete happenings, as concrete as his speaking to ordinary pilgrims and visitors. Hallucinations normally involve confusion and sharp distortions of reality and perception. But elder Paisios's experiences, like other such reports, were lucid, orderly, and highly coherent. Hallucinations are furthermore accompanied by anxiety and mental disturbance.[3] That was far from the case with this contemporary anchorite. On the contrary, these extraordinary experiences brought him exquisite feelings of peace and spiritual well-being that had a transformative effect on his life.

I remember the reaction of Professor John Rossner after I narrated such stories from Mount Athos at a conference in Montreal on the interface between science and religion. As the moderator, he stood up and with a strong and authoritative voice he made some poignant observations:

"What you said about miraculous happenings on Mount Athos and other monasteries, of the manifestation of dead saints to the living and so on, is very important," he stated. "This is the kind of thing that early Church and Roman historians, including even the eighteenth-century skeptic Gibbon, have said: That early Christian literature claims that the Christian movement spread not because of teachings and preachings— they were not allowed to do that—but because people had mystical experiences in which the dead saints and martyrs appeared to the living and taught them about the reality of the spiritual world. This of course is not understood by contemporary Christianity very much. These monasteries and places out of the way are like preserves from history, really! And as Kyriacos said, trying to bring forward this spiritual tradition is like bringing up something that is a lost treasure from the bottom of the ocean. . . . These kinds of events are indeed still part of the lives and traditions of contemporary monks and hermits of Eastern Christianity. And we don't know this treasure is there. If you try hard enough you can find it in history books. Our problem is that theologians in the West are not learned enough in history to find it. And they don't recognize that the origins of the Christian movement were spiritistic and shamanistic. And when they come across things like these in places like Mount Athos or in little villages in Russia or Greece, they can't make sense of them. They are incapable of understanding why an old woman is considered a holy woman and the archbishop comes and sits at her feet in the village because she has had experiences of dead saints and angels and consequently becomes a channel of information. They can't realize that that is the way Heaven talks to the living."

There was no trace of doubt in Father Maximos's mind that elder Paisios's experiences were concrete materializations of divine, supersensible realities. I was pleased that he was in the mood to narrate more such vignettes from the life of his late elder.

"One day," he went on, "old Paisios had many guests visiting him. I was not personally present that day but he told me about it. 'I was,' he said, 'very tired and desperate and wondered what kind of a hermit I was anyway. Over one hundred people had passed by that day. I couldn't even do vespers. I didn't even know what saint we were supposed to celebrate the next day. The whole situation was intolerable.' Exhausted, old Paisios retreated to his hermitage not knowing what to do, not knowing how to resolve this dilemma. 'Father Maxime,' he told me once, 'my greatest enemy is my reputation. Woe to the monk who becomes famous. He can never find peace of mind. People will begin to weave all sorts of stories about him that are often not true. Before he knows it, he finds himself entangled in all sorts of situations.' He had become so well known that just about everybody who arrived on Mount Athos wished to meet him. His hermitage became the first stop of their pilgrimage.

"Distraught and feeling desperate," Father Maximos continued, "old Paisios sat down with tears in his eyes. Suddenly, while in that state, he noticed a tall priest standing at the entrance of his cell. The stranger said: 'Greetings, Father!' Old Paisios was surprised and asked his unexpected visitor 'And who are you?' The stranger answered, 'I am the martyr Saint Loukinianos and my name is commemorated by the Church tomorrow. Because you don't remember which saint is celebrated tomorrow I came in person to remind you. I was asked to instruct you not to lose heart. You must continue to offer your services to your fellow human beings in need. It is God's will.'

"The life of elder Paisios," Father Maximos added, "was full of such experiences which he carefully kept secret. Alas to you, however, if he ever confided something to you and by chance you mentioned it to somebody else and he found out about it."

"His fame reached as far as America," I pointed out. I first heard of elder Paisios in 1990 from the Orthodox priest of Bangor, Maine, who referred to him as "the Lion of the Holy Mountain."

Increasingly nostalgic over his apprenticeship with elder Paisios, Father Maximos began narrating another episode from that "golden age" of his monastic career. "I still remember the Christmas of 1981 when I went to join him for the *agrypnia*. As the two of us chatted for a while, during a break, he said to me what a great gift the love of God is and how it resides inside human beings like a burning flame. 'One day,' he said, 'so much grace fell upon me that I couldn't walk. I just knelt down and I was concerned in case somebody saw me and erroneously thought that I was hurt.' The love of Christ was burning with such intensity inside him that he felt as if his bones were melting away like a candle made of bees' wax. Then he said, 'The great love I experienced that day led me to a deep sorrow for the world.'

"It seemed to me," Father Maximos reminisced, "that such experiences turned elder Paisios into a repository of God's Grace. Since then he devoted himself entirely to helping to alleviate the suffering and sorrow of the world."

When I asked Father Maximos whether he felt that elder Paisios was still guiding him, he replied that in fact he was closer to him now than ever before and that he would always have him as his guide. Carried away by his memories, he described to us what took place at the end of his first encounter with elder Paisios while he was still a student at the university.

"We came out of his hermitage and began saying good-bye. When we took turns kissing his hand something extraordinary took place. Everything around us began to emanate an exquisite fragrance. Old Paisios immediately sensed what was happening and urged us to leave at once. He asked us to speed up our pace and not say a word to anybody about what we experienced."

"Why did you have to hurry?" I asked, puzzled.

"Because old Paisios didn't want people to talk about phenomena happening around him. Anyway, not knowing what was going on, we started running toward Karyes, the administrative center of Mount Athos. As we ran we felt intense joy, something beyond description or comprehension. We just couldn't understand how it was possible to have such feelings of utter happiness and bliss. We couldn't understand why everything around us was so filled with that fragrance, the mountains, the air, the rocks, the trees, everything."

"Signs from Heaven," Stephanos mused as we reached the highest elevation after Palechori and began to descend toward Limassol. From that high point we could see the village of Agros on the slope of the opposite mountain, surrounded by terraces covered with vineyards and blooming almond trees. For a moment I felt sentimental about my boyhood, when my father would send me and my sister to relatives to spend a few weeks there during the hot summer months. Agros was my father's village, which he left behind at the age of twelve when my grandfather, unable to support a large family, sent him to Nicosia on foot, sixty miles away—there were no roads to speak of at that time—to begin making a living for himself.

Before we reached Limassol, Father Maximos gave us a few more details from the life of his late elder. "He was born," he went on, "in 1924 at Pharassa, a small town in Asia Minor, that same region of Cappadocia where several of the early fathers of the Church came from. He was baptized by elder Arsenios, the then priest of Pharassa, who was also graced with divine gifts and is considered today as one of the major twentieth-century saints of our church.

"The baptism took place a few days before all the Greeks from that region were forced to leave Asia Minor as a result of population exchanges during the aftermath of the Greco–Turkish War of 1922. An interesting incident took place during the baptismal ceremony," Father Maximos went on to say. "When the time came to give the infant a name, elder Arsenios realized that the infant he held in his arms was extraordinary. He raised the boy high and, seeing with the eyes of his soul, declared that the infant was destined to become a vehicle of God on earth and an instrument of the Holy Spirit. He pronounced, 'He will do what I do and he will become a monk like myself.' "

"Well, he was right on the mark," Stephanos commented from the back.

"To the letter," Father Maximos added.

When Father Maximos told us this story, an unorthodox thought crossed my mind. Does that mean that the infant which Saint Arsenios baptized was the soul of some great saint born at that time for a special divine mission? Does that mean that this incident supports the belief entertained by some early Christian thinkers like Origen (anathematized three hundred years after his death by the established Church under the orders of Emperor Justinian) on the preexistence of souls? And if the infant did not preexist as a soul, given what Saint Arsenios pronounced, does it mean that God discriminates as to who becomes a saint and who an ordinary sinner? Ever since Emperor Justinian denounced such "Origenist" notions, they had become taboo subjects within Christianity. Of course, one could argue that Saint Arsenios, given his spiritual gifts, could see into the future that Father Paisios was destined to become a vehicle of the Spirit and a monk like himself. There is no suggestion in his words that Father Paisios's soul preceded his birth. However, this "mainstream" interpretation left me with great doubts. Where is the absolute fairness of God if an infant who has just been born is already destined by God to become a great saint? As I did not wish to interrupt Father Maximos's flow of reminiscences, I kept those controversial thoughts to myself. I resolved, however, to do some more reading and reflection on this when I returned to Maine.

"Well," Father Maximos continued, "young Paisios began showing his deep piety as he was steadfastly initiated into the mysteries of Christian spirituality. Very early in his life he began to systematically fast and engage in long prayers."

"He must have had these propensities right from infancy, as stated by Saint Arsenios," I suggested.

"Elder Arsenios was graced with the gift of prophecy and could foresee what was going to happen," Father Maximos said. He then went on, "Let me tell you of an episode from elder Paisios's early life. When he was fifteen years old he got into an unusual habit. Each afternoon he would withdraw into a forest near his village and pray for hours, shedding many a tear. Because of his young age and inexperience he was not aware that his tears were the means through which the energy of Divine Grace was working inside him. He just felt this exquisite sweetness when he prayed to the Christ with tears in his eyes. But his parents became deeply concerned. They thought his behavior was abnormal."

"That's not surprising."

"They did try in vain to persuade him to at least cut down on the amount of time he spent alone in the forest. When a cousin from Athens visited the village, his poor parents thought that they had found the opportunity to bring some sense to their son. The cousin told young Paisios that Jesus was a very good man like the ancient philosophers, but still, just a man. Therefore, praying to him was foolish and served no purpose.

"Young Paisios," Father Maximos went on, "was demolished and scandalized. After all, his cousin was from Athens and educated whereas he was just a poor village youngster. With great sorrow he agreed to stay away from the forest. But a couple of months after his cousin left he became restless once again. Inside him the flame of faith in God was burning. He returned to his retreat and resumed his prayers. His soul was craving union with God. Old Paisios told me jokingly, 'Well, I said to myself, it did not matter whether Christ was God or not. At least he was a good man. It just made me happy to pray.' However, the words of his cousin planted doubts in his heart. Then one afternoon something extraordinary happened to him. While praying, he saw Christ in front of him right there in the forest."

"Was it a mystical vision of the Christ?" I asked.

"No. Elder Paisios insisted that it was Christ Himself who literally appeared in front of him. He had a material body and was seen by the elder with his ordinary vision. It was a living experience, just like the experiences he later had with dead saints. In this manifestation Christ held an opened Gospel and what He said to him was spoken verbatim in the way it was written in the Gospel. Addressing him by his first name Christ told him: 'I am the Resurrection and the Life. Whoever believes in Me will not taste death.'

"This direct experience of the Christ," Father Maximos continued, "was as far as I know the first entrance of young Paisios into the realm of supernatural revelations and was a turning point on his path toward monasticism."

Father Maximos then shared with us some more details from the early life of his venerated elder. His formal education remained on the level of elementary schooling which, however, did not prevent him during his eremitic life from writing, like Saint Paul, epistles to his disciples giving them instructions on spiritual matters. After his death these letters and other documents were published.[4] During the Second World War when the Germans invaded Greece he was drafted into the army and served in communications. It was after the war that he abandoned the world and journeyed to Mount Athos to become a monk.

"Once there," Father Maximos continued, "he had a burning desire to meet living saints. So he literally combed Mount Athos in search of God-realized elders."

"Did he find any?" I asked.

"Yes, several," Father Maximos replied. Then he went on to tell us that elder Paisios's most important elder was the Russian hieromonk Tychon, a celebrated saint, an "angelic presence" who attained sainthood while on Mount Athos. Before meeting elder Tychon, however, he traveled to Egypt and lived near the ancient monastery of Saint Catherine at the foothills of Mount Sinai, the place where Moses received the Ten Commandments. His hermitage was an hour away from the monastery.

"He told me," Father Maximos said, "that when he first arrived there he had such a passion for the ascetic life that he brought along with him only a piece of bread and a pair of scissors. He broke the scissors in two, turned them into knives, and used them to carve little crosses and icons that he of-fered to the Bedouins who provided him with the little food he needed. He stayed in the desert all by himself with hardly any human contact or support for two whole years, doing nothing but praying. Then he returned to Mount Athos where he became an apprentice to elder Tychon at the monastery of Stavronikita. Eventually, after elder Tychon's death, he ended up once again living and praying by himself in the hermitage where he spent the re-mainder of his life. That's the place where you met him, Kyriaco."

"I heard stories," I said, "that elder Paisios had a special relationship with wild animals. Is it true?"

Father Maximos nodded and claimed that was the reason why he was not afraid to be alone with elder Paisios at night at his hermitage when all around the area there were wild boars, wolves, and a variety of snakes. He then explained to us elder Paisios's special relationship with the wild king-dom.

"When human beings reach the stage when they become a repository of God's Grace, then animals instinctively recognize that as the state of the first humans prior to the Fall. Friendship is reestablished between humans and the rest of nature. In such a state even wild beasts cannot harm you. Do you see what I mean?" Father Maximos asked, turning toward me.

"I think so," I replied, and speculated on the possible ecological im-plications of what he had just said. Stephanos asked whether the attain-ment of sainthood brings to an end the age-old warfare between humans and nature that has ravaged our planetary environment. Father Maximos replied that in fact that is the prerequisite for ecological survival. The evi-dence he said is the very life of saints like that of elder Paisios.

"We have so many examples of this phenomenon in the biographies of great saints throughout the ages. Some of them even lived in the company of lions without being harmed. I remember the first time I met old Paisios, I naively asked him where he kept the snakes as I had heard all kinds of stories about his love for them. And do you know what he told me?" Father Maximos said laughing. " 'I have them stored right in here,' and he pointed to his heart. 'When you become a confessor,' he added, 'come and I will tell you all about them.' "

"Did you ever see any real snakes?" I asked as we reached the outskirts of Limassol, from where we could see the open sea.

"Actually I did. One day I was terrified to notice a huge snake inside his cell doing acrobatics from a beam. He took it in his hands, placed it outside, and said, 'Now you go. We have guests and you must not disturb them.' One day he welcomed a pilgrim with a reprimand. 'What have I done to you to hurt me so much today?' Everybody was astonished. 'Father, this is the first time that I have ever met you. How could I have done you any harm?' the visitor responded. 'You committed a terrible deed today. You hurt me deeply.' 'But what did I do, Father?' 'You killed my friend.' 'Your friend?' 'Yes, my friend the snake.'

"Do you see what happened? On the way to his hermitage these pilgrims had spotted a snake crossing the road and one of them killed it with a stick. Old Paisios, being graced with the gifts of the Holy Spirit, saw with the eyes of his soul what that pilgrim did."

"He was a clairvoyant," Stephanos pointed out.

"Among many other things," Father Maximos added.

Stories circulated of how, on many an occasion, elder Paisios was seen in two places at the same time, a phenomenon known as "bilocation." He was also reputed to have been able to speak to a group of French pilgrims in their own tongue when he had no knowledge of French, to have healed people from incurable illnesses, and to have miraculously appeared in places of accidents to rescue people. When asked to confirm these rumors, elder Paisios denied everything and claimed that all those miraculous happenings that people attributed to him were in fact performed by the Holy Spirit. He vehemently rejected any credit for himself. Elder Paisios explained that the Holy Spirit would often appropriate his image and perform those miracles that people attributed to him. In fact, all he did was pray ceaselessly and therefore could not have been present where people claimed to have seen him. In his own subjective experience, he said, the episodes that people attributed to him were nothing more than lucid images that appeared within his mind while these events unfolded. But it was the Holy Spirit that performed the miracles by borrowing, as it were, elder Paisios's physiognomy.

Within the Athonite tradition there are innumerable stories of saints actually being teleported instantly to other locations. According to Father Joseph, another elder I met on Mount Athos, when human beings reach a certain state of purification, the Holy Spirit ". . . reveals to them un-known and secret mysteries through supernatural interventions. . . . It re-veals to them the secrets of nature and His kingdom. He heals them from illnesses and transports them instantly to faraway places and shows them various episodes of the past and the future. Above all he helps them out in their spiritual development and elevates them to a life consistent with their true nature."[5]

"Here is another episode with animals that came to my mind," Father Maximos said. "Old Paisios lived for a while near Konitsa, a remote moun-tain village in northern Greece. One day as he left the monastery where he stayed at the time and walked through a wooded area toward the vil-lage, two large bears charged at him. There were bears in that area then. But the moment they reached him they mysteriously froze. He had with him a piece of *antidoron* [a small, sanctified piece of bread ritualistically offered after church services], which he cut in half and gave to the bears. Then he grabbed them by the ears, one on each side, and walked in this manner into town. The villagers couldn't believe their eyes. Then he de-cided to put the bears to work. He loaded them with provisions and, hold-ing them by the ears, guided them back to the monastery to unload."

We stopped our conversation as we entered Limassol. Both Stephanos and Father Maximos were born and raised there and lamented on the rapid growth of the city soon after the Turkish invasion of Cyprus. That was when Limassol replaced occupied Famagusta both as a port and a ma-jor tourist town.

"Father Maxime," I asked. "Before we meet your mother, I have one last question about elder Paisios. Why did he request at his deathbed to be buried at Sourote?" This is the women's monastery right at the edge of Mount Athos.

Father Maximos smiled broadly and pointed out that old Paisios was the elder of that monastery. Throughout his life he had periodically left his hermitage and traveled to Sourote to counsel the nuns that he was deeply fond of. Father Maximos mentioned in a humorous tone that some Athonite monks were scandalized when they heard the news that elder Paisios wanted to be buried at a women's monastery. They wanted him to stay on Mount Athos forever. "But old Paisios was unconventional!"

Father Maximos then mentioned that there are similar stories about other anchorites he knew from his time on Mount Athos. "Remind me," he said as we got out of the car, "to tell you at some other time about elder Porphyrios."

8

aNGels aND DemoNS

The apartment where Father Maximos's mother and stepfather lived was within walking distance from the harbor in a working-class neighborhood of Limassol. This was the place where Father Maximos grew up. We were to stay there for an hour or so before heading toward Lania, our destination. "Tell me, Father Maxime," I asked as we walked up the steps to the third floor where his mother was waiting for us, "how did you end up as a man of God when you grew up with parents who were at that time committed atheists?" Father Maximos laughed, claiming that it was, of course, the result of Providence. "More specifically it was my grandmother who would hold me by the hand as a boy and secretly take me to church to introduce me to the mysteries of the *Ecclesia*."

On several occasions I had the opportunity to talk with Father Maximos's mother, a dynamic and extroverted woman, about her son's early life. Based on those conversations, and from what Stephanos and I gathered by talking to Father Maximos himself, I began to get a glimpse of the abbot's early life.

When he was about three years old, Father Maximos wrapped himself in a black dress belonging to his grandmother and, walking up to a group

of visiting women, friends of his mother, extended his right hand and requested them to kiss it. He confidently declared to them that one day he
was going to become a bishop. That day his stunned mother discovered
that her little boy had constructed an altar in the attic of their apartment.
Using paper icons and incense containers made of tin cans, he, together
with one of his playmates, regularly conducted secret liturgies. His parents
had a fit, threw everything out, and forbade him to ever step into a church.
What made matters particularly painful was the fact that both of his parents were card-carrying communists, especially his father, who was an active member of the party.

As a teenager Father Maximos had to sneak into church with fear in
his heart. One day his father was informed that his son, his only son, was
attending a religious service. Frantically he rushed to church, grabbed his
then thirteen-year-old boy by the ear, and brought him home. He threatened him with further punishment had he continued his flirtation with
the "opiate of the people." Father Maximos's father had hopes that his son
would one day study engineering in England, where relatives lived or, better yet, get a scholarship from the party and study in Russia. He had hopes
of seeing his son become a graduate of Moscow University, thoroughly
schooled in the wisdom of Marx and Lenin, and he fantasized that someday his son would play a part in the ongoing great proletarian revolution.

When Father Maximos's father died in a freak accident, the result of
an unlikely tornado that ravaged Limassol, young Father Maximos began
his regular and relatively unencumbered love affair with religion. It was
the beginning of his monastic career, a career that his mother vigorously
opposed, even going so far as to seek help from the then bishop of Limassol. "Give him a good spanking," he advised her, "and lock him in his
room." When that did not work, she sought the help of the school principal, who urged her to have her son evaluated by a psychiatrist. Eventually,
however, she learned to accept it.

When Father Maximos returned to Cyprus as a monk and was appointed abbot of the Panagia monastery, his mother and her women
friends became his regular patrons. They followed the crowds for confession and communion, kissing the hand of the abbot in accordance with established custom. The old icons of Marx and Lenin that had decorated his
mother's living room were tossed away and replaced by those of the Holy
Virgin, Jesus, and a score of patron saints.

"One day I went to see the members of the party," his mother told me
once. "They were all friends of my late husband and had known my son
as a boy. I asked them why they were so much against Father Maximos,
writing nasty articles in their paper about him. They were surprised. 'And
why do you care?' they asked me with blank faces. 'Do you know who he

is?' I asked them. When they learned that Father Maximos was in fact 'Andrikos'—that's how they knew my son as a boy—they were shocked. They promised to stop their editorials against him. But I vowed there and then never to vote for them again."

We stayed at the apartment close to an hour as planned, chatting with Father Maximos's mother and stepfather and looking at some old photos. Later we were joined by his sister, who lived next door. They were all so proud of him. Father Maximos related to his immediate family with humor and laughter as they reminisced about the past. To be with them was a real break from his more serious mission and responsibilities. Then, after his mother gave us packages of pastries that she baked for the monks, we resumed our journey to Lania to attend the town meeting.

The village was about forty-five minutes north of Limassol at a higher elevation, halfway between the coastal city and the summit of the Troodos Mountains. It was a clear day, and as we drove up the mountains we could see on our left the Akrotiri Peninsula with its salt lake in the middle. Like a shoe protruding into the Mediterranean Sea from the underbelly of the island, Akrotiri is part of the British sovereign bases set up in 1960 as a result of the agreements that turned the former colony into an independent republic. Not far from Akrotiri we could see the village of Kolossi surrounded by orange groves and vineyards, a stopover for tourists thanks to its medieval castle. That was the place, it is said, that in 1191, King Richard the Lionheart spent his wedding night with his betrothed Berengaria on a return journey from the Crusades. The island was ruled at that time by a petty Byzantine tyrant who held the English king's future wife hostage when the ship carrying her was marooned in Limassol due to bad weather. According to the chronicles King Richard roared like a lion with anger when he learned about it. With a few hundred archers he took over Cyprus, placed Isaakios Komnenos, the Byzantine governor, in chains, and married his queen at the Kolossi castle. Not being particularly interested in holding Cyprus, he handed it over to the Knights Templars. It was they who imported to the island the institutions of European feudalism which lasted until the fall of Cyprus to the Ottoman Turks in the sixteenth century. It is said that before leaving the island King Richard sampled Cypriot grapes and pronounced one type to be "very good." Since then the islanders have called it verygo. The Lionheart's adventures in Cyprus were the beginning of a romance between England and Cyprus, so much so that Shakespeare made it the setting for his Othello at another medieval Cypriot castle, an imposing structure now part of Turkish-occupied Famagusta, Emily's hometown, the only abandoned and barbed-wired city in the world.

A small crowd was waiting for us at Lania, the mountain tourist town with its traditional coffee shops and narrow cobblestone streets. I saw surprise in Father Maximos's face when someone began ringing the church bell as he approached the church and women carrying rose water sprinkled him, throwing rose petals over his head as he entered the church. After a short prayer service, the local priest welcomed Father Maximos with a flamboyant but mercifully short speech. It was an honor and a blessing, he said, to have a monk from Mount Athos of Father Maximos's reputation visit them. Father Maximos was then shown the ancient icon that was recently discovered near their village. He made a long prostration, crossed himself, and kissed it. Before leaving the church he suggested to the local priest that he place an oil lamp in front of the icon and keep it always lit. "Saints," he reminded them, "like to have a lamp lit in front of their icon." We were then escorted into a local coffee shop for refreshments and to talk business.

The townspeople wished to recreate the monastery that in centuries past used to be at the very spot where the icon was discovered. That was also the reason why Father Kallinikos had been brought over from Mount Athos to be the new abbot. Father Kallinikos, a monk in his early sixties, was once a successful architect who at some point in his career decided to abandon the world and enter Mount Athos in search of God. He and Father Maximos were old acquaintances and delighted to meet each other again.

Father Maximos, however, had other ideas about what kind of monastery should be created at Lania. After listening to details of how the icon was discovered and how they decided as a town to collect several thousand pounds as "seed" money to start construction, Father Maximos suggested that it might be good to visit the place for an on-the-spot inspection. It was about fifteen minutes by car through a dirt road up the mountain from the center of the village.

When we reached the plateau at the top of the mountain where a small chapel overlooked the village, Father Maximos walked about the grounds and asked questions about who owned the surrounding vineyards. He then delivered a pep talk to the thirty or so townspeople present. After congratulating them for their work and initiative, he proceeded to elaborate on the value of having a monastery not far from the village. He told them about the spiritual benefits to the villagers, that a monastery radiates positive, angelic energies that cover the entire area and that it provides an opportunity for local people to engage in spiritual work themselves. This, he said, is what usually happens when monasteries, usually built in remote areas, are created near villages or towns. It is like building a spiritual university so people may learn experientially the reality of God. "But in addition to the obvious spiritual benefits," Father Maximos told the small crowd of men and women, "a monastery will bring other rewards to the area, both cultural and economic. It will become a center of pilgrimage for large numbers of people." There were looks of satisfaction on all the faces as Father Maximos said those words.

But," he said further, "this place is better suited for a women's monastery."

I noticed the faces of the men around us dropping. Father Maximos took a deep breath, let some of the men express their disagreement, and then went on to convince them that indeed a women's monastery next to their village was a more viable option. It is better, Father Maximos explained to us later, for a women's monastery to be near a village to give them protection from possible intruders and help from the villagers for some heavy chores that traditionally have been allotted to men, like plowing the fields and taking care of plumbing. As for Father Kallinikos, Father Maximos had plans for him to become the abbot of another abandoned monastery at Mesa Potamos (Inner River), a remote and isolated region deep in the woods of the Troodos Mountains. A wealthy and devout Cypriot had pledged seven million dollars to rebuild that abandoned monastery.

Before we left, Father Maximos promised the mayor and his councillors that by the following spring they would be able to have their monastery. "All you need to do," he told them, "is set up a few cells for four or five nuns. There is already a chapel so an architect can draft the architectural plans for a more permanent structure in no time. Once people see the physical setup of the monastery and the architectural plans, they will then contribute generously. That's how it usually works." Father Maximos was speaking from experience.

"Where are we going to find the nuns?" asked the mayor.

"Don't worry about that. That's my job. I'll help you find them," Father Maximos reassured him.

When we got into the car for our trip back to the Panagia monastery after waving goodbye to the villagers, I turned to Father Maximos and murmured, "Now I know why some parents are after you." At that Stephanos, who sat in the back and was mostly quiet during our adventure at Lania, burst out in uncontrollable laughter.

The following morning Stephanos and I, at the invitation of Father Maximos, entered his office to resume a discussion that we had started the day before upon our return from Lania. It was about demons and angels and how in the lives of Athonite monks these forces are taken for granted and experienced as reality, not hallucinations.

The topic had presented itself to us, so to speak, when Father Maximos mentioned the name of elder Porphyrios, the late charismatic elder and extraordinary wonder-worker who had been an Athonite monk before leaving the Holy Mountain to serve as a priest in a community outside Athens. The discussion on demons and angels was triggered when I asked him specific questions about Porphyrios's life. As Father Maximos had known elder Porphyrios personally, he began narrating an episode from the life of this wonder-worker.

"A hieromonk and a good friend of mine from Mount Athos," Father Maximos began, "was attacked one night by a demon while he was praying. The demon grabbed him by the neck, trying to strangle him. They wrestled on the ground and before he was able to disentangle himself the demon struck him with his fist right here on his chest." Father Maximos pointed with a clenched fist at the center of his chest.

"My friend experienced extreme pain at the chest but he thought that was all. Neither old Porphyrios nor my friend knew of each other. They had no relationship whatsoever. Furthermore, my friend didn't tell others of his experience. You can imagine his surprise then when, very early the following morning, he got a long-distance call from old Porphyrios. 'You managed well with him last night, Father,' old Porphyrios said. 'However, the punch he gave you caused some damage to the upper part of your lungs. You must have a doctor take care of it.' And that's precisely what he did. He visited a doctor in Thessaloniki and had his lungs checked. They found a problem with the upper part of the lungs, exactly where old Porphyrios had pointed out to him. How did he know?"

"Father Maxime," I asked, "why did the demon attack your friend in such a physical manner?"

"Perhaps because he was reciting the Prayer with his *komboschini.*"

"I don't get it. Does that mean that the closer you come to God through prayer, the more likely it is for a demon to attack you?" I promptly reacted.

"Look. All of these matter unfold within the Providence of God. They can be seen as spiritual exercises. Such episodes take place in order for us to realize that we are dealing with an existent entity. We are not dealing with evil in the abstract, as many people assume. How should I explain it to you?" Father Maximos said and spread his hands out.

"Should we assume that a demon is like a person?" Stephanos asked.

"No, not a person. Only God is a Person. Yet, a demon, though not a person, is also not evil in the abstract. It is a fallen angel, an existent entity that is a real objective force that can cause mischief," Father Maximos emphasized. "Monks who are novices are targets of attacks. This usually happens within the first month of their monastic life. It happened to me. When I was a novice, one used to come and grab me by the neck. Then I would run to old Paisios for advice. He instructed me not to be afraid of him and not to answer him when he talked to me, for the demon used to scream and scare me with death threats. He talked endlessly and promised to slaughter me like a lamb." Father Maximos laughed as he reminisced about the incident. "One time old Paisios gave Satan such a strong punch in the face that he felt sorry for him. That day he did not take communion, believe it or not, because he felt remorse for Satan, who moaned with pain after he was hit by old Paisios. 'The poor fellow!' he said."

"It seems to me that a demon is rather weak to do any permanent damage," Stephanos pointed out after we calmed down from laughter.

"Not necessarily," Father Maximos replied. "Demons can cause serious problems to people."

"You mean to monks," I interjected.

"No, not just to monks. Only a few days ago we had such a problem in a tourist village here in Cyprus. A Russian couple in their early twenties were literally grabbed by a demonic force and thrown out of their house. So far it has happened twice to them even though they have no relationship with either the Church or with monastic life. They were neither believers in God nor in the devil. Yet they had experienced this demonic attack, not in their dreams and fantasies but in their fully awakened state. It was a shattering experience for them."

Father Maximos argued that it is dangerous to demythologize the demonic by considering it as nothing more than a creation of people's imagination, or as bad energy. He insisted that demons are something real. "An episode comes to my mind from the life of elder Joseph the *Hesychast* [practitioner of quietude]," Father Maximos went on to say. "He lived as a hermit in a cave on Mount Athos. One day he was visited by a friend and his companion. He only had two very small rooms with two beds. The elder decided to offer his own bed to his friend and the other room to the other pilgrim. He chose the outdoors for himself and planned to hold an *agrypnia*. So while his friend slept on the bed, elder Joseph spent all night long praying outside. Unfortunately, demons attacked the hermitage during the night and clobbered his friend. By morning he was covered with bruises. When the elder returned and saw what had happened he tried to calm his guest. 'Don't be afraid,' he told him. "That beating was intended for me, but the demons were confused and mistook you for me." Father Maximos laughed as he finished his story. "Sometimes these matters are quite entertaining." Then in a more serious tone he went on to add that in the final analysis Satan has no power over us, and that the only way he can cause problems is when we show fear. The best tactic is to ignore him.

I pointed out that stories about demonic attacks go contrary to modern ways of thinking. It is difficult for contemporary, educated people to believe in the reality of demons. Father Maximos responded that the biggest success of Satan was to convince everybody that he does not exist. But those experienced with spiritual work are very much aware of his existence and the mischief he constantly creates everywhere.

I remember how difficult it was for Emily to accept such a notion, which she considered a primitive way of looking at evil. In one of our debates, as we walked by the banks of the Stillwater River which flows in front of our house, I asked her whether she believed in the reality of energy. Naturally, she replied. After all, her doctoral dissertation was on Maine healers and "energetic therapies." I then asked her, "Do you accept the reality of positive and negative energy? For if you accept that, can you also accept that such negative energies can be shaped within a form compatible with our cultural beliefs, mythologies, and preconceptions?" Emily's response was: "If you put it this way it becomes easier for me to consider. Just don't call it Satan!"

The reality or nonreality of demons and angels may in fact be an empirical question that should interest not only theologians but also scientists. To make my point clearer I brought home a report from the *New York Times* about what happened to a French village. I read to her:

> An exorcist has been called in to rid the Delain village church of devils, which he said had sent candlesticks flying, forcing ecclesiastical authorities to close the building until further notice. . . . Witnesses said . . . that a candle went flying, splitting in two, and that statuettes and vases were broken inexplicably. Also the altar was moved by four inches, apparently unaided. The Mayor of Delain, Thierry Marceaux, said, "There was no collective hallucination, or 50 people will have to be sent to the lunatic asylum." . . . The Roman Catholic Church, like many Christian churches, teaches that the Devil is real and evil spirits exist. But modern theologians have been playing down Satan's influence as they have accepted psychological and psychiatric explanations of abnormal behavior.[1]

I told Emily that one would think that scientists would rush to that village to study the phenomenon. But who would risk their reputation to investigate such a report? It is safer to either ignore it or assume that such phenomena are simply unreal and unworthy of scientific exploration. But what if they are real? Does that mean that what Father Maximos says and what the Church teaches about the reality of angels and demons is based on empirical fact and not just on the outcome of a mythological representation of good and evil?

I asked Father Maximos whether "evil energies" can acquire concrete form and materialize within the context of our cultural preconceptions on the basis of what we subjectively imagine this energy to look like.

"It is true," he answered, "that early Christians in Europe thought of the devil as a black satyr with horns and tails, whereas Christians in Africa painted the devil as white in their iconographies. Yet, it is not exactly as simple as that," he went on as I noticed some hesitation in his voice.

"But doesn't our culture provide the image, or the parameters if you will, of how this evil energy or force is perceived by our minds?" I persisted.

"But Kyriaco, this entity does not have a stable image. Satan changes his image continuously in order to scare and deceive us."

Father Maximos's response brought to my mind the experiences of Jesus in the desert and how Satan tried to disorient Him. Similarly I thought of the legions of demons that attempted to distract the Buddha's concentration as he sat under the Bodhi Tree seeking enlightenment.

"What I meant to say," I tried to clarify my point, "is that our own cultural beliefs determine how Satan appears to us."

"Fine. But keep in mind that Satan, although not a person, is a real entity who, for purposes of deception, does not maintain a stable image. When he appears to human beings in ways that he can be seen, he constantly metamorphoses his appearance. This is one of the signs that we can use in determining whether a vision that we observe comes from God or from the devil. Things that are from God do not change in form or appearance for the purpose of spreading fear or confusion in us. When for example a saint, or Christ, or the Holy Virgin appears to you, their form remains stable while they present themselves to you. Do you remember how old Paisios held a conversation with Saint Efymia for eight hours? She never changed her image while she was with the elder. Satan's appearance on the other hand constantly shifts. He never keeps a stable form because his goal is to confuse and deceive you."

Father Maximos then went on to illustrate this point by narrating the case of a young man who had visions of Christ. However, with further spiritual counseling it turned out that the "Christ" he was in contact with was in fact a demonic force masquerading as Christ, causing him much confusion and grief.

I went on to raise the question that if Satan is so clever, wouldn't he know that his image-changing gives him away? Wouldn't he maintain only one form to confuse us more? Father Maximos nodded but went on to say that Satan's aim is to confuse us in any way possible. That is why we need a spiritual guide to help us through such difficulties. However, on the basis of his own experience and from what he learned from his elders, Satan behaves in ways that he outlined earlier, by shifting his image in order to confuse and disorient.

As Father Maximos completed his story, a monk entered the room, made a prostration, and informed his elder that the architect for some planned renovations at the entrance of the monastery was waiting for him at the *archondariki*. "Please tell him that I'll be there shortly," Father Maximos said, not wishing to terminate our conversation.

"Father Maxime," Stephanos asked. "Do you think there are locations that are charged with demonic energy?"

"Absolutely. I realized this fact two months after my ordination." Father Maximos paused for a few seconds, then he proceeded. "I was twenty-three years old when I temporarily left Mount Athos for Thessaloniki. I used to do a lot of walking, fast-paced walking. I kept my gaze on the pavement, watching the feet of other pedestrians so I would not crush them while reciting the Prayer.

"I remember one day," Father Maximos continued, "I had to stop at a red light. As I approached that intersection, waiting for the light to change, I literally felt engulfed by a very bad sort of energy, a demonic energy. I didn't know what it was. I turned around and noticed it was coming out of a basement that was used as a nightclub. I got these chills that one usually gets when such presences are around. And I was certain that the rush of bad energy was coming out of that basement."

"Maybe it was a place for drugs and prostitution," Stephanos suggested.

"Maybe. Whenever sins are committed in a particular location, the space around it is charged with demonic energy. And this demonic energy has an effect on people who spend time there. It is very important to keep this in mind," Father Maximos warned. "That is why churches are decorated with icons. They radiate angelic energy which has a positive effect on us."

"Is it possible, Father Maxime, to transform a place that is charged with negative energy?" Stephanos asked again.

"Of course! Didn't we do that on the boat to Patmos?" Father Maximos was alluding to the pilgrimage of the previous summer to the famous Aegean island where John the Evangelist is believed to have written the Apocalypse. The boat was chartered exclusively for the three-day voyage, and seven hundred disciples of Father Maximos were on that boat, including Stephanos and Erato. Alas, my good friend Stephanos, being of fragile constitution, suffered a minor "apocalypse" of his own. He was severely seasick all the way to Patmos and all the way back to Cyprus.

"The moment we carried out the *agiasmos* [ritual of sanctification], the dance hall on the boat, which was earlier used for cabaret shows and drunken parties, was transformed into the Holy Mountain. We brought icons of Christ and the Holy Virgin. We placed them there, creating an altar, and we carried the liturgy. Automatically that space was sanctified, transformed from a nightclub into a holy church. Everybody felt it."

"Except me," Stephanos quipped.

"Can spaces that have been sanctified sustain this angelic energy?" I asked. "I assume that repetitive rituals of sanctification will increase this effect, as in churches and temples."

"Yes, exactly," Father Maximos nodded. "This is particularly the case with spaces devoted to God. These places become known as a result of the healing miracles that take place there. Even in those places where the actual church is no longer in existence, the effect can be felt years, even decades, later. There are plenty of examples here in Cyprus, even in Turkey. As you know, during Byzantine times Asia Minor [present-day Turkey] was full of Christian churches and monasteries. Cappadocia, the country of Basil the Great and elder Paisios, was noted for its hermitages covered with wall paintings of saints and caves where saints spent their earthly lives. Even today, Muslim Turks in this area of Cappadocia claim to have witnessed extraordinary phenomena. In fact, several years ago an elder from Mount Athos visited the town in Cappadocia where he had lived as a child. While there he searched for the place where the village church was once located. Sadly, he discovered that the church, devoted to Saint John the Baptist, was torn down. The elder sighed and murmured, 'Oh, dear Forerunner [John the Baptist], we left and you left with us.'

"There were several Turks present who escorted them. One of them knew some Greek and overheard what the elder said. 'No that is not true,' he said. 'You left but he stayed. Every year during August we hear bells ringing and chants and we smell the church incense.'

"These phenomena are not fantasies or hallucinations. They are real," Father Maximos insisted. "The lives of saints are filled with such extraordinary episodes. That means that it is possible for a physical place to disappear, but angelic energies in the form of a guardian angel of a particular church or monastery may continue to exist."

"I have a question, Father Maxime," Stephanos interjected. "Does a demon physically assault you due to the fact that he was unsuccessful in damaging you spiritually? I gather from everything I hear that in order for a demon to harm you, he has to attack you spiritually. It is only when he fails on the spiritual level that he attacks you on the physical plane."

"Yes, that is true," Father Maximos replied but with a certain hesitation. "However, one should be very careful not to rush to conclusions about such phenomena. It is not a sign of virtue to see a demon and suffer an attack. An experience of this sort may deceive you. You may begin to fantasize that you are holy. You can say to yourself, 'Oh, if I have been attacked and have wrestled with demons I must have reached heights of spiritual attainment.' This is not necessarily the case."

In fact, Father Maximos himself had suffered such attacks. He confided to Stephanos that some time back a demon had tried to chew a piece off his leg, leaving behind some scars. During another incident a demon allegedly pushed him down the stairs. Such purported incidents seem to be quite common among circles of Athonite monks and hermits.

"Magicians," Father Maximos went on to say, "can have similar experiences, such as seeing demons, wrestling with demons, and so on. If these magicians induce demons to do certain things for them but they fail, then the demons turn against those who summoned them. So it is not necessarily a sign of virtue to wrestle with demons.

"You know," Father Maximos continued, "this issue about Satan is not a trivial matter, I mean one that can easily be dismissed. You cannot understand authentic spirituality unless you become aware of the way Satan works. As I said earlier, he is not just evil in the abstract. Satan hates God. He is dominated by a single passion, the passion for destruction. The more people follow him, the more he increases his hell, making it virtually impossible to save himself."

"Is it possible, Father Maxime," Stephanos asked again, "for a human being to hate God with the intensity of Satan?"

"Oh yes! Definitely. I have known such persons myself. I have known people, even young people, who love Satan, believe it or not. They feel erotically attracted to Satan and even pray to him. A young fellow from Thessaloniki, an otherwise nice fellow actually, who was a devil worshiper came to see me. He asked me, 'Who has more power, God or Lucifer? Who is the ruler of this world? Definitely not God.'

" 'Let me see how you react if I read some prayers for you,' I challenged him. I was really surprised when he actually knelt in front of me. I then began reading extracts from Saint John Chrysostom's book of prayers against demons. The moment I began reading he collapsed with spasms, foam coming out of his mouth. I was really afraid and began trembling since I hadn't done such an exorcism for a number of years. I was trembling so much that I couldn't even focus on the book. There were three other people present, one of them a doctor. 'Keep reading, Father,' he implored me, 'keep reading.' "

I suggested that perhaps the man suffered from epilepsy, but Father Maximos insisted that the incident was clearly not a case of epilepsy, but demonic possession. He went on, "After that experience, I persuaded this fellow to come to confession and then I made him do penances so the evil spirit would leave him. I asked him to chant every night a *troparion* devoted to Archangel Michael that says, '*Opou episkiase e charis sou Archangele ekeithen tou diavolou diokete dynamis. . . .*' [Wherever your grace is spread, Oh Archangel, it drives out the power of Satan. . . .] Archangel Michael is superior and has power over Satan.

"It was a real struggle to attend to that fellow and to heal him from demonic possession. I instructed him to practice the Prayer, 'Lord Jesus Christ, Son of God, have mercy on me,' but he could not mention the name of Christ. He would get stuck on the 'Lord. . . .' and wouldn't go any further. He complained, 'Father, I can't. I feel burned.' "

"So what happened to him?" I asked.

"He is okay now. He finally got healed. He is a student at the University of Athens."

"He must have gotten involved with satanism," Stephanos speculated.

"Naturally. Such problems don't happen out of the blue. He once said to me, 'You know I have such a strong urge to grab a priest, cut his tongue, and take his eyes out.' It was his obsession to slaughter a priest," Father Maximos said laughing.

"Perhaps a lot of inexplicable horror crimes that we read in the papers may be due to such experiences," I suggested.

"That's what they are," Father Maximos replied. "You know, by temperament I was skeptical about such stories myself. But I had to change my mind when I began hearing about these matters during confessions of people who were under the spell of demonic energies. As a rule they faced such problems because of their involvement with black magic."

"How often do you hear of such cases?" I asked.

"Four times since coming to Cyprus," Father Maximos replied, bringing forward four fingers of his right hand. "You can't imagine the stuff they told me! The last one who came for confession was sent to me by old Paisios, just before he died. This fellow went to Mount Athos for help after the spirits he was summoning to carry out magic went out of control and started attacking him. He had a reputation in Greece of being a very effective and powerful medium. He learned his trade when he got involved with a Brazilian cult.

"As a young man," Father Maximos explained, "he was a sailor in the Greek merchant marine. On a trip to Brazil he met some people who got him involved with sorcery. One night he took part in one of those frenzied dances and became intoxicated. After staying in Brazil for several years during which he learned these black arts, he returned to Greece and set up shop in a town near Thessaloniki. He was very successful. Every night he used to read from magical texts and invoke spirits to do things for his customers. But at some point he lost control and the spirits, demons in reality, turned against him. One day he decided to have communion but without first confessing his involvement with these spirits. The moment he took holy communion he collapsed with paroxysms, foam coming out of his mouth. It was after this episode that old Paisios sent him to Cyprus so that we might try to help him out."

"Father Maxime," Stephanos asked, "is it possible for a person like him to summon demons that can heal people?"

"Yes, sometimes it is possible. It is not always easy to recognize when something comes from God or from Satan. As Saint Paul wrote, Satan can transform himself into an angel of light. As I said, one of the properties of the evil spirit is its incredible capacity to deceive. Being the spirit of deception it can mimic what the Grace of God can do. So, inexperienced and naive people can easily be fooled."

I pointed out that it was very difficult for me to accept that an evil spirit can perform genuine healing phenomena since, by definition, healing must come from God. Father Maximos explained that these are mysteries beyond our comprehension and that naturally everything is within Divine Providence. They could happen to give us lessons that we may need to learn.

"Unfortunately," he continued, "in these troubled times we see plenty of examples of naive people being deceived by self-proclaimed saints and wonder-workers who, with the help of demonic spirits, cause phenomena to happen that impress the gullible. The devil too is capable of miracles, you see. Just yesterday afternoon three young men from Limassol came to the monastery with someone whom they considered a living saint. These fellows wished to introduce me to this man from Eastern Europe who, they claimed, healed the sick and performed miracles. I knew intuitively that it was a fraudulent case but I said nothing until I met him. Frankly, I had never seen the likes of such a saint before. There were golden chains hanging from his wrists, he wore earrings, necklaces with all kinds of occult symbols, and the like. He also wore a very shiny blue shirt, may God forgive me for speaking like that. I challenged 'his holiness.' 'Are you the one who does miracles and is considered to be a saint?' I asked him. 'Yes, I am,' he replied.

"What shocked me," Father Maximos went on, "is how educated people like those young men, who studied in American universities, could become so easily duped by such an impostor. When I started to question his sainthood, he became irritated. Then when I pointed out that saints don't behave like that, he really became upset and walked out of the room. The spirit of deception, you see," Father Maximos explained, "has egotism and pride as its primary attribute."

"Saints will never call themselves saints," Stephanos pointed out.

"They wouldn't be saints if they did. Compare that case with the life of Saint Simeon the Stylitis. When he decided to practice asceticism he climbed up on a marble pole and spent his time there praying by himself. The elders wondered whether his bizarre behavior was of God or of Satan. It never happened before that a hermit would climb up on a pole and sit there as a form of *askesis*. They were in a dilemma. If his action was indeed the result of an inspiration from God, to demand of him to step down from his column would be to prevent him from carrying out his spiritual exercise in reaching God. They held a meeting to decide what to do. They concluded that in order to test whether his behavior was of God or not they would go under the pole and begin to provoke him, urging him to come down. They would accuse him of being deceived by the devil and that's why he chose to sit on that pole like a lunatic pretending to be a saint. Based on his reaction they would then decide whether his strange behavior was inspired by God or not. When the elders assembled at the base of the pole and started yelling at him he immediately climbed down, made a prostration in front of them, and asked for forgiveness. Witnessing his humility, the elders then instructed him to climb back to his pole and continue his ascetic practice. They concluded that his action was not inspired by the spirit of deception.

"The foremost attribute of saintliness is humility," Father Maximos repeated as he leaned back in his chair. "People who are boastful, who are incapable of accepting any personal criticism, cannot be saints."

"Those who question their own sainthood are the saints themselves," Stephanos pointed out.

"Absolutely. People who claim that they are saints are into delusion. They have been under the influence of the spirit of deception, not of God. This is a sign that we must always keep in mind. By merely allowing the thought to come into our mind that we may be holy, this is a clear indication of delusion."

Father Maximos then went on to say how surprised he was to learn that there were so many people today that become victims of such charlatans. The most troublesome development, he mentioned, was the fact that many people considered him some kind of a magician. "They come here at the monastery to find out whether someone cast a spell on them, why they were abandoned by their lover or their husband and so on. At first I couldn't figure out why they would come to me with such problems. Then I realized that they thought of me as some kind of a sorcerer capable of undoing spells." Father Maximos shook his head and chuckled in his characteristic way.

"What do you tell them in such cases?" I asked.

"What do you think? I tell them that there is no magic to resolve their problems, that they need to do spiritual work. I tell them that if they have a problem with demonic energies then they can follow the prescriptions of the *Ecclesia* to heal themselves: confession, participation in the mysteries, fasting, charity, prayer, and *askesis* in general. That's the way to do it."

"So, there you are. You offer them a recipe on how to cast out the spell," I pointed out in a light tone. "But are they receptive?"

"Hardly. Most people crave a quick fix. They are too lazy or unwilling to invest any effort of their own. They assume that if I read some magic formula over their heads, their problems will disappear. No need for them to change their ways. No need for them to engage in systematic prayer and *askesis*. Of course, some do follow the therapeutic guidelines of the *Ecclesia* and see results."

Once more we were interrupted by a knock at the door, and a monk reminded Father Maximos that the architect was still waiting in the *ar-*

chondariki. Father Maximos excused himself and asked us to remain there since the business he had with the architect was to be brief. The plans had already been laid out for the creation of a library and a museum for rare artifacts saved in the monastery for hundreds of years. The project, which was to cost over two hundred thousand dollars, was the gift of a well-known businessman and philanthropist.

For the next half hour I chatted with Stephanos. We walked outside and enjoyed the sun as we waited for Father Maximos's return. When he completed his errands and came back to the office, our conversation shifted to guardian angels, a theme which, like demons, is at the heart of Athonite spirituality.

"It is a given in our religion that there are spirits sent by God to do His work. These benign spirits accompany us in this world, protect us, and offer us support. They are spirit guides. And, according to God's revelation in the Bible, not only do human beings have their own guardian angel but nations have them, too."

"Nations?"

"Yes, of course. For example, in the Old Testament prophet Daniel learned from God that the nation of the Persians had their guardian angel just as the Hebrews had their own. Not only does every nation have them, but also every city, every town, every locale, and particularly every temple devoted to the worship of God."

"So, there is no nation on earth which is not being looked after by God," I pointed out.

"If that were not the case, then God would not be God."

"The reality of angels is confirmed also through the experiences of saints throughout the Christian movement," Stephanos pointed out.

"And through ordinary people," I added. "In America, fascination with angels and reported encounters with angels has become a national pastime."

"Angels are omnipresent," Father Maximos claimed with an air of certainty that characterized him when speaking about spiritual matters. "Many elders and saints of the *Ecclesia* reach the spiritual stage whereby they are able not only to sense the presence of their guardian angels but also to see them and have conversations with them. I read about the life of a saint who was so familiar with his guardian angel that whenever he would enter a house he would let his guardian angel go first. I don't know if anyone of you has read about the life of Father Iacovos," Father Maximos asked. Neither Stephanos nor I had heard of him. "Well, he was a humble priest from the island of Ebvia who had the innocence of a child and talked openly about his experiences. One day as he was conducting the liturgy, the eyes of his soul opened up and realized that the sanctuary was packed with angels. It was so packed that he felt there wasn't enough space for him to move about. He gently asked them to make some room so that he could conduct the liturgy." Then Father Maximos went on to tell us more anecdotes about angels that were related to the life of this contemporary saint. He mentioned that it is possible for Christians to become accustomed to the presence of angels and suggested that it is prudent and spiritually beneficial to make conscious contact with one's guardian angel through prayer and *askesis*.

"Our guardian angels will be present," Father Maximos went on to say, "during the time when our souls will exit this world and abandon the material body. They will be there at that moment to offer us solace and support during that difficult transition and then help us adjust to the realms of the spirits when our soul will be directed toward God. It will be at that point that the soul will become conscious of its eternal condition.

"The *Ecclesia*," Father Maximos said further, "recognizing the reality of angels through the witness of the saints and the teachings of the scriptures, incorporated into its liturgy special prayers and invocations to summon these spirits for the benefit of our souls. You will notice that during the liturgy the priest recites, among other prayers, *Angelon erenes piston odygon fylaka ton psychon kai ton somaton ymon para tou Kyriou etisometha*. In other words, we are asking God to send us an angel of peace to guide us and be a guardian of our souls and bodies."

"I assume," I interjected, "that whether an angel is ready to assist us or not depends on our own receptivity."

"That goes without saying," Father Maximos replied. "There are angels and there are demons. The activation of both is dependent upon our own cooperation. It is the same with the Grace of God. When a human being is ready to cooperate with God, then the Holy Spirit penetrates the heart and sanctifies that person. Likewise, when a person rejects God and cooperates with Satan, then such a person becomes his instrument and demonic energies penetrate the person's heart like poison.

"You may have noticed," he continued, "that during the baptismal ritual and before the immersion into the sanctified water we read many prayers over the head of the infant or the adult to be baptized. The priest blesses and seals the person who is being baptized with the symbol of the holy cross so that he or she may be able to overcome the satanic energies. The priest asks the person to repeat three times that he refuses the works and worship of Satan and is then asked to symbolically spit on Satan three times. This act is followed by a declaration that from then on the baptized person will follow Christ and the teachings of the *Ecclesia*. In the case of an infant, it is the Godparent who performs this ritual.

"The act of crossing oneself is basic to the ritual of baptism," Father Maximos explained. "You must realize that the symbol of the Cross is the par excellence most potent weapon against satanic energies. I have been a monk for nearly twenty years and I can testify that, based on my relatively short experience, I have been time and again a witness to the awesome power of the Cross."

I asked him whether he could tell us of a case during which he witnessed such power. Father Maximos replied that he had many stories, but the one that came to mind was the following:

"It happened one Sunday after the liturgy at a church in Thessaloniki. I was in town that day to carry out some errands for our monastery. Nobody knew me in that church. I just went there on that particular Sunday. I was to complete my errands the following day and head back to Mount Athos. I was in the sanctuary helping the priest put things in order when I heard a lot of commotion in the middle of the church. There were many people around a woman who was completely out of herself. She was making very loud, howling screams. Several people tried to hold her as she screamed and kicked violently, foam flowing out of her mouth. I walked out of the sanctuary to see what was going on. Without her seeing me and without anybody telling her who I was, she began hurling insults at me. She then suddenly changed her tone and began addressing me by my name, but in a childish manner."

"How?" I asked. Father Maximos grinned and mimicked the voice of the woman.

"She called me 'Maximaakiii . . . , Maximaakiii. . . . come to me my baby. . . .' I was afraid that I was dealing with a powerful diabolical energy which had taken possession of the poor woman. There was no way she could have known my name. It was the spirit in her that knew my name. So immediately, and before I came close to her, I placed my hand under my cassock and stroked the Cross that I always have on me. Within the Cross I had placed a small piece of Saint Arsenios's remains, given to me by old Paisios as a talisman. The moment I touched the Cross the woman started screaming and hurling insults. She had spasms and kept screaming 'Don't touch that, don't touch that, you are burning me!' Keeping my hands on the Cross, I approached her while the others restrained her and I began to pray. The poor woman calmed down and finally came to her senses. Embarrassed, she looked around and apologized to me. She could not remember exactly what she was saying before."

"Was she cured?" Stephanos asked inquisitively.

"At that point the unclean spirit left her because it was 'burned' by the cross. The woman experienced relief. But you know, in cases such as these, it is not that easy to induce a demon to leave the individual permanently. It required much more work until she was finally cured of the demonic energy that had overtaken her. Without the power of the Cross she would not have been healed.

"That's why it is necessary for Christians to realize the extraordinary power of the Holy Cross as a symbol for spiritual protection," Father Max-imos added and leaned back in his chair. "Nothing, but nothing can stand in front of the Cross of Christ. I have repeatedly experienced this power of the Cross. No demon can stand in front of you while you hold the Holy Cross and while you invoke the name of Christ. When you do that the power of Satan is annihilated. That's why people need to learn how to properly cross themselves and not to do so mechanically. When you ha-bitually make the sign of the Cross before anything you undertake, it is as if an extraordinarily powerful energy marches ahead of you, offering pro-tection along the way. The Grace of God, through the Holy Cross, guards and supports us as human beings. This way we open ourselves and give the opportunity to the holy angels of God to help us and sanctify us. No dia-bolical spirit can then touch us or cause us any harm."

"Father Maxime," I asked, after we chatted more on the power of the Cross to undermine diabolical energies, "what is the origin of Satan ac-cording to the Christian spiritual tradition?"

Father Maximos went on to present us a conventional exegesis based on scripture, according to which Satan is considered a fallen angel. "The Holy Bible does not reveal to us exactly how and when the angels came to be, ex-cept that they existed prior to the creation of this world. According to the scriptures, angels are spirits sent by God to help humanity. We are told that originally there were ten orders of angelic beings. One order of the holy an-gels fell out from its relationship with God. How exactly we don't know. Based on the testimony of the saints and some extracts from scripture we may conclude that a basic cause of that fall was pride. Satan wanted to become God without God. In doing so he was completely emptied of God's Grace. The other nine orders, however, remained loyal to the Creator. Among them are the Cherubims, Seraphim, Thrones, Archangels, and so on."

Father Maximos then pointed out that, according to tradition, the tenth order has been replaced by the monastic order. That is why, he claimed, the *Ecclesia* calls monasticism the "angelic order." When one becomes a monk or a nun it is said that one is enlisted into the monastic angelic order. He clarified, however, that in reality only those monks and nuns who have at-tained a certain stage of spiritual development can be considered as be-longing to the angelic order. "Wearing the robes is not enough."

"Is it possible for a fallen angel to be redeemed and return back to God?" I asked.

"Unfortunately, it seems highly unlikely. Not because God does not want these angels but because they themselves do not wish to do so. It seems that they reach a point of no return, so to speak. They have become God-haters and therefore unable to master enough energy and momen-tum for the journey back to God. This is the essence of Hell. Their con-dition seems to have become stabilized with the fall of humanity."

"You speak of demons as if they are persons. But are they?" I asked, raising this issue once again.

"As I mentioned earlier, demons are not just evil in the abstract sense of the word. They are concrete entities but not persons. That is why we must never think of or call a human being a demon. For this reason, when people act in a hostile manner toward us we should always keep in mind that they are made in the image of God. They are our brothers and sisters. Their hostility toward us may be the result of demonic energy. But we must separate the person from that energy."

Father Maximos then in his characteristic way illustrated his point with a story. He talked of Abba Theodoros, an ancient elder. A monk under the supervision of this elder was verbally abused by two other monks. "That monk," Father Maximos said, "showed great patience and did not respond to these provocations. Abba Theodoros was impressed and asked him to explain how he managed to maintain his tranquillity in spite of the harassment. The monk replied, 'Am I to pay attention to these animals?' Then Abba Theodoros went to his cell and shed bitter tears for the spiritual fall of that monk who on the outside appeared so virtuous and patient but whose heart was completely perverted."

"But wasn't it natural for the monk to feel that way?" I reacted.

"For monks, or for everybody else for that matter, such thoughts are inexcusable. We must never see our fellow human beings as anything other than the image of God. Monks are expected to see the image of God when they encounter any human being. We must never see human beings either as demons, donkeys, dogs, or anything else, regardless of what they do to us or what their behavior toward us is like. It is for this reason that monks, when they meet, habitually kiss each other's hand. It is a ritual to remind us that the one we have in front of us is God Himself."

"I would have a difficult time maintaining such an attitude under extreme provocations," I murmured. "How should one respond under such circumstances?"

"The spiritually safest position is that suggested by Saint Silouan," Father Maximos replied.[2] "He teaches that when someone curses us, we should remind ourselves, 'I am responsible for this reaction. I brought it upon myself. I must be worthy of this curse.' You know, this can be a cause of a lot of inner peace. Saint Isaac the Syrian instructs that persons who keep their minds in such a state can easily get along with their worst enemies.[3] It's true and you ought to try it."

"Couldn't such an attitude be interpreted as pathological?" I asked.

"It would be so if you didn't really mean it because you have not reached that state of understanding and selflessness. But if you are sincere and you genuinely mean it, then it is a sign of true spiritual well-being and health. Such a predisposition arms the individual with extraordinary spiritual force. Not feeling comfortable in the presence of some people is indeed a sign of our spiritual imperfection. We must tell ourselves that it is we who have the problem, not the others."

"But who is perfect?" I asked, not expecting an answer.

"The perfected human being," Father Maximos replied, "is that person in whose heart there is room for everybody. Saint Isaac teaches that perfect love is shown by the person who prays even for demons and sheds tears at the thought that there are beings that are separated from God. Can you think of greater evil than that manifested by demons? Impossible. And yet, the great elders loved even the demons, not as evil but as suffering entities."

Father Maximos continued sharing his observations with us about the function of demons within the realms of creation. "Demons have the authority to act freely within creation. However, they have freedom only to the extent that we allow them to have influence over us. They have no authority to do whatever they wish. Alas to us if that were the case. We wouldn't exist. Black magicians can converse with demons and utilize their power. A magician can get an object and, through the power of demons, can charge it with their energy. In a similar manner, but from completely the opposite direction, a priest can get a glass of water and by reading some well-established prayers, he can sanctify the water and charge it with the energy of the Holy Spirit. That water can then be used to sanctify our homes. Symbols have enormous power not usually recognized by laypeople. This is also the reason why the Cross offers such an effective protection against diabolical energies."

To illustrate this point, Father Maximos then proceeded in his typical way to share yet another story from the life of elder Paisios. A man reputed for having extraordinary psychic abilities which he learned by becoming a member of a magical cult visited elder Paisios. He demonstrated his power by smashing a rock the size of a fist into dust by sheer power of concentration. He was able to do this by summoning demonic spirits. After witnessing this feat, elder Paisios grabbed a fistful of dirt and with his saliva made clay out of it, which he shaped into a ball the size of his fist. He then marked the sign of the Cross on top of it and challenged this magician to repeat that phenomenon. According to Father Maximos, who was present, the magician was unable to reenact his feat. His power was gone.

Father Maximos remained thoughtful for a few seconds, giving us time to think these matters through. "I know that what we have been discussing today may seem too fantastic from the point of view of ordinary reality and common sense," he mentioned with some hesitation in his voice. "Yet, such extraordinary realities are found in the life and the experiential testimonies of the saints throughout the history of Christianity. They are also revealed to those who engage in a serious search for the discovery of God."

invisible intruders

Father Maximos, sitting at the head of the main table in the *Trapeza*, the monks' dining hall, picked up a spoon and hit an empty glass in front of him. It was the signal that the evening meal was officially over. He did that as soon as he noticed that the last person had swallowed his last bite. Monks and guests all stood up at once while the monk assigned to read from a text stepped down from the podium. It is part of Athonite practice that during meals a monk is assigned the task of reading a story from the life of a particular saint while everyone else eats in silence, listening.

The reader, a young novice, bowed in front of his spiritual elder as the latter blessed him by making the sign of the Cross over his head. Then Father Maximos offered him a piece of bread that he had sanctified by making the sign of the Cross over it. The young monk then kissed the bread and the abbot's hand and proceeded to have his own dinner by himself in the kitchen. While everybody remained standing and crossing themselves, Father Maximos recited a short prayer in a soft, barely audible voice, blessed the leftovers on the table, and walked out onto the open, long corridor overlooking the yard. Each monk then waited in line and proceeded, one at a time, to receive Father Maximos's blessings individually. Once this ritual was over they moved on to work at the various tasks related to the operation and functioning of the monastic community. Evening vespers, the finale of the day's cycle, was to take place in an hour. After the service each monk would retreat to his cell and, before going to bed, engage in various spiritual exercises assigned to him individually by Father Maximos. Everything was well-organized and cemented by long-established tradition. It was interesting to see these monks go through such ritual cycles without any complaints, when one takes into account that prior to dressing themselves in their black monastic robes they lived full lives in the secular world. They repeated these rituals day after day, year after year, without any sign of boredom, without an apparent desire to walk out of the monastery and return to the world they had left behind. For Father Maximos the answer was simple: They found what they were looking for, the God within. So, why leave?

"Come, Kyriaco," Father Maximos said after the last monk had received his blessings. "Leave the dishes to others and let's go for a walk."

I had volunteered to help Father Nicholas and Father Nektarios in the kitchen, but they urged me to leave everything to them and join their elder for a walk. Father Maximos stepped into his office for a minute and came out holding two long walking sticks. He handed one to me and we set off. He always held a stick while walking in the mountains, a habit he had developed during his years on Mount Athos, where he covered long distances over rough terrain.

"I really love hiking in the mountains. But unfortunately I don't have many opportunities to do so here in Cyprus," Father Maximos complained as we stepped outside the main gate. "On Mount Athos I used to walk from one monastery to another for hours and hours. It was a sheer delight. But here I have too many responsibilities. Unfortunately, walking is a luxury I can't afford. Look at me, I am getting fat." Then with a laugh he went on to claim that there is a definite advantage in looking a bit on the heavy side.

"In what way?" I wondered.

"So that people have no fantasies that I am an ascetic, or even worse, a saint," Father Maximos joked.

We walked in silence for a few minutes, cherishing the last glimpses of sunlight and breathing the uncontaminated, pristine mountain air. An exquisite fragrance was oozing from the wet earth as a result of a hearty shower during the afternoon. The wind blew away the last clouds and we could already notice the trembling light of a few stars as the sky became increasingly darker. We walked up the mountain through the forested road and turned the next curve, beyond which we could no longer see the few lights of the monastery below us. We stayed on the main road to make certain that we wouldn't lose our way in the dark.

"Father Maxime," I began as we walked at the center of the road, "the other day you said something that puzzled me."

"What did I say?"

"That the *Ecclesia* is an arena of an ongoing battle, an ongoing warfare, spiritual warfare as you put it. This is military language."

"Why did it puzzle you?"

"I was under the impression that the *Ecclesia* is a harbor of peace and healing, not a battleground."

"Of course it is a harbor of peace and healing. Let me explain so that you don't get scandalized. You have to realize that the *Ecclesia* is available to us as a vehicle for our salvation. Such a pursuit implies a struggle against those forces that labor to block our ascent toward God."

"I assume you mean satanic forces."

"What else? We need to learn how to engage in this spiritual warfare in order to prevent such adversary forces from sabotaging our ascent toward God. This is what Apostle Paul and the other elders of the *Ecclesia* taught us. That we need to become experienced warriors of this relentless spiritual struggle." Father Maximos paced a few more steps and continued. "We need to become aware of the machinations and duplicitous ways of these forces so that we don't end up becoming their victims."

Father Maximos looked pensive. Then, seemingly changing the subject, he continued. "People are confused. They think that the aim of our existence is primarily to become good human beings, or to become moral, socially well-adjusted, and well-balanced personalities."

"I thought becoming good is what the *Ecclesia* is all about."

"No, not only that. This pietistic notion is not the essential purpose of the *Ecclesia*. It is a gross misconception. What the *Ecclesia* primarily teaches," Father Maximos said emphatically, "is the means through which a human soul may attain *Christification*, its saintliness, its union with God. The ultimate goal is to become perfect in the same way as our Heavenly Father is perfect, to become one with God. Christ didn't come into the world to teach us how to become good fellows, how to behave properly, or how to live a righteous life in this world. Nor did he come to offer us a book, even if this book is called the Bible or the New Testament."

"Well?" I probed as Father Maximos stood still for a few seconds and looked upward toward the heavens, marveling at the Milky Way. With no moon and no artificial lights anywhere near, the night was perfectly crystal clear. Father Maximos remained silent for a few seconds. Then he went on.

"He came to the world to give us Himself. To show us the Way toward our salvation," he replied as we resumed our walking. "Don't you remember what Athanasios the Great said? 'God became human so that humans may become God?' "

"Yes, yes, I know," I rushed to add. "It's the motto of Eastern Orthodox mysticism. So, Christ showed us the way toward God while Satan is the force that tries to prevent us from reaching our destination," I added. "But how is it done? How are the ways and means of Satan?"

"By means of what the elders call *logismoi*," Father Maximos replied.

"You mean thoughts?"

"*Logismoi* are much more intense than simple thoughts. They penetrate into the very depths of a human being. They have enormous power. Let us say," Father Maximos went on to clarify, "that a simple thought is a weak *logismos*. We need to realize, however, that certain thoughts, or *logismoi*, once inside a human being, can undermine every trace of a spiritual life in its very foundation. People who live in the world don't know about the nature and power of *logismoi*. That is, they don't have the experience of that reality. But as they proceed on their spiritual struggle, particularly through systematic prayer, then are they able to understand the true meaning and power of this reality."

I realized that Father Maximos was elaborating about a phenomenon that was very similar to the notion of *elementals* which I had written about extensively in my previous work. I have encountered this term in other spiritual traditions but under other names, such as "thought forms."[1] The theory of *elementals*, or "thought forms," is based on the assumption that thoughts and feelings are forms of subtle yet concrete energy that we constantly produce, affecting others as well as ourselves. Likewise, we are influenced by thought forms or *elementals* that others, individually or collectively, incessantly produce and which float in the environment. *Elementals*, therefore, have an ontological existence and must be thought of as objectively real "things" and not simply as subjective states of mind. These *elementals*, positive or negative, affect us constantly as real energies. Negative *elementals* can be thought of as the equivalent of conventional devils that can even appear in a shape that is imprinted within a particular cultural imagination.

Since my intention was not to engage Father Maximos in discussions and debates on comparative spiritual traditions and metaphysics but to learn from him about the Athonite spiritual tradition, I decided not to raise this issue. Instead, I probed him to elaborate further on how the elders of Athonite spirituality understand the power of thought in the form of *logismoi*. I had an intuitive feeling that Father Maximos's understanding would offer novel and in-depth insights into this matter that would be relevant not only for spiritual seekers but also for therapists dealing with the psychological problems of their clients. I was fascinated that this notion of "thought forms" was at the center of monastic spiritual practices and worldview of the mainstream Eastern Christian tradition.

"To tell you the truth," Father Maximos continued, "when I first heard about this notion of the *logismoi* on a visit to Mount Athos as a lay pilgrim, I was also puzzled. In the particular monastery that I visited they used to pray for six hours continuously, from sunset to after midnight. Then they had divine liturgy for another one to two hours. I had noticed that by one in the morning, a group of ten monks stood in line outside the cell of their elder. When I inquired what was going on there, I was told that they were awaiting their turn to confess their *logismoi*. I wondered, how was it possible for these monks to confess their thoughts? I had assumed that *logismoi* were just ordinary thoughts, and since we have thousands of thoughts every day, how were these monks able to confess them?"

I told Father Maximos that his puzzlement made sense to me. I explained that based on some research carried out at the University of Minnesota, the average human being has about four thousand distinct thoughts in a sixteen-hour day. It means that over a life span of let us say seventy years, this amounts to a total of about one hundred million thoughts.[2]

"Do you mean to say that it is possible to measure something like that?" Father Maximos replied and stopped his walk for a second. I reassured him that contemporary psychological science can indeed accomplish something like that.

"When I later became a monk and was under the sway of *logismoi*, I understood what those monks were doing. You see," Father Maximos continued, as we warmed up and accelerated our pace, "the spiritual warfare that goes on undetected by ordinary people is carried out through the *logismoi* that constantly assault our hearts and minds. These are the forces that prevent us from experiencing the reality of God."

Father Maximos clarified that not all *logismoi* are negative. Sometimes *logismoi* can be good and may be sent to us by God. It is through spiritual guidance and discernment that we will be able to differentiate one type from the other.

"But how exactly do *logismoi* prevent us from reaching God?" I persisted.

"Let us say that a *logismos* is a thought of a special quality and power intensity," Father Maximos replied. "There is something mysterious about a *logismos*. Its impact is similar to the sting of a needle when you go to the doctor to receive a shot. When negative *logismoi* manage to enter into your spiritual bloodstream they can affect you in the same way that a needle, full of poison, penetrates you and spreads the deadly substance throughout your body. Your spiritual world becomes contaminated and you are affected on a very deep, fundamental level. Your entire spiritual edifice can be shaken from its very foundations. Sometimes the intensity of a single *logismos* is so great that human beings under its spell may feel totally helpless. They may employ all of their powers to defend themselves against such intruders but to no avail."

"Do saints suffer from such *logismoi*?" I asked. "I would assume that since they are considered to be at the doorsteps of *Theosis* they would be freed from such assaults."

"On the contrary. They also have to face them but they are masters over them. Saints are, in fact, constantly assaulted by *logismoi* but they don't allow them to take residence within their souls."

When I later discussed this issue with my friend Erato (Stephanos's wife) who was well-read on the life of saints, she pointed out that eldress Gabrielia, the twentieth-century foot doctor who looked after lepers in India, claimed that *logismoi* for saints are like flies that enter an empty room. There is nothing there for them to sit on, nothing to attract them, so they leave.[3]

For a few minutes we walked without speaking as Father Maximos breathed deeply a few times. He enjoyed the walk and I felt good that I was the excuse he could use to take such a long intermission from his overburdened schedule. Our conversation seemed to energize him.

"I have noticed that some people, particularly young, oversensitive souls," Father Maximos said, breaking the silence, "suffer so much from these *logismoi* that it often leads them into psychopathological conditions. They reach such states partly because of their ignorance of the nature of *logismoi*. Such persons who may be attacked by a perverted, or let us say a sinful *logismos*, are unable to realize that such a *logismos* does not necessarily emanate from within themselves, but is directed toward them from the outside. They feel guilty and begin what the late Paisios used to call 'the repetition of those whys.' They become obsessive. Oversensitive persons become even more sensitive and blame themselves with all kinds of questions: 'Why do I have such a thought, why?' Such people are in dire need of proper instruction on how to handle the *logismoi*," Father Maximos pointed out. He went on to say that the most dangerous *logismoi* are those sent by demonic spirits that get support and get activated by our own passions. *Logismoi* coming from demons are extremely devious and duplicitous.

"In order to push us toward a sinful act," Father Maximos continued, "demons will send us a *logismos* that will put us at ease. It will convey the message that it is fine to commit a particular act because God is compassionate and merciful and will, therefore, forgive us anyway. Then, once the act is committed, the *logismos* that God is a punishing father will invade our mind like some kind of a merciless judge who will toss us into the eternal fires of damnation. I have noticed that the cause of so many mental pathologies and breakdowns that people suffer from is the direct result of such destructive *logismoi*. I would go as far as to argue that people suffering even from schizophrenia and similar severe disorders are victims of intense and obsessive *logismoi* from which they are unable to free themselves.

"The holy elders," Father Maximos went on, "as experienced spiritual warriors described and outlined for us in great detail the nature of this struggle. They set down for us a methodology on how to cope with the *logismoi* that are unavoidably encountered by every human being, including the saints."

We stopped and sat by the side of the road on a wooden bench planted there by the forest service for the comfort of hikers and nature lovers. In front of us lay the dark expanse of the mountains, mute and majestic. Above us were the starry heavens. The night was unusually warm and we sat there for quite some time gazing at the abyss below. Father Maximos fondled his *komboschini* and for a few minutes seemed deep in thought or perhaps prayer. I broke the silence with my usual questioning. "So, what kind of methodology did the holy elders invent in order to master the *logismoi*?" I asked.

He bowed his head and reflected for a few seconds. "Before we get to the methods," he replied, "we need to bear in mind the current state of affairs of our existential predicament. As we discussed earlier, there was a time when the first humans lived in full accordance to their true nature. In such a state all their energy, all their powers, were totally harmonized and focused around one motion, the motion toward God. Their *nous*, that is their heart and mind, had but a single and exclusive preoccupation, ceaseless prayer. At that state their sole experience and focus was what the elders call the *Theoria*, that is, the vision of God.

"Adam and Eve, as the primordial humans, disrupted this relationship of oneness with God through the Fall. They consequently became trapped and entangled within this world of the three dimensions, of matter, of egotistical passions, of sin. They ceased being in a constant prayerful state, their essential and true function by nature. The entire Creation suffered as a result of this split between humanity and God.

"So what we now have," Father Maximos explained further, "is this phenomenon of the ceaseless production of *logismoi* instead of ceaseless prayer. The *logismoi* are alien to our original condition, to the original working of our *nous*. The moment we were cut off from God, we entered into a state of existence dominated by worldly concerns, by *logismoi*. Our *nous* became scattered to the things of this world."

"Are you implying, if I understand you correctly, that human beings are not disturbed by any *logismoi* in the depths of their true nature, in the very essence of who they are?"

"Yes, that's right. By nature the true function of the *nous* is to engage in ceaseless prayer, which is a state of continuous contemplation of God. All the *logismoi* that we constantly generate are in reality not innate to us but are acquired since the Fall. They are both a symptom and a manifestation of our distance from God. It is, in fact, the *logismoi* that maintain our separation from God.

"All of us as human beings suffer from this inherited, primordial illness of the Fall. This is the meaning of the so-called original sin. It is the inheritance of that disruption from God which opened the way to the constant bombardment of our hearts and minds by the *logismoi.*"

Father Maximos insisted on several occasions that the notion of original sin as some kind of a violation of a moral taboo is a childish way of thinking about this issue. Original sin means, according to the experiential tradition of the holy elders, the original separation and alienation of the entire human race from God.

This discussion of original sin and the paradisiac state of primordial humans brought to my mind a panel discussion on the nature of myth that I had participated in at my university a few days before I boarded the plane for Cyprus. The panel was organized by a group of Marxist colleagues. The topic of the panel, typical of Marxist orientations and concerns, was about whether myths are inherently "reactionary." I am certain that the reason the organizers invited me to be on that panel was to have some kind of balance in terms of what was to be presented. The traditional Marxist position, not necessarily fully shared by my Marxist colleagues, was that myths, particularly religious myths, are forms of mystifications that obscure people's understanding of their real class position in society. Myths are typically considered by traditional Marxists as forms of "false consciousness" that inevitably, like religion, would wither away with the attainment of full and mature communism. Human beings would then have no need for myths since myths are symptoms of the exploitation of one class by another.

I remember how I began my brief presentation by pointing out that, unlike Marxists, I would start my argument with a different premise. Our understanding of ultimate reality is unavoidably mythic since reason, by itself, can never provide us with satisfactory answers as to the mystery of our human existence. We can never employ our rational faculties to travel beyond the original explosion that created our universe. All human knowledge, including science and philosophy, is therefore grounded on mythic, or better still, on mysterious foundations. The way to evaluate myths should not be on the basis of whether they are true or false, reactionary or nonreactionary, but whether they are life enhancing or life destroying. Nazi myths, for example, are clearly life destroying myths. Cultural myths, on the other hand, which help people cope creatively with the exigencies of human existence by cultivating love and compassion, can be considered life enhancing myths.

These ideas crossed my mind as Father Maximos talked of Adam, Eve, and the Fall. Such stories, I thought, must be seen as metaphors that suggest great truths about human existence, truths that cannot be pinned down by rational formulations, Marxist or non-Marxist. The idea of the

Fall as understood by the Athonite tradition that Father Maximos represented, I reasoned, was life enhancing insofar as it helped individuals on their advance toward God. It motivated individuals like the monks of the Panagia monastery to focus their energies wholeheartedly in the direction of healing the split between themselves and God. I wasn't certain, however, whether Father Maximos himself would have agreed on the stand I took vis-à-vis myths during the academic panel discussion. The Church has traditionally treated these primordial creation stories as literal historical facts. This is something singularly impossible to accept for a person steeped in modern thought. It would be analogous to believing as an empirical historical fact that the world was created a few thousand years ago or that God needed a rest on the seventh day because He got tired after laboring for six whole days. At this point in my life, however, whether Father Maximos considered such biblical stories as literal historical happenings or metaphors of deeper truths was not important to me. What was important was that as far as he was concerned, the individuals who use these stories as frames of orientation for self-transcendence and union with God are the great saints and prophets throughout the ages of the Judeo-Christian experience. Their lives and spiritual attainments, therefore, prove the value of the notion of the original split as a frame of orientation for spiritual struggle and *askesis*.

"What is the best way to overcome the *logismoi* and reestablish the original unity with God?" I asked Father Maximos again, bringing my mind back to the present. "Could it be ceaseless prayer?"

"Yes, to a great extent it is so, but it is more than that. The holy elders, being the scientists of spiritual practice, have taught us through their experience how to cope with the constant bombardment of our hearts and minds by *logismoi*."

Without further elaboration Father Maximos suddenly stood up. "I think we should be heading back." I noticed some concern in his voice that we were already late. We hastened our pace. There was enough light from the stars to help us stay on the main road without getting lost in the woods or falling off a cliff.

The road ahead was suddenly illuminated by the lights of a truck that stopped next to us. It was Father Efstathios, one of the older monks of the monastery, returning from a trip to Paphos. He had driven there in the morning in order to buy a year's supply of almonds from a wholesaler. There were rumors and concerns that due to the drought the price of almonds was about to rise steeply. Since the monastery was renowned for the production and sale of a special sweet made of almonds, it was prudent to buy the raw material ahead of the price rise. Father Efstathios was surprised to find us on the road at that hour and asked whether we needed a lift. Father Maximos preferred that we continue our walk. We were only forty minutes away from the monastery.

"Well, besides prayer, what did the holy elders teach about how to cope with the *logismoi?*" I asked as the lights of Father Efstathios's pickup truck disappeared around the next curve and the first lights of the monastery appeared in the distance below us.

Father Maximos thought for a moment and then elaborated. "The holy elders," he claimed, "identify five stages in the development of a *logismos*. Of course, I am speaking of a *logismos* that goes contrary to God's laws. The first is the **assault stage**, when the *logismos* first attacks our mind."

"How does it happen?"

"Let me give you an example. A thought enters our mind in the form of a suggestion urging us, let us say, to steal. It is as if this *logismos* knocks at the door of our mind and tells us: 'Look at this pile of money. Nobody is looking. Take it.'

"When such a *logismos* strikes, no matter how sinful it may be, it does not render us accountable," Father Maximos explained. "The quality of our spiritual state is not evaluated on the basis of these assaults. In simple language we commit no sin. The holy elders throughout the ages were relentlessly tempted and assaulted by similar and even worse *logismoi.*"

"After all," I interjected, "Jesus Himself was tempted by Satan during His retreat into the desert."

"Exactly. This clearly shows that when human beings are attacked by such *logismoi* they ought to feel no guilt whatsoever. They are totally innocent and not responsible for these *logismoi*. The great saints faced legions of negative *logismoi*. No human being has ever lived without being assaulted by myriads of *logismoi*. Only the dead are free of *logismoi.*"

"I am not sure even about them," I blurted out and laughed. "Do you have such *logismoi* yourself?"

"Constantly. I assure you I feel assaulted by the most crazy, the most irrational, and the most bizarre *logismoi* you can imagine. Yes, I do have them all right."

"Such *logismoi,*" Father Maximos went on to say, "have nothing to do with the quality of our soul. They are the unavoidable symptom of the Fall. People are often terrified by the number and nature of the *logismoi* that attack them, and they become obsessed with questions such as, 'Why do these thoughts come to me? Why me?' When they adopt such an attitude, Satan begins to truly do them harm. These obsessive questions are nothing more than an expression of egotism. I tell such people, 'You have such *logismoi* because you are human, period.' It is natural to have such *logismoi*, natural, that is, in the fallen state. We are human beings, not angels, and as such we are unavoidably marked by the imprint of the Fall. We are, therefore, bound to have such *logismoi*."

"So what does one do under the circumstances?"

"The saints are our guides," Father Maximos replied. "They were constantly bothered by myriads of *logismoi*. But they did not succumb to them. Do you know why? Because they reached the state of *apathia*, the state beyond egotistical passions. In that state it is as if the *logismoi* are hitting against a wall. And we are all aware that when we reject a *logismos*, not only are we not defeated but we also score a spiritual triumph."

"So the *logismoi* play a useful spiritual function, after all," I suggested. "Perhaps it is part of our training on our ascent toward God."

"What you just said reminds me of an episode in the life of a holy elder," Father Maximos mentioned. "There was this elder who had two young monks under his spiritual supervision. One day he asked them to spend some time with him in his hermitage so that he could check on their progress. At night, when they woke up for prayers, the elder noticed that some strange insects were hovering all around the younger monk. Every time this young monk managed to chase the insects away, he was graced by a radiant wreath over his head. The elder soon recognized that his disciple was being invaded by *logismoi*. But because he had the strength to chase them away and not allow them to penetrate further within his heart and mind, he was offered by the Holy Grace a spiritual victory."

"Why can't we say then that these *logismoi* are sent to us by God as a form of spiritual exercise?" I persisted.

I noticed a grin on Father Maximos's face. "As I said before, the holy elders claim that the *logismoi* may come either from God or from demons. But for the inexperienced novice it is often difficult to distinguish between the two. So as a general rule they suggest that they be ignored, because the more people become obsessed by their *logismoi*, the more they run the risk of suffering from psychopathological symptoms."

"Is it not possible that we may also chase away a *logismos* that comes from God, erroneously assuming it comes from Satan?" I asked.

"Even under such circumstances be certain that God is not going to misunderstand us or be offended," Father Maximos reassured me. "In cases where one is unsure, it may be best to consult with an experienced spiritual elder. The following, however, is a rule of thumb one can use to verify the origin of *logismoi*: Those *logismoi* that come from God generate in us inner peace and joy. On the other hand, *logismoi* that come from demons cause much turmoil and unhappiness.

"Let me give you an example on how difficult it is sometimes to ascertain the source of a *logismos*," Father Maximos went on to say. "When

Saint Silouan as a young novice lived at Saint Panteleimon, the Russian monastery on Mount Athos, he decided one day to leave the monastery and go live like a hermit in the desert, a much more austere existence. On the surface this *logismos* appeared to be admirable—to abandon the monastery where life was not so harsh and begin to live alone in the desert like the old prophets so that he might advance more quickly toward sainthood. Although externally this *logismos* seemed to have its origin in God, in reality it was from the demons, with the precise aim of blocking his ascent toward God. After isolating him in the desert, the demons would have assaulted him with all their destructive power. They would have led him, young and inexperienced as he was, to lose courage, become disheartened, and eventually abandon the spiritual struggle. Fortunately he consulted with his elder, who counseled against his decision to become a hermit at that early stage of his development.

"Saint Silouan's case, you see," Father Maximos continued, "underscores a fundamental principle for the serious spiritual explorer. That is the need for guidance from an experienced teacher. Serious spiritual work is full of mystery and no one should proceed alone. I would say that for all practical purposes, it is almost impossible. A person working alone without spiritual supervision will most probably be deceived."

"I see some serious logistical problems with what you just said. Millions of people are serious spiritual seekers. Yet very few have or can have access to a spiritual guide, someone who is a possessor of the Grace of the Holy Spirit. What will happen to the others, the vast majority of humanity? Does God treat people unequally? I am confident this is not the case, otherwise God would not be God."

"It does not mean," Father Maximos clarified, "that in order to be effective, the spiritual guide must necessarily be endowed by the Holy Spirit with gifts such as clairvoyance, prophetic vision, and other abilities. The mystery of spiritual guidance is predicated on the fact that both the spiritual mentor and the disciple form a sanctified dyad situated within the Body of Christ. Then the Holy Spirit works in such mysterious ways that it allows the disciple to benefit from the kind of advice that is required for spiritual development. The Holy Spirit often works through the spiritual guide in more subtle than concrete ways."

"But under such conditions isn't it possible to have the emergence of abuse and erroneous advice from the spiritual elder?" I asked.

"We are human beings and mistakes are unavoidable. That is why before someone establishes a relationship with a spiritual guide, they must first explore and inquire whether such a person is really representing, without distortions, the experience of the holy elders. If persons have faith in the mystery that is being activated in the name of Christ, then we can say with confidence that the Grace of the Holy Spirit will not abandon them. Therefore, even if a human error is committed it is eventually corrected. God will bring together the necessary circumstances so that the damage will be repaired."

"That's true faith," I marveled as we approached the outer gate of the monastery. Alas, it was closed. We pressed the button but there was no answer. The monks were still at vespers and nobody could hear us. Father Maximos, who usually carried a key with him, had left it in his office. We sat outside on a bench next to a public telephone booth and resumed our discussion as we waited for vespers to be over.

"So what is the second stage in the development of a *logismos*," I asked after going over in my mind the basic characteristics of the assault stage.

"The second stage according to the holy elders is what they called **interaction.** It implies the opening up of a dialogue, an actual exchange with the *logismos.* When a *logismos* urges you, for example, to steal that pile of money, you begin to wonder, 'Should I or should I not? What's going to happen if I steal it? What's going to happen if I don't steal it?' This is risky and dangerous. However, even at this stage there is no accountability on the part of the individual, no sin committed as yet. The person can indeed examine such a *logismos* and consider several options without being accountable. But, if the person is weak by temperament, then defeat may be the most likely outcome of that exposure to the *logismos.*"

It was getting chilly. I stood up and paced up and down a few times to warm up as Father Maximos continued. "The third stage in the progression of a *logismos* is the stage of **consent** as we would say. You consent to commit what the *logismos* urges you to do, in this particular case, to steal money. You have made a decision. That's when guilt and accountability start to emerge. It is the beginning of sin. Jesus was referring to this stage when he proclaimed that if you covet a woman in your mind you have already committed adultery in your heart. The moment this decision is allowed to take root in your heart, then you are well on the way to actually committing the act in the outer world."

"So, actions begin first in our minds," I added.

"Yes, but we must be careful," Father Maximos warned. "We are still at the stage of consent and desire. Action has not taken place, as yet. This spiritual war is still on the mental level. It is an important point to keep in mind. In such a case, if a person manages to invoke the name of God and to confess, they can avoid the next stage. It is still possible, through God's providential intervention and love, to liberate oneself from the stage of consent."

"I can think of another possibility," I interjected. "That's when an individual, due to circumstances, is unable to engage in the act. A person may desire fervently to embezzle money or commit adultery but it does not mean that they are in a position to do so."

"Quite right. Even in this case the individual is still on the third stage of consent. Yet since the person has succumbed to the temptation, he must be concerned because repeated surrender to the *logismos* will eventually lead to its actual implementation. The enemy of our salvation will concoct favorable circumstances for this purpose, believe me. And when the *logismos* floods a person's heart, surrender becomes virtually unavoidable. Then the actual act takes place . . . ," Father Maximos went on to say as I interrupted him.

"Before we get to the next stage, please clarify this point for me. According to the teachings of the holy elders, are human beings equally accountable whether, let us say, they fervently wish to steal or when they actually steal?"

"No. You still have a ways to go from the stage of fervent desire to the actual commitment of the act," Father Maximos replied. As he thought of something he chuckled. "Your question reminds me of an anecdote from the life of Saint John Chrysostom. During his time in the fourth century, some very austere Christian zealots, lacking any spiritual experience themselves, insisted that when human beings succumb to a *logismos* it is as if they had already committed the act. They misinterpreted, you see, Jesus' words about adultery. Saint John tried to no avail to convince them that this was not the case. Yes, sin is committed in one's mind through the *logismos*, but it occurs at a different stage of commitment. Therefore the accountability is of a less serious nature.

"While he was patriarch of Constantinople," Father Maximos went on, "he invited these zealots to a lavish banquet. He instructed his cooks at the patriarchate to prepare the most sumptuous dishes. He also sent a message to his guests not to eat during the day because there would be plenty of good food at the table. They did as he instructed and arrived ravenous to the banquet. Then the cooks began bringing the warm and delicious food to the table. Before they began eating he asked them to rise for the customary prayer. Everybody stood up while his deacon recited the Psalms. It went on and on. Twenty minutes passed by and the deacon continued reading from the Psalms. His hungry guests, the food steaming in front of them, wondered whether that endless prayer would ever come to an end so they could sit down and eat. They were salivating with desire. Finally the prayer was over. Saint John then told his guests, 'You may now leave.' They were shocked and confused. 'Why do you all look so puzzled?' he asked them. 'Didn't you see the food?' 'Yes, we did.' 'Didn't you desire the food?' 'Yes, we did.' 'Hasn't all of your mind and body changed as a result of that desire?' 'Yes.' 'Well,' he said to them, 'then it was as if you ate the food!'

"So with this practical joke," Father Maximos went on, "Saint John Chrysostom was able to convince those austere but spiritually inexperienced Christians that there is a great distance between committing a sin in one's heart and actually committing it in action."

"Does it matter what the reasons are that render you unable to carry out the act?" I asked.

"Not at all. The holy elders knew from their own experience that even if you had already committed the sinful act in your mind by setting up all your strategies, but for whatever reasons were unable to carry it through, you were the victorious beneficiary. In such cases their counsel was to remember and give thanks to God for His providential intervention on your behalf through the prayers of the saints and through your own works."

"So a person always has an opportunity not to proceed to the next stage," I pointed out.

"Absolutely so," Father Maximos retorted. Once again we remained silent for a few minutes. He then proceeded to describe the nature of the next stage.

"In the event that a person is unable to free himself from the previous stage, then there is defeat. He becomes hostage to the *logismos*. The moment the person succumbs, the next time around the *logismos* returns with greater force. It is much more difficult to resist then. And so it is with the next time and the time after that. The holy elders called it the stage of **captivity**. That's when the person can no longer retreat and proceeds along with this act which now becomes a habit that is repeated time and again."

"Psychologists would call it addiction," I interjected.

"The holy elders base their conclusions and discoveries on their personal experiences. They are the psychologists in the truest sense of that word."

"It may be so," I agreed. "After all, modern psychology does not even accept the reality of the soul, the *psyche*."

Father Maximos shook his head and sighed before continuing. "Finally, the holy elders identify the end stage in the evolution of a *logismos* as that of **passion** or obsession. The *logismos* has become an entrenched reality within the consciousness of the person, within the *nous*. The person becomes a captive of obsessive *logismoi*, leading to ongoing destructive acts to oneself and to others, such as in the case of a compulsive gambler. The holy elders have warned us that when we become dominated by such passions it is like giving the key of our heart to Satan so that he can get in and out any time he wishes. We see a lot of our brothers and sisters struggling desperately to overcome their obsessive passions and addictions but without much success. They are fully aware that what they do is self-destructive. They are capable of reasoning with clarity of mind, but their heart is captive. They cannot eject from themselves that negative energy that possesses and controls them."

"So what can be done about these people? Are they beyond hope of freeing themselves from their destructive passions?" I asked.

"Through the Grace of the Holy Spirit everything is possible, including their healing," Father Maximos replied. Then, like a good teacher, he summarized the five stages.

"So, we have five stages in the evolution of a *logismos*," he concluded, spreading out the five fingers of his right hand. "**Assault, interaction, consent, captivity,** and **passion**. These are more or less all the stages. They unfold and grow within us sometimes gradually, sometimes like an avalanche."

"So far," I went on to point out, "we have not talked about how to confront such destructive *logismoi*, how to prevent their evolution from the stage of assault to the last stage of passion or addiction."

As I completed my sentence the outer gate of the monastery opened up. It was Father Arsenios with his perennially wide smile who realized that his abbot and I were locked outside. "Why don't we discuss this topic some other time," Father Maximos suggested. "It's rather late now and we are both tired." We stepped inside the yard and walked up toward our cells.

strategies

ather Maximos spent most of the morning in his office chatting with two fellows in their mid-twenties. They had arrived at the monastery two weeks earlier and were staying in a cell reserved for visitors. I assumed at the time that they were potential novices exploring the option of a monastic life. But Stephanos, being a kind of lay father figure to the younger monks and therefore having intimate knowledge of the goings-on in the monastery, informed me confidentially that the newcomers had a very severe drug problem. They had arrived with the aim of freeing themselves from their deadly addiction, and were not primarily concerned with the salvation of their souls. Father Maximos was their therapist and the monastery was serving as a detoxification center of a sort.

I was sitting on the bench outside my cell reading when Father Maximos came out of his office and waved at me to join them. It was then that the two young men volunteered to reveal in graphic detail how they had become addicted to drugs. One had just completed a two-year jail sentence for possession and use of cocaine. The other, a tall former Olympic athlete from Greece, had an even greater problem. "Bad company," he said, led him into all sorts of mischief and eventually to heroin addiction.

He was sent to Cyprus by his desperate parents after they heard from a Cypriot friend of Father Maximos's reputation as a charismatic elder.

Had it not been for the hospitality and care they received at the Panagia monastery and Father Maximos's spiritual guidance, they would have been back on the streets, they both told me. When I asked them whether they considered the possibility of becoming monks they emphatically replied that they had no such intentions. Their temporary stay at the monastery was for purely therapeutic purposes. While staying there, however, they had to follow the routine activities of the monks, including waking up at three-thirty every morning to attend long services, practicing the Jesus Prayer, fasting, and working in the gardens. This regimen apparently worked well for them, and while in the monastery the young men did not suffer any withdrawal symptoms. Father Maximos later told me that he was concerned that a brief stay at the monastery may not be sufficient for their long-term rehabilitation. An additional concern was how serious a problem drug addiction had become on the island, and how little the government was doing about it. He felt that he had to do something himself.

That afternoon Father Maximos asked me to drive him half an hour down the mountain to the construction site of the Holy Shelter, a drug rehabilitation center that had started a year earlier at Father Maximos's initiative. During the ride he described the circumstances that led to the creation of the center.

About a year and a half ago Father Maximos began to regularly visit an imprisoned young man in an attempt to help him with his drug problem. This fellow was about to be released but there was no agency which could at that time take up his rehabilitation. Hearing this, Father Maximos did what he knew best, he prayed for him. Then an unusual incident took place at the monastery which he considered a form of divine intervention and an answer to his prayers.

"It was very early in the morning, on the sixth of January, 1996, when a wild dog rushed into the monastery the moment the gate was opened. The dog was out of control. He bit Father Arsenios on the leg, and when Father Isaac tried to intervene he bit him on his right arm. It was terrible. Finally we managed to chase him out of the gate and shut it firmly. The dog would not leave and kept howling and barking outside. It was Epiphany and we were concerned about the safety of people coming for the morning service. So we called the police. Their response was that their job was not to handle stray dogs and that we should instead contact such and such an agency. So we did and what do you think their reaction was? They warned us not to harm the dog and to make sure that we fed him properly. Before arriving at the monastery they called several times to find

THE Mountain of Silence 133

out, not whether anyone was harmed, but about the welfare of the dog." Father Maximos chuckled in his usual way.

"After that experience, I thought that if there is so much concern about the well-being of wild dogs, why isn't there any concern about the welfare of drug addicts? If there are homes for stray dogs, how about a home for those recovering from drugs?

"That episode with the dog," Father Maximos went on, "gave me the idea to begin the search for money in order to create a drug rehabilitation clinic. The first thing I did was to give a talk in Nicosia. To my great surprise, that very night many people volunteered to make donations and four thousand pounds [eight thousand dollars at that time] was raised. I had no idea what to do with that money. The following day I received a telephone call from a sixty-five-year-old woman who was a refugee. She had inherited five thousand pounds and wished to donate it for the project. So, we put all the money we had collected, by then nine thousand pounds, in a special account.

"The following Saturday," Father Maximos continued, as I cautiously steered the car down the rough dirt road, "I offered confession to pilgrims all day long. It was late in the afternoon when I finished and walked down the steps in a state of exhaustion. A woman, who I thought wished to see me for confession, was waiting for me. I said to her, 'My dear lady I am very tired. Please come some other day.' I could hardly stand on my feet. 'But, Father,' she persisted, 'I want to talk to you about a very important matter.' 'I am really sorry but I just can't help you,' I replied. I saw that there were two other women sitting on the steps and I assumed they had come for confession also. 'Father,' she announced, 'we would like to make a donation for the center you are creating.' 'Thank you very much. But could you please give the money to Father Arsenios. He will give you a receipt.' 'But, Father,' she insisted, 'I am talking about a lot of money.' I thought she meant something around a hundred pounds. 'Father, you don't understand,' she said. 'I am talking about half a million pounds!' [a million dollars at that time]. I froze. She repeated, 'Did you hear me? Pounds, not drachmas.' 'Are you serious,' I asked, 'or is this some kind of a joke?' 'Do you see these two ladies sitting on the steps?' she replied. 'Don't you know who they are?' How could I have known that they were the wives of Greek shipowners? They had heard about the project and come to Cyprus to help out. That very day they pledged a quarter of a million pounds each.

"The next day," Father Maximos went on as I drove and shook my head in disbelief, "a very wealthy Cypriot and his wife visited the monastery. When they heard about the donation they themselves pledged an additional quarter of a million pounds without even being asked."

"Unbelievable!"

"Kyriaco," Father Maximos said in earnest as he turned towards me, "wealthy friends of that couple pledged another one hundred thousand pounds. Within the span of just a week, a million pounds were collected without any effort on our part."

Father Maximos added that the monastery had donated its best parcel of land, several miles down the mountain, for the project and that construction had now entered the completion stage. "The only problem left," he added, "is to find donors for the operating expenses."

"That's a serious problem. What are you going to do about that?" I asked as we approached the construction site.

With a wide smile on his face, he replied, "Pray some more." Father Maximos firmly believed that when people pray sincerely, from the heart, for the good of others, the Almighty always responds in one form or another.

The drug rehabilitation center was in the middle of an ancient olive grove, a serene place befitting the purpose for which it was being created. The two-story, square building was almost completed, looking like a monastery with a large yard in the middle and traditional arches all around. Father Maximos was particularly meticulous about aesthetics and he made certain that the building would blend with the surrounding countryside. "You know," he said while showing me around, "this place would have made a wonderful seminary."

"Well, pray some more and you never know, some donor may appear out of nowhere," I joked.

The two workers putting the finishing touches on the building were delighted to see Father Maximos and offered us soft drinks. They brought forward two chairs and Father Maximos and I sat on the side of the building under an aged olive tree. According to one of the workers, who came from a nearby village, that tree was estimated to be about eight hundred years old. We sat there, sipping the orange sodas and enjoying the sight of ancient olive trees as if looking at a magnificent oil painting.

"Perhaps," I suggested, "this may be a good time and place to resume our unfinished discussion about the *logismoi*. So far we have not discussed the way we should defend ourselves from negative *logismoi* and how to deal with them once they take over our minds."

Father Maximos remained pensive for a few seconds. "I remember when a pilgrim asked an Athonite hermit about this problem of *logismoi*. 'Father, I am troubled by a torrent of *logismoi*,' he complained, 'particularly when I am in church during services. I have so many negative *logismoi*, blasphemous *logismoi* against God, against the mysteries, against the priests, that I want to run away. I can't tolerate it. I feel that I am on fire.

What can I do?' The hermit pointed to the sky and replied, 'Do you know what these things resemble?' As they were talking they heard a military plane zooming over Mount Athos. . . ."

"I thought that the Greek government does not allow planes to fly over the Athonite peninsula," I interrupted.

"This was before the enactment of that law. Anyway, 'that is what these *logismoi* resemble,' the elder explained to the pilgrim. 'The airplane which creates all that noise and disturbance cannot land on Mount Athos because we have no airport here. If we don't allow a *logismos* to land inside the depths of our hearts and minds, then even if we see it and hear it, even if it bothers us for a while by its presence, we should never be afraid of it. We must not wail and beat our chests because an airplane passed over the roof of our house. Only when that airplane crashes on our house should we worry,' " Father Maximos joked, making a humorous grimace.

"So the holy elders," I added, "claim that the best strategy to cope with troublesome *logismoi* is simply to ignore them."

"Precisely. Our first defense against destructive *logismoi* is complete **indifference.** This is the healthiest and most productive method to head them off right at their inception. Ignore them completely. Never open up a dialogue with these intruders. Do not interact with them either out of curiosity or out of overconfidence. It is a tactical error. It's like starting a dialogue with a mortal enemy who is much more clever than you. If you pay attention to a *logismos* you must realize that it will become increasingly bolder. It will begin to invade your heart with louder and louder noise. The best strategy in confronting a *logismos*, therefore, is to completely disregard it. Do not focus on what it tells you and urges you to do."

"This is a sound principle that one could employ not only in terms of intrusive *logismoi* but also when being provoked by others."

"Yes, very much so, as long as you keep in mind that human beings are not *logismoi* but producers of *logismoi*. Just imagine," Father Maximos went on as he tried to illustrate the method of indifference, "that you are inside your home with the doors and windows firmly shut and someone in the yard is shouting obscenities and daring you to come out and fight. He cannot get inside. He is just outside hurling insults at you. He threatens and verbally assaults you with every conceivable curse in order to provoke you to respond and come out of the house. The best strategy for you is to shrug it off. Don't focus. Don't pay attention. Just stay inside, knowing that you have nothing to do with that person. Let him shout as much as he wishes. He cannot harm you as long as you stay in the house with doors and windows firmly shut. Again, the holy elders called this attitude of the mind the strategy of indifference. It is the best method for a person to fight off *logismoi*. Just keep them out."

"But aren't there situations when you simply cannot ignore a *logismos*, when you must react?" I asked.

"You know, of course, that for every rule there is also the exception. In cases where negative *logismoi* touch upon fundamental principles of faith, such as the reality of God, then perhaps the contrary strategy may be followed, active opposition."

"I would have assumed that particularly under such circumstances, silence should be the best strategy," I stated.

"No, not always. Let me clarify why. Suppose a *logismos* troubles you with the persistent insinuation that there is no God. You go for communion and the *logismos* comes to you saying 'What are you doing here? There is no God. What kind of nonsense is this, drinking wine and eating bread and calling it the blood and flesh of Christ. Is this some kind of cannibalistic ritual, a remnant of a bygone era? These customs are concoctions of the priests to stay in business.' Or suppose they tell you that the Bible is not a divinely inspired text, but just a book that keeps people ignorant and docile. Then you must respond with counterarguments such as, 'Okay, if you say there is no God, then can you explain to me how the Universe came into existence?' In matters of fundamental principles of faith you may face the need to react.

"Obviously this approach," Father Maximos continued, "is easy for those who have reached the stage of *apathia*, they have emptied and cleansed themselves, that is, from earthly passions and desires. Such people who actively engage themselves against the *logismoi* can debate and defeat them. After all, Jesus Himself did not ignore Satan when He faced him in the desert. He answered him back. He employed the **adversarial** method by using exactly the same strategies as those employed by Satan. For example, Satan made references to various extracts from the scriptures and then Christ answered with other extracts from the scriptures. And by using this method He was victorious.

"But of course, this strategy," Father Maximos added, "is not recommended for novices. As a rule, it is better to maintain an attitude of complete indifference from the start."

Father Maximos stood up and stretched. He suggested that we take a stroll to enjoy the rays of the setting sun as they shone through the leaves of the olive trees.

"What if, in spite of all my efforts," I went on to ask as we paced leisurely, "I cannot chase away the negative *logismos* and I am at the verge of surrendering to it and consenting. What then?"

"In such cases the holy elders suggest a game that you can play with your mind."

"A game?"

"Yes. Inject into your mind what they call a **splitting logismos**. That means grab onto another *logismos* and shift your focus on that. A hermit told me once that he chased a particularly bothersome *logismos* by counting the number of candles that were on the chandelier hanging from the middle of the church.

"So," Father Maximos went on, "in cases when the *logismos* refuses to retreat, the advice of the elders is to shift your focus to something else, even to something foolish or irrelevant. It is a ploy to trick the mind. Think of something ridiculous instead, for the sake of undermining the power and energy of the *logismos* that torments you. By using this method you can gradually reduce the energy and the force of the *logismos*. Next time it returns it will be weaker."

"As for me," I commented, "physical exercise, like fast-paced walking in the woods of Maine, is an effective way of handling such *logismoi.*"

"Good. Nature always has a healing effect on us, particularly trees."

"In fact," I added, "eldress Gabrielia[1] suggests that if you feel tired, go and hug a tree. You will be charged with renewed energy."

"Good. I must also say," Father Maximos went on, "that the holy elders consider manual work an effective and practical method of fighting off the *logismoi.*"

"Is this the reason why the monks, when not praying, are always working?" I asked. I noticed that there was no time reserved for leisure activities or entertainment. Whatever leisure time there was in the daily cycle of the monks at the Panagia monastery was spent either on studying or praying. The purpose of that rigor, Father Nikodemos explained to me the other day as I helped him in the library, is to prevent the mind from being distracted with matters of this world that disrupt the flow of Grace within the individual. Every moment must be used productively through ceaseless prayer for "the acquisition of the Holy Spirit."[2]

"The work that the monks do in the fields, looking after the orchards and the vegetable gardens, is not aimed only at material sustenance," Father Maximos added as he pointed with an expansive gesture at the fields around the Holy Shelter. "It is also a form of spiritual practice." He then reflected for a second or two. "This reminds me of an episode in the life of the Great Antonios, the third-century desert father. When he abandoned city life and went into the desert to live by himself in that total silence, he was confronted with the problem of *logismoi* that began to attack him. Inexperienced as he was at the time, he felt lost and confused. He was drowning in his *logismoi*. Not knowing the ways of spiritual warfare, he became deeply depressed and desperate. He relentlessly prayed to God to teach him how to overcome the myriads of *logismoi* that tormented him. At one point as he prayed, he saw further away another hermit who was also praying. He noticed that the other hermit would pray for a while, and then stand up, grab a pickax, and work the land, cleaning the place, breaking rocks, weeding, making baskets, and so on. He would then stop and begin praying again. Then back to work. The cycle would be repeated time and again. That other hermit was in reality an angel sent by God to instruct the Great Antonios how to cope as a hermit. It was that experience which taught him that physical work, particularly work with the land, is beneficial for persons suffering from *logismoi* which they are unable to overcome by other means. Through physical labor persons can gradually overcome the *logismoi* and begin to recover their mental and spiritual health."

"If I am not mistaken," I pointed out, "conventional psychotherapy has also recognized the beneficial effects of certain kinds of activity such as working the fields. In fact I read somewhere that in Cuba they implemented a policy of putting inmates of mental asylums to work because, following the Marxist ideology, they believed in the redemptive power of labor. According to Marx," I said, "one cannot be a whole person without being creatively employed."

Father Maximos pointed to the fields around the center and explained that part of the rehabilitation program for the inmates of the Holy Shelter would be to work the fields. "So here is another area," he mused, "where Marxists and hermits share something in common." Then, in a more serious tone, he continued, "It is really a terrible thing to see people under the spell of a destructive *logismos* that has captured their minds. Sometimes it is really unbelievable. I meet people during confessionals who beat on their chests and with bitter tears declare: 'I don't want to do this thing, I don't. I will be destroyed, I will be lost.' And the moment they are out of the confessional they immediately go and do exactly that which they vowed even minutes earlier that they didn't want to do. Do you know why? Because their minds have become hostage to a *logismos*. So, in those cases, the splitting *logismos* could perhaps work for them."

"You have not mentioned prayer so far," I pointed out. "Isn't that a way of protecting oneself from troublesome *logismoi*?"

"That goes without saying. This is the most effective method, of course. It is the most powerful weapon at our disposal as Christians. And the most important of the prayers is the *Efche*, the repetitive invocation of the name of Christ, the '*Lord Jesus Christ, Son of God, have mercy on me.*' Keep in mind that participation in the mysteries and tradition of the *Ecclesia* is a form of spiritual nourishment that penetrates our inner world and empowers our soul to overcome the *logismoi*. This kind of spiritual work is what we call in one word *askesis*, meaning prayer, fasting, confession, communion, the study of the word of God and of the life of saints, sleepless nights in all-night vigils and so on. All this work leads to the strengthening of the soul through its embrace, as it were, by Divine Grace. That is the path that the soul takes in order to attain spiritual health." Father Maximos remained pensive for a while.

"There is a detail we must keep in mind in reference to the repetition of the Prayer as a method of overcoming the *logismoi*," Father Maximos said softly as we turned back to where the car was parked. "A person should not resort directly to the Prayer immediately after being assaulted by troublesome *logismoi*."

"Why not?" I asked puzzled.

"I know that what I am about to say may sound paradoxical. But an automatic recourse to the Prayer could have the opposite effects. It may lead a person to extreme psychic turmoil and to a loss of self-mastery. Old Paisios used to tell us that when confronted with a *logismos*, whoever resorts to repeating the Prayer very rapidly resembles a terrified soldier in the heat of battle. He holds his rifle tight to his chest, paralyzed with fear. To reassure himself that he is not afraid he repeats 'Holy Virgin help me, Holy Virgin help me.' And he shakes from head to toe, sitting there completely immobilized and unable to fight or even to breathe."

Father Maximos laughed. "That reminds me," he mused, "of the dentist we had on Mount Athos. The moment he would take a look into our mouths he would sigh, start crossing himself, and begin lamenting. 'Holy Virgin! May you help us. May God place His hand here.'

"Before a person begins to pray, when confronted with a troublesome *logismos*, a rational mastery over the situation must be developed. Again, if at all possible, the best way is to employ the strategy of complete indifference."

"So when should one pray then?"

"Pray, but not while in a state of panic. Not right at the moment when you are waging war against a *logismos* that immobilizes you. Under such conditions you become highly vulnerable to the machinations of the enemy. Prayer does its work at the deepest recesses of the human heart and leads to true spiritual health. But prayer should not be an alternative to using our reason and willpower in confronting the *logismoi*. It should not be practiced in a state of panic. Otherwise we will behave like the paralyzed soldier of old Paisios."

"I like what you just said," I pointed out. "It shows that systematic spiritual practice need not be an alternative to reason, personal initiative, and freedom, as some critics of religion have been saying all along."

"Of course it should not be a replacement of reason," Father Maximos reacted. "Speaking of old Paisios, I am reminded of an episode that makes me laugh every time I think of it. He and I were having vespers at the small chapel next to his hermitage. He then went inside his room to talk to a pilgrim while I was in the sanctuary. Suddenly through the window I saw old Paisios rushing out, looking sick. I noticed that he was throwing up and I rushed to help him. 'What is the matter, *geronta* [elder]?' I asked. 'Are you sick? Shall I get you some water?' 'Oh, it's nothing,' he said, 'it's nothing. I am not sick.' 'But what happened?' I asked. 'What can I tell you,' he sighed. 'I just heard some things. . . .'

"What happened, you see," Father Maximos explained, "is that the fellow who went to see him must have described something he committed and old Paisios imagined the sin in his mind and couldn't take it. He became sick. Another day," Father Maximos continued, "I began to tell him what I had heard during confessions. He interrupted me. 'Stop. Enough. I can't listen to this anymore. Every time I hear about such sins I feel that whatever food I eat during the day comes back to my mouth.'"

"How could he be so sensitive?" I wondered. "I would assume that someone with so much spiritual training would not be so affected."

"He was not affected. The mind of a human being that is purified of lower passions will not allow a base *logismos* to get inside, to get imprinted on the mind. A person on that level, out of curiosity, as was the case with old Paisios, may say to himself, 'Let me see what it means to have such and such a *logismos*.' In that specific case it was a very provocative, banal *logismos*. Old Paisios just couldn't fathom it. His body rejected it outright.

"The clean person, liberated from sinful passions, will not tolerate such *logismoi* even as a painting on canvas, as an image in his mind. On the other hand the person whose mind succumbed and became captive to base *logismoi* commits sins with 'maniacal intensity,' as Saint John Chrysostom put it. That person's mind is under the spell of passion, totally hostage to sin. Like a drug addict he is attracted to it and cannot do otherwise."

When we got into the car and started the drive up the dirt road back to the monastery, Father Maximos repeated that regular and systematic prayer is the best practice for the attainment of spiritual health. It assists the mind to defend itself against intrusive *logismoi*. "When our heart is guarded by prayer," he said, "then no image or negative *logismos* that comes our way gets imprinted on it.

"The holy elders," he continued, "were witnesses of ghastly, sinful scenes but they were not scandalized. They were not propelled into sinfulness. Nothing would touch them personally. Yet they shed bitter tears for the predicament of human beings, created in the image of God but falling so low, and prayed for them. Persons who pray regularly, you will notice, acquire with time mastery over their lower passions. Prayer, you see, works in a mysterious way within the mind and heart of people, gradually exposing them to God's divine love. The moment human beings taste of the power of God's love, then every other experience within this world becomes trivial by comparison."

"Is prayer by itself sufficient in a person's spiritual development?" I wondered.

"As I mentioned to you earlier, in addition to prayer, the reading and study of holy texts, like the word of God in the Gospels, and the life and work of the holy elders, is of crucial importance. They help so that our mind gets nourished with spiritual meanings that can displace the meanings of anger, envy, greed, and such other base emotions."

Father Maximos went on to argue that through the reading of divinely inspired literature we create spiritual antibodies in our psyche that can combat the destructive mental viruses of negative *logismoi*. Texts like the Bible and the works of the holy elders were written under the inspiration and guidance of the Holy Spirit. The person who studies them partakes of this Divine Grace in a mystical way. The soul is nourished with Grace even if the person who reads such literature does not understand the meaning of what is being read. "Just by reading this material," he claimed, "the individual becomes spiritually empowered by the Grace embedded in the words themselves."

"The same principle must also apply to people attending sacred rituals," I suggested. "They may not understand what is being said but the spiritual energies that are being generated affect them in subtle ways."

"Exactly. In addition there are other ways to purify oneself from negative *logismoi*. For Christians, as I said before, it is participation in the mysteries of the *Ecclesia*. In addition to baptism, which is usually given early in life, the most important of these mysteries are those of confession and communion. Through confession a human being becomes humbled, and through humility one reaches true *metanoia*, the transformation of one's mind in the form of deep repentance. It leads to the removal of egotism, which is the very root of the *logismoi*. Furthermore, through the sacrament of Holy Communion the person communes with Christ. When people reach the true state of humility, the *logismoi* cannot touch them. Legions of *logismoi* can attack them without affecting them, as in the case of the saints.

"Of course," Father Maximos added, "the *logismoi* play an important role in the spiritual development of human beings."

"I am surprised that you are giving the 'devil' his due," I exclaimed with a laugh.

Father Maximos went on to elaborate. "Quite often, negative *logismoi* serve God's plan. Not that God Himself sets them up, but because it may be the only way for proud individuals to attain humility. The *logismoi*, you see, can offer us extreme grief, bitter experiences, and pain."

"I've read the work of an Athonite elder," I added, "who claimed that whoever does not become humble by his own volition is humbled by the devil."

"Yes, this saying is well known on Mount Athos. Satan is ever ready to help us out. That's why we learn to keep our heads down."

It was almost dark when we approached the monastery, and the lights were on. Having only a few more minutes together alone, I hastened to complete our conversation on the strategies to overcome the *logismoi*.

"Father Maxime, we have not yet talked about steps that can be taken to liberate minds taken over by destructive, negative *logismoi*. What happens when you are trapped by an obsessive addiction?"

"Well, the most urgent task is to immediately cut yourself off from the causes of the passion."

"More easily said than done," I retorted.

"The holy elders," Father Maximos explained, "teach that upon making a proper diagnosis of what the causes of a problem are, one should proceed to cut oneself off from them."

"But if you could do that, then it would not be a problem."

"Let me give you an example. Suppose you are a recovering alcoholic and you believe that you have, more or less, overcome your drinking problem. Well, if you do not wish to start drinking again, you must stay away from anything that reminds you of alcohol. Don't visit a bar and assume that you will have orange juice. Don't go to parties where people drink. Stay away from the very cause of your addictive passion. Don't become bold, believing that you can resist because you now feel strong. The holy elders suggest that you must avoid the places where your passion has its origins. Stay away at all costs. Change location. Don't remain in places that remind you of the episodes that led to your captivity. Anything that reminds you of your passion is potentially a trap."

It was very interesting for me to hear Father Maximos discuss these issues of addiction that coincided perfectly with contemporary therapeutic principles. Father Maximos, in an earlier conversation I had with him, called addictive passions *philepistrofa*, which means that they have a tendency to return to the person who, in the past, was under their sway. One of his lay disciples, for example, confessed that as he was watching television late at night, he accidentally turned the channel to a station showing a porno film. He remained up all night watching it. Father Maximos instructed him to get rid of his television set at once. The reason was that this individual, in his youth, had lived a life of debauchery. He therefore ran the risk that by watching such movies, his sex addiction, like in the case of the recovering alcoholic, would return with a vengeance, creating havoc in his personal and marital life. Father Maximos explained to me that those who did not have such a problem in their past would not be as vulnerable as people under its impact. Passions, he repeated, are *philepistrofa*; they love to return.

"All this is fair and good, Father Maxime," I interjected, "and it is all sound advice. But isn't it also a bit too simple? After all, a person with addictions has a problem with self-control to begin with."

"You are quite right. A person with such problems needs help from an experienced counselor. Naturally, from our point of view, there are healing methods prescribed by the *Ecclesia*: participation in the mysteries and regular confession that could lead to the purification of the heart through deep *metanoia*. If a person engages in these practices systematically, then they have nothing to fear. Sooner or later they will be freed from the troublesome addiction. Even if they fail repeatedly, the time will come when the heart will be healed. It will become increasingly purified."

"Father Maxime," I asked as I switched off the engine outside the gate of the monastery and turned towards him, "you keep talking about the heart frequently. What is really meant by this term within the Athonite spiritual tradition? I have some confusion about the meaning of 'heart' and '*nous*.'"

"The word '*nous*' sometimes has two meanings. '*Nous*' is often equated with the heart, and by heart we mean the center and totality of the mental and psychological powers of the individual. This is what Christ meant when He said, 'Blessed be the pure at heart for they shall see God.' At other times, however, mind is simply identified with what is now understood as the intellect, or logic. These distinctions are important for several reasons. What we notice often is that the mind or logic of people can be clean but their hearts may be impure. It means that persons in certain situations may have good judgment or think clearly. The very same individuals, however, can commit acts that they clearly know to be reprehensible because their heart is impure. The heart, the center of their psychonoetic existence, is a hostage to their *logismoi*."

"I have one last question," I said while entering the monastery as evening vespers were about to begin. "Can we say that the heart is what is commonly understood as the subconscious where people store their unfulfilled desires? Is the heart the depository where what Freud called 'repression' takes place?"

Father Maximos shrugged. "The holy elders were not using such terms. So I cannot really say much about it. But as I understand it, the subconscious is a storage space into which human beings pile up, so to speak, those memories and experiences they don't want to be aware of. You may call it whatever name you wish, but one thing is clear to me. From the point of view of the true spiritual life we must eradicate the subconscious."

"Eradicate the subconscious?" I exclaimed as a group of curious monks surrounded us, listening with great interest to our exchange.

"What you called 'repression' is totally unacceptable in real spiritual medicine," Father Maximos replied. "In the spiritual arena of the *logismoi*, we aim at the transmutation or metamorphosis of our passions, not the actual storing of them into the so-called subconscious.

"Now let us take sexuality, for example," Father Maximos continued. I was taken by surprise. I had assumed that sex was a sensitive if not taboo subject with ascetics. "We monks do not try to repress our sexual passions by storing them in our subconscious. I remember reading an interview given by a married priest who stated that the central problem of the monks is sexual. That, in order not to think about sex, we work all day long in the fields, clean the yard, wash the floors, and so on." Father Maximos scoffed and shook his head as the monks that surrounded us burst into laughter. "This is sheer nonsense. So what do we do at night? Continue to wash the floors and dig ditches in the fields, or gobble up pills to overcome our insomnia?

"Woe to those monks and nuns," Father Maximos went on after we stopped laughing, "who shovel into their subconscious their sexual passions. In such a state they would tremble and sweat in the presence of the opposite sex. There is no spirituality in that. What happens, and what we aim at, is the transmutation of erotic energy from earthly attractions to God, the way human beings were in their primordial natural state."

"Eros turns into *agape*," I muttered.

"Right. Such persons love all human beings without distinction to their sex. Such persons do not have much to do with what belongs to the after-the-Fall state of humanity. Do you understand? The love of God totally transforms human beings through Grace. Therefore, we monks as a rule, and ideally of course, do not repress our desires in our subconscious. What we attempt to do is to force ourselves to bring everything out from the subconscious and clean it up."

He paused for a second and, looking around at the faces of his monks, he continued. "When someone is professed a monk, his spiritual elder warns him: 'Look! The moment you decide to join the monastery, you accept withstanding hunger, thirst, humiliation, and injustices.' The spiritual elder will sometimes subject the novice to some difficult exercises. He may set up certain conditions and circumstances in order to provoke and aggravate him. He is like the physician who gives us a medicine to cause us to vomit in order to get rid of the poisons that we have swallowed. It is the same with the medicine offered us by our spiritual elder. You have to vomit the old ways of thinking and feeling. This will not happen unless you touch some sensitive chords. That is how you acquire real humility."

"I have not witnessed such harsh exercises in this monastery," I re-marked, and nodded at Fathers Arsenios and Nikodemos, who were among the monks listening to our discussion. In fact, I was impressed with the gentle way in which Father Maximos and other elders I met dealt with apprentices.

Father Maximos laughed. "With the help of the Holy Spirit each per-son will be given the type of exercises appropriate for their situation."

"Is that true also for the laypeople and nuns for whom you act as a spir-itual guide?"

"Naturally," Father Maximos nodded. "We have learned to employ certain methods that allow us to get to the depths of our being, that which you called the subconscious, and to help others explore the depths of theirs. According to the spirituality of the holy elders, the subconscious must never remain dark. The aim is to purify it, distill it, and make it trans-parent. We must never repress our weaknesses and passions. The aim of the *Ecclesia* as a method of healing is to sanctify the human individual, the whole person."

"So," I murmured, "if the work you do here led to the repression of de-sires. . . ."

"We would all be psychopaths, neurotics, and schizophrenics, Kyriaco! For how long can you repress your passions? Lunacy, that's what is going to be the inevitable outcome, and that's why the saints are truly liberated in their very being. They are the freest people on earth. Once they reach that state they can never be affected by the sins of the world. They are not ter-rified by them. They are not human beings fortified behind their prejudices and repressions. You may go meet saints and tell them the most horrendous sins. They will not be touched in their innermost core. Persons who have repressed their passions will get angry, will get into the punishing mood. If you tell them that you committed some sinful act, they will become very upset and judgmental. They will become intolerant without a trace of com-passion. Do you know why? Because they themselves are suffering. They have a lot of repressed emotions and anger inside them, a lot of repressed *logismoi*. Such persons are moralistic and pious, but they are no saints. Their hallmark is not utter humility." With that last remark we heard the rhythmic sound of the *symandron* calling us for vespers.

Father Maximos's last comments on the utter humility of saints and the presence at the Panagia monastery of three Russian monks praying next to me during vespers shifted my mind to prerevolutionary Russia. Standing there in the darkness, watching the Russian monks praying with their *komboschini* as they made endless prostrations in front of the mirac-ulous icon of the Holy Virgin, brought to my mind a story by Leo Tolstoy who, like Fyodor Dostoyevski, was deeply affected by the eremitic legacy of the *startsy* (elders). Both writers were frequent patrons of the Optina monastery, the leading spiritual center of Russia, later destroyed by the communists. Tolstoy must have been familiar with tales of wondrous incidents related to the lives of these Russian hermits. Mesmerized by the chanting, my mind shifted to nineteenth-century Russia.

In this story that came to mind, Tolstoy wrote of the encounter between a Russian Orthodox bishop and three hermits. The bishop was traveling by boat with other pilgrims from Archangel to the Solovetsk monastery. On the way he heard rumors that on an obscure little island along the way there were three old hermits that had spent their entire lives trying to save their souls. The bishop became intrigued and implored the captain to stop the ship so that he could visit them. The captain reluctantly agreed and dropped anchor near the island. The bishop was then placed on a boat and with a group of oarsmen sent ashore. The three hermits were dressed raggedly with long white beards to their knees. In total humility they welcomed the bishop, making deep bows. After he blessed them he asked them what they were doing to save their souls and serve God. They replied that they had no idea how to serve God. They just served and supported each other. The bishop realized that the poor hermits didn't even know how to pray, since all they did was lift their arms up towards heaven and repeat "Three are ye, three are we, have mercy upon us." The bishop considered it his ecclesiastical duty to teach the illiterate hermits the Lord's Prayer. They, however, were poor learners and required a whole day of instruction. At dusk and before returning to the ship, the bishop even offered them a short and simple lesson on Christian theology.

But lo and behold! During sunset as the boat left the island all the passengers saw a sight in the distance that filled them with fright. The three hermits were running on water as if it were dry land. When they came by the side of the ship they implored the bishop to remind them of the Lord's Prayer because, poor fellows, they had already completely forgotten it. The bishop crossed himself in awe and told the hermits to continue their own prayers, for they had no need for instruction. Then he bowed deeply before the old men and asked them to pray for him as they turned and ran back across the sea to their island. "And a light shone until daybreak on the spot where they were lost to sight."[3]

escape from hell

A festive atmosphere stirred the Panagia monastery on the morning of March 25, as monks and pilgrims celebrated the appearance of the Archangel Gabriel in front of Mary, when he announced the good news that she was the Chosen One for the virgin birth of God's only Son. But for the Greeks, the Annunciation was even more significant because it coincided with the outbreak of the war of independence against the Ottoman Turks in 1821. Over the decades, this worldly, patriotic event had come to overshadow the religious significance of this date. In Cyprus in particular, with its chronic political problems, it was a time to pump up nationalist passions and ethnic pride, a time for parades, flag-waving, and flamboyant, fiery speeches with churches traditionally serving as focal venues for nationalist fervor.

No other date in the Greek Orthodox ecclesiastical calendar, I wrote in my notebook that morning, symbolized more disturbingly the merging of religion and nationalism, a deadly mix and a development officially condemned by enlightened religious leaders such as Patriarch Bartholomew of Constantinople. In a recent encyclical he had denounced nationalism as a dangerous heresy, contrary to the ecumenical spirit of

Christianity.[1] "But few seem to be listening to such warnings," I jotted down before stepping out of my cell to join the celebrants.

To my great relief the atmosphere at the Panagia monastery was radically different from what went on everywhere else on the island. There was no trace of nationalist fervor; the festivities revolved exclusively around the Annunciation. No one delivered patriotic diatribes, no one thundered against the Turks, no one urged the congregation to "never forget." On the contrary, the celebrations at the monastery had begun the night before with an all-night vigil, an *agrypnia*, offering salutations and hymns to the *Theotokos*, the Mother of God.

But was this surprising considering Father Maximos was the archetypal nonpolitical, nonideological hieromonk? Unlike the majority of higher clergy on the island, he stubbornly refused the relentless pressures he underwent to be entangled in local nationalist fervor, political upheavals, and partisan intrigues. As an Athonite monk who had made a conscious choice to abandon the world, he focused strictly on his spiritual mission. By doing so he protected the monks under his supervision from the passions and vagaries of this world. Neither radios nor television sets were allowed inside the Panagia monastery. Even newspapers were not permitted to circulate among the monks and novices. It was Father Maximos's belief that all these worldly distractions were harmful to those who had embarked full-time on a serious quest for deification in Christ.

To be so provocatively nonpolitical in Cyprus, where nationalism reigned supreme, was a subtle, unrecognized political message in and of itself. But Father Maximos's politics were confined to fasting and all-night prayer vigils for Divine assistance as a way of averting the war with Turkey that so many prophesied with disturbing regularity. "The first step toward a lasting peace with the Turks," he insisted, "is to find peace within ourselves. Then outer peace will be its natural consequence."

The island's social and political system was so deeply flawed and plagued by so many insoluble problems, Father Maximos told me once, that only through God's help could we have a chance to cope and find solutions. For what is not possible by humans is possible by God. It was the same motto I had heard from the lips of a Hindu abbot, Swami Swaroopananda of the Sivananda order, a few years earlier during an evening of informal conversations on Paradise Island on how to save the world from its path of self-destruction. After hearing Emily's enthusiastic ideas on the significance of peace education and the need to create "international eco-peace villages" that can act as oases of peace in troubled spots of the world, the Hindu abbot from Israel, after politely acknowledging the value of such enterprises, shook his head. The problems of the world, he pointed out, are just too monumental and complex to be tackled by human intelligence alone, unaided by Divine intervention. He therefore suggested that it was imperative that people develop the habit of systematic prayer for God's assistance. It was a suggestion that Father Maximos would have fully understood and endorsed.

Because it was a national holiday and unlike ordinary days, the church at the Panagia monastery was packed with pilgrims. Very early in the morning women and men began arriving with their children, bringing along special offerings of oversized loaves of wheat bread, bottles of olive oil, and *kollyva*—plates of boiled wheat mixed with seeds of pomegranate and sesame, crushed almonds, and raisins. Bread, olive oil, and *kollyva* were brought for sanctification in order to commemorate deceased relatives. The *kollyva* and the bread are distributed to the congregation after the service, who in return say, "May God forgive his/her soul." It is the custom in the Orthodox Church that the departed must be remembered periodically with memorial services toward the end of the liturgy. This happens routinely at the request of relatives who wish to commemorate their deceased loved ones. The purpose of the memorials is to pray to God for the salvation of the departed and their restoration into Paradise.

Saint John Chrysostom and other early fathers of the *Ecclesia* taught that the mere mentioning of the names of the departed during the Eucharist benefited their souls. It therefore became customary to periodically conduct memorials for the departed souls during church services.

I remember how intrigued I became when I came across a statement by the abbot of an American monastery implying that he could "see" the impact of such memorials on the souls of the departed. As if to corroborate what Saint John Chrysostom had said in the fourth century, this American abbot claimed that during memorial prayers

> a subtle bond of communication is established between them and those who remain on earth. I myself usually see the departed during the rituals I perform on their behalf. As the ritual progresses I often see them in their new . . . home and perceive the effect of the energies being directed to them. Frequently their loved ones also either see or feel them near during the ceremonies. I have seen long-standing grief eradicated completely after the sorrowing ones attended a memorial service.[2]

That passage flashed through my mind when I noticed Father Maximos stepping out of the sanctuary to lead the chanting during the memorial service. Unlike on ordinary days, he was dressed in ceremonial purple vestments and held a scepter with one hand and a long censer with the other. Father Maximos stood in the middle of the church, surrounded by monks and pilgrims, solemnly facing the altar. A table with the offerings on it lay in front of him. Lit candles made of beeswax were placed at the center of each loaf of bread. Murmuring prayers with a bowed head, he moved the censer back and forth, filling the air with fragrance, a fragrance that I had been conditioned to automatically identify with church services. In a soft, mournful voice accompanied by the other monks, he began chanting the familiar hymn:

"Blessed are You, O Lord, teach me your Statutes.

"The choir of Saints has discovered the fountain of life and the door to Paradise. May I also find the way through repentance. I am the sheep that is lost: O Savior, call me back and save me.

"Blessed are you, O Lord, teach me your Statutes.

"Of old You created me from nothing and honored me with Your divine image. But when I disobeyed Your commandment, O Lord, You cast me down to the earth from where I was taken. Lead me back again to Your likeness, and renew my original beauty.

"Blessed are you, O Lord, teach me Your statutes.

"I am an image of Your ineffable glory, though I bear the scars of my transgressions. On Your creation, Master, take pity and cleanse me by Your compassion. Grant me the homeland for which I long and once again make me a citizen of Paradise.

"Blessed are You, O Lord, teach me Your statutes.

"Give rest, O God, to Your servants, and place them in Paradise where the choirs of the Saints and the righteous will shine as the stars of heaven. To Your departed servants give rest, O Lord, and forgive all their offenses."

After a few more chants, Father Maximos read in a low voice more prayers for the departed souls. "O God of spirits and of all flesh, You have trampled down death and have abolished the power of the devil, giving life to Your world: Give rest to the souls of Your departed servants in a place of light, in a place of repose, in a place of refreshment, where there is no pain, sorrow, and suffering. As a good and loving God, forgive every sin they committed in thought, word or deed, for there is no one who lives and is sinless. You alone are without sin. Your righteousness is an everlasting righteousness, and Your word is truth."

I had listened to that memorial chant time and again since my early childhood, but it was the first time that I really focused on its meaning. I realized that the lyrics of the chant expressed key elements of the mystical Christian tradition, the notion that the soul is cast off from God from time immemorial and the expressed hope for its ultimate restoration to its original condition through the Grace of the Holy Spirit.

As Father Maximos began to read the list of names of the deceased, many pilgrims began wiping their tears. I kept watching and listening and,

true to my professional habits, I dwelt on the social significance of such rituals. It was a rationalist *logismos* that crossed my mind against which I
could offer no resistance. Religious rituals, I thought, perform a useful
function for society and individuals in that they contain the level of anxiety and fear that are unavoidably experienced by people confronting the
tragedies inherent in the human condition. A sociologist would have reasoned that such memorials were actually for the welfare of the living and
not for the departed. Such ceremonies cause emotional release of grief
and foster interpersonal solidarity. Furthermore, ceremonials like these re-
inforce the moral fabric of society. But it was the potentially mystical
meaning of these memorial ceremonies that interested me. And it was that
aspect of the memorials that Father Maximos could speak about, based on
his personal experience.

When I later confessed my *logismos*, his response was that such secular explanations are only partial truths. Quoting the works of the early fathers of the *Ecclesia*, Father Maximos insisted that a real mystical event
with spiritual consequences unfolds during rituals commemorating departed souls. He spoke with such force of authority on the matter that he
left me hardly any room for doubt. Perhaps, I reasoned, Father Maximos's
interpretation may be on a superior level of apprehending reality than that
of my sociologically conditioned mind.

Outside in the courtyard, once the service was over, the loaves of
bread and the *kollyva* were distributed by the mourners to all those in at-
tendance. "May God bless her soul," I wished a man and his three teenage
daughters as they offered me a bowl of *kollyva* and a piece of sanctified
bread that they brought over to commemorate the recent death of his wife,
the girls' mother.

After the *kollyva*, pilgrims were freely offered tea, coffee, and pastries
at the new *archondariki*. Then it was time for fellowship. Several visitors
were close relatives of the monks and would visit the monastery on such
holidays in order to chat with their sons and brothers. On such occasions
the monks' other activities were suspended so they could spend more time
with their visitors. It was also a time for the monks to learn a few things
about the world beyond the boundaries of the monastery. "I am glad my
son is here rather than on Mount Athos," a black-clad mother of a monk
told me. "At least here I can see him once in a while," she sighed as she
drank from her teacup.

At the *archondariki*, where as many as a hundred people had gathered,
I was pleased to see Stephanos, whom I hadn't seen for several days, and
the deeply devout and spiritual Erato, his wife. My friend Antonis, who
first introduced me to Mount Athos, was also present. He had decided to
spend the weekend at the monastery for spiritual renewal.

Following lunch, Father Maximos asked the four of us and Maria, an energetic and outspoken social worker friend of Stephanos and Erato, to join him at a private guest room. Fathers Arsenios and Nikodemos also joined us. I made certain that my minirecorder was in a fully functional form with new batteries and a clean tape.

The special guest room was better furnished than the larger *archondariki*. We sat in the comfortable velvet armchairs as Father Arsenios served us tea. In addition to several large icons decorating the walls was a picture of elder Paisios standing outside his hermitage. Next to him was a large portrait of elder Ephraim, another contemporary charismatic elder from Mount Athos. Facing them on the opposite wall was also a large, framed photograph of elder Porphyrios. Their pictures were able to be displayed publicly because all three had died recently. In accordance with Athonite tradition, only after a holy elder leaves this world is it permissible to have his picture displayed in public or books written about his life. Father Maximos believed that such displays were important insofar as they demonstrated the fact that the presence of saints among us has been an ongoing reality within the *Ecclesia* from its ancient beginnings to the present. While drinking tea I tried to steer the conversation to further elaboration on the significance of memorial services. To that end I asked Father Maximos whether he had any thoughts on what happens to those souls that have no one to pray for them. "What's their fate?"

Father Maximos placed his teacup on the table in front of him. He recognized the provocative insinuation of my question and with a grin on his face began to argue that the liturgy itself is for the benefit of the entire human race, the living and the dead of all the generations throughout time.

"Do you mean," I asked, "that all the billions of people that have ever lived and are now living benefit spiritually from the prayers during services?"

"But of course."

I interpreted his response to imply that the prayers human beings engage in create a benign, angelic energy field that benefits the entire human race. I reminded him, however, that the memorial carried out that morning was conducted for specific persons whose relatives wished them to be commemorated during the liturgy. "What happens," I persisted, "to those anonymous others who have no one to pray for them, no one to remember them? In one hundred or two hundred years there will be nobody thinking of us just as we don't think of those who died two or three hundred years ago. What then?"

Father Maximos reflected on my question for a few seconds and then he replied. "Let me tell you of a true story that just came to my mind. Perhaps this will shed some light on what happens when we pray for the departed. It took place in Russia, before the revolution. There was this priest who had a problem with alcohol. He would often go to church drunk, scandalizing the faithful. The parishioners sent a delegation to the local bishop, imploring him to intervene and do something about it. The bishop accepted their requests and reprimanded the alcoholic priest. Unfortunately, the poor fellow had no control over his addiction. So the bishop finally told him, 'Look, Father, since you are unable to quit drinking, then you must quit being a priest. From this moment on you are no longer authorized to administer the sacraments.' The bishop defrocked the alcoholic priest. Feeling guilty, the priest accepted the verdict and humbly walked out.

"During the night," Father Maximos continued, "while the bishop was alone in his room in prayer, he had an extraordinary vision. He saw thousands of angry people in an open field threatening to harm him. When he returned to his normal state he was shocked and wondered what the significance of such a vision could be. Was it perhaps some kind of fantasy, a hallucination? He calmed down and then went back to his prayer. But he reexperienced the same vision. In it he saw people screaming and demanding that he bring back the priest.

"The following day the bishop summoned the defrocked priest to his office. He asked him 'What's going on with you? What did you do?' 'What did I do, my bishop?' the poor man muttered with confusion. 'We just talked about it yesterday.' 'But you must have done something else,' the bishop insisted and asked him to report in minute detail how he spent his days as a priest. 'You know, Your Eminence,' he said, 'because of this problem with alcohol I felt great remorse and guilt. So, in order to compensate for my problem I made it a habit of going to the cemetery every single day to conduct memorial services for the dead. I prayed for their souls since I could do nothing for mine. That's all I did.'

"The bishop realized," Father Maximos went on to say, "that the people in his vision were the souls of the departed who demanded the return of that priest so that he may continue his prayers for them. That Russian priest knew none of the people buried there."

"Was this perhaps some kind of dream?" Maria, the social worker, hastened to ask.

"No, it was a vision. He was not asleep," Father Maximos replied. Then he went on. "In this story we see that God, who does not judge with human conceptions of justice, appreciated the greater good that the priest was performing for the departed souls, considering it more important in comparison to the minor evil of his personal addiction."

As Maria kept raising challenging questions, Father Maximos tried to

make things clearer. "Let me tell you of another case so that you are better able to understand how spiritual laws operate. Do you see that picture?" Father Maximos asked, and pointed at the portrait of elder
Ephraim. "He was one of the greatest elders and ascetics of the twentieth
century, a real contemporary saint, one endowed with extraordinary divine
gifts.

"Elder Ephraim," Father Maximos continued, "went to Mount Athos
when he was only twenty years old. Right from the start he became a subordinate to Father Nikeforos, a hermit who lived at Katounakia, a rugged region of Mount Athos. They were compatriots from Thebes. Unfortunately,
Father Nikeforos was a notorious elder with a reputation for being a very
harsh and authoritarian man. I can't describe to you the difficulties that
elder Ephraim had to go through during his apprenticeship with this elder.
Father Nikeforos was merciless, had no discernment, no trace of human
sympathy, no compassion. Other elders who knew him well used to say, 'We
would go there to visit Father Ephraim, but we could not tolerate his elder
for more than fifteen to twenty minutes so we had to take our leave.' One
elder went as far as to say that 'PapaNikeforos' may have looked like a man
but in reality he was a wild beast."

"Perhaps he was mentally ill," Maria suggested.

"Who knows? Perhaps he was," Father Maximos replied.

"Or perhaps he was possessed," Antonis joined in.

"I would not exclude that possibility either," Father Maximos said
softly, and continued. "Many times elder Ephraim reached the point
when he prepared to leave him. Not only was he being tormented by this
elder but the conditions for real spiritual work did not appear to be present. It was impossible for them to sit down and eat without PapaNikeforos
shouting and screaming. It was a life of martyrdom."

"But why did he stay with him? This is not normal," Maria protested,
raising a question we all had in our minds.

"Well, it's a mystery and a paradox. Elder Ephraim confided in me,
when I asked him the same question, that every time he decided to leave
him, he felt the Grace of God abandoning him. One day a different elder
asked him, 'How are you Father Ephraim?' 'Good,' he replied wryly. 'And
how is your elder?' Father Ephraim sighed and replied, 'He torments me,
Father, he torments me.' Guess what happened? Because of those words
against his elder he felt Grace withdrawing from him for the next six
months. During that period he mourned the loss of Grace and felt absolutely miserable. Imagine! Can you fathom something like this?"

None of us could understand such a state of mind since none of us
knew what it means to be abandoned by Grace. "It sounds like masochism
to me," Maria muttered.

"Elder Ephraim felt the loss of Grace," Father Maximos continued, "because he had negative thoughts, negative *logismoi* about his elder. Every time he thought of leaving him he had the same experience of Grace abandoning him. Forty-two entire years passed by in this insufferable state. He entered Mount Athos at age twenty and he was sixty-two when PapaNikeforos died. 'Forty two years,' elder Ephraim said to me once, 'and he never called me by my name. He always addressed me with heavy words and curses.'

"Toward the end," Father Maximos continued, "PapaNikeforos did go crazy. The older he got the more paranoid he became. Then elder Ephraim was forced to lock him up in his cell so that he wouldn't kill himself or someone else. Elder Ephraim used to tell us, 'Forty-two years, but they were seconds.' He said to me, 'Do you understand what I am telling you? Turn forty-two years into seconds in order to imagine that I lived not only days of martyrdom, not only hours, not only minutes, but also seconds.'

"When PapaNikeforos died," Father Maximos went on, "they conducted the funeral rites. Elder Ephraim, as the subordinate, and as was customary, made a prostration and for the last time kissed the hand of his deceased elder. At exactly that moment Divine Grace spoke to him and said, 'What you did all these years was the Will of God.' And the elder replied, 'And you only tell me this now when he is dead? For forty-two years I wailed and implored you, day and night, to tell me what to do. I was burning inside, and now that he is dead you tell me this is your Will? What if I had left?' Then God answered: 'Had you left you wouldn't be where you are now. In fact you would be lost.' It was spiritual development that elder Ephraim was after. This is what he wanted and this is what he got. He used to tell us how in the final analysis his elder actually benefited him spiritually. He really meant it."

Father Maximos stopped for a few moments and smiled as he looked at our faces that mirrored incredulity. Then he proceeded. "There is more to this story. One day while elder Ephraim was in deep prayer, he had a vision. With the Grace of the Holy Spirit he realized that his elder, upon his death, was cut off from God and was suffering in Hell."

"It does not surprise me," Maria quipped, and we all laughed.

"But right at that very moment," Father Maximos continued, "elder Ephraim undertook a mercurial spiritual undertaking that lasted for years, a struggle of prayer, fasting, and charity, in order to free his elder from Hell. He fell to his knees and implored God's mercy to spare his deceased elder and free his soul from that tormented state. For the next four years elder Ephraim prayed continuously for the sake of his late elder. Every time he prayed he saw the soul of PapaNikeforos moving away from Hell until he was completely liberated. He exited Hell thanks to the prayers of his disciple that he had tyrannized for four decades."

"I still cannot see how that is possible," Maria said, and shook her head in disbelief.

"You see, Maria, the *Ecclesia* has the power, through the prayers of the saints, to save the souls of the departed. Believe me, the *Ecclesia* does have that power. Of course, for those exposed to the life of Mount Athos, elder Ephraim's story is not so extraordinary. During his older years and until his death elder Ephraim was revered by those who knew him as a living saint and a wonder-worker, just like elder Paisios and Porphyrios," Father Maximos said, pointing at the photographs of the other two venerated elders and contemporary saints.

I noticed that Stephanos and Erato, as well as Antonis and Fathers Arsenios and Nikodemos, although marveling at what Father Maximos had related to us, showed no particular puzzlement with such uncommon tales. They had been exposed to Athonite spirituality for too long to be plagued by wordly doubts and questions. Erato, who by temperament was a quiet woman but deeply knowledgeable about spiritual matters, went on to add that elder Ephraim's experience was similar to other cases in the history of Christian monasticism.

"In fact," she said, "I can think of an identical case, the life of Saint Paisios the Great."

As soon as Erato mentioned the name of Saint Paisios, Father Maximos turned towards Father Nikodemos and asked him to fetch a certain ecclesiastical book from the library next door. When the young monk returned carrying the thick, oversized text, Erato leafed through it and located the story about the fourth-century anchorite. Father Maximos then asked Erato to read the vignette, which was similar to the case of elder Ephraim but with a reversal of roles.

According to the story, the disciple of an elder, after committing numerous transgressions without experiencing any remorse or *metanoia*, suddenly died. His elder, deeply concerned about his student's fate, implored God to reveal to him what happened to this lazy and unrepentant subordinate. God then informed him that he was suffering in Hell. The elder felt great sadness and began to fervently pray for his disciple's deliverance. In his despair he sought the help of Saint Paisios, who lived in the desert and had a reputation of being a great elder and saint endowed with extraordinary gifts of the Spirit. After denying having such gifts, Saint Paisios agreed to pray with the elder for the salvation of the soul of that unrepentant disciple.

"Saint Paisios raised his hands towards the heavens," Erato read, "and prayed: 'Oh Creator of everything, please hear the prayers of your undeserving servants and demonstrate your infinite compassion by freeing the student of this elder from the chains of Hell.' "

Erato went on reading to us that after this invocation, both Saint Paisios and the elder of the deceased disciple experienced an identical vision that they later corroborated among themselves. The vision offered them details of how that disciple was finally freed by Christ from the torments of Hell. "Then the elder," Erato went on reading, "asked the great Paisios to reveal to him what kind of spiritual struggles he engaged in that allowed him to have this extraordinary gift. According to the chronicler, Saint Paisios humbly replied: 'Forgive me honorable father but no work that I have performed is worthy of such a gift. It is Divine Providence that arranges such matters as a response to those who ask for help from the bottom of their hearts. Divine Providence heard your prayers and realized the great love that you showed toward your student. You have thus followed the example of the compassionate God who revealed to us this truth, that no virtue is superior than selfless love for which one sacrifices even his life for his friends. It is this love which you demonstrated towards your disciple and it is for this reason that the Lord listened to your prayers.'"[3]

I mentioned that regardless of the factual nature of these experiences, such stories were very interesting theologically in terms of how the Athonite Christian tradition, as seen by its most ardent practitioners and charismatic elders, envisioned Hell.

"First of all, let me clarify something. We call it Hell," Father Maximos interjected with an emphasis on the We. "In reality what we mean is that the soul experiences estrangement from God. The soul of Father Nikeforos was cut off from God in similar ways as that of the disciple freed by Saint Paisios."

"Fine. But based on what you related to us today I can identify four basic dilemmas that stand out for someone unfamiliar with the culture and ethos of Mount Athos," I argued, looking at Maria who nodded approvingly as if she could read my thoughts.

"Let's hear them," Father Maximos said with the usual smile on his face.

"In fact, I jotted them down as you were speaking," I mentioned as I began to read from my notebook. "My first concern is whether these experiences are real. I mean the story of the Russian bishop visualizing dead people screaming at him, elder Ephraim seeing his own elder in and out of Hell, and that of Saint Paisios liberating the unrepentant disciple, or whether they are mere fantasies or hallucinations. Secondly, and forgive me if I am repeating myself here, what happens with those people who end up in Hell but have no one like elder Ephraim or Saint Paisios that could rescue them from Hell through their prayers? Thirdly, do these stories imply that Hell is not a permanent state and that one can escape from it? And fourthly, based on elder Ephraim's experience, is it spiritually beneficial to remain loyal to such an elder, no matter what? What do we learn from such an elder/disciple relationship and the struggle for *Theosis*? Doesn't such an abusive relationship go contrary to basic principles of human rights?"

Father Maximos shook his head while the rest of the group, particularly Maria, awaited his response with heightened anticipation. Antonis pointed the finger at me and jokingly said that I had never ceased being a rational academic in spite of all my years of studying mystics and monks.

"How about taking the first question," I suggested. "Is it possible that elder Ephraim saw things about his elder in Hell or did he have a vision that was a projection of his own active imagination? How could one accept and believe that elder Ephraim's experience was authentic and grounded on reality and not on delusions or hallucinations?"

"Now, without theological criteria and prerequisites," Father Maximos responded, "everything must be rejected as an illusion or hallucination, including the reality of God Himself."

"What sort of theological criteria and prerequisites are you referring to, Father?" Maria interjected.

"First of all you must accept and believe in the reality of God. You must also believe in the reality of spirits and spiritual planes and subplanes that are different from and beyond that of the earth. Furthermore, you must accept that saints have real experiences of other realities. The experience of elder Ephraim, for example, was not unique to him. All saints throughout history have had similar experiences. From Abraham and Moses and Saint Paisios the Great all the way to the present, saints have had dialogues and conversations with God. You must accept that, at least as a possibility, before we go any further. Elder Ephraim was not a mentally deranged person. He was an extraordinarily gifted saint, a scientist of spiritual realities, not a mentally unbalanced person. His spiritual gifts were well known on Mount Athos among those who came in contact with him. He did not see that vision one time only. It was a repetitive vision that lasted for four years. Furthermore, he witnessed how his prayers gradually had an impact on his elder's soul. Every time he prayed he saw the soul of his elder rising higher and higher away from that hellish condition. In other words the soul of his elder was gradually becoming more and more receptive to God's grace. This continued until his complete and final restoration in God."

"The theological significance of this story is that it goes contrary to conventional beliefs about hell and damnation," I commented. "Hell in this case does not appear to be a necessarily permanent state. A human soul can in fact achieve liberation from that condition."

"Of course that is possible," Father Maximos said emphatically, as if it were self-evident. "We are naturally speaking of people who are receptive to sanctification. There are always those who are simply not amenable or receptive to such assistance. You can pray for demons as much as you want. In my opinion they are incapable of accepting Grace, although elder Paisios did pray for the salvation even of demons."

"The obvious question that comes to my mind," Maria interjected, "is that second concern that Kyriacos already raised in regard to that tyrannical elder who was saved because of the prayers of his obedient disciple, elder Ephraim. What about other people, ordinary folks, who have nobody to pray for them, who simply lack these spiritual networks and connections? It seems to me that there is an obvious inequity here that is inconsistent with God's total love for all creatures."

"But we have just talked about this. Haven't we said that the *Ecclesia* prays for all the departed? Furthermore there are the special days that we reserve specifically in order to pray for the souls of those who have gone. These services are devoted to the departed souls of the entire planet."

"Orthodox and nonorthodox alike?" Maria asked again.

"The prayers embrace and affect the entire human race," Father Maximos replied.

"So, these prayers," I interjected, "have an influence on all the people who have departed. If they are receptive, they are helped in their ascent towards God. It means, if I understand this well, that what we consider as Hell is something relative. One can be in a state of Hell that can be deeper or shallower."

"I am not sure about that. Hell is Hell. I am not aware of any deep or shallow Hell. We first need to understand what Hell means."

"I thought it is a state of being cut off from God."

"It is that, of course. It is ignorance of God, but it is not only that. According to the holy elders, Hell is the experience of God, not as light and eternal Grace but as eternal fire instead. God, however, is not eternal fire. It is human beings who create the distortions, not God. It is therefore the souls of human beings that need to be healed so that they may be able to have the vision of God as light and not as fire that torments."

Father Maximos was presenting a vision of Hell radically different than the one injected into Western consciousness as pots of boiling oil and burning brimstone. I was intrigued, as I have always felt that there was nothing more alienating for contemporary-thinking Christians than the "hell and damnation" theologies. Such dogmas led them by the droves to other religious traditions that do not entertain such grim visions of the world-to-come. Recently propelled by this same realization, a Church of England commission repudiated the idea of Hell as a place of "fire, pitchforks and screams of unending agony," describing it instead as annihilation for those who turn away from the love of God.

Rejecting the medieval understanding of Hell, the report went on to state that "Christians have professed appalling theologies which made

God into a sadistic monster and left searing psychological scars on many." The report also went on to identify several reasons for this change of position in the Anglican Church. Amongst them have been ethical protests from inside and outside the Christian faith against a religion of fear, and a growing realization that the picture of a God who consigns millions to eternal torment is alien to the revelation of God's love in Christ.

Yet the report ended with a note that I felt raised just as many questions. "Hell," it stated, "is not eternal torment, but it is the final and irrevocable choosing of that which is opposed to God so completely and so absolutely that the only end is total non-being."[4]

Total non-being? From my understanding of the order of things, even humans who rejected God "so completely" could not enter into a state of "non-being." Wouldn't that contradict the fundamental principle that the soul is immortal? Furthermore, doesn't God's absolute mercy and compassion presuppose that souls be given further chances to escape from their veritable hell and misery? And doesn't God's total compassion and absolute love necessitate their eventual restoration in their divine state? I suspect it was this inner logic that propelled elder Paisios to pray for the salvation even of demons, and Saint Silouan to state that he could not rest in peace with the notion that even a single soul may be lost. How can I be happy in Paradise, lamented this contemporary Russian saint from Mount Athos, when even one of my fellow humans remains tormented in eternal Hell?[5] Can we then conclude, I wrote on the margin of the page where I read that passage from the life of Saint Silouan, that the soul in Paradise cannot be in a state of total bliss as it ought to when even a single human rots in eternal damnation? Is Paradise then incompatible with such a morbid notion?

I was about to raise these issues with Father Maximos when Stephanos, who up to that point had remained silent, raised his own question. "Father Maxime," he asked, "how can we differentiate delusion from authenticity? We as human beings, no matter how advanced we may be, carry within us the possibility of delusion. You may have a vision of God or you may hear the voice of God, as was the case with elder Ephraim, and yet you may still think that it is a form of misperception or hallucination. How can you differentiate an authentic experience of God from an unauthentic experience? Many people today claim that they hear the voice of God, that they see the Holy Virgin, Christ, and so on."

"I have known people who come and tell me that they hear messages from God, they hear this and they hear that, and I am pretty certain that they are deceiving themselves," I interjected.

"That's what I had in mind when I raised this question," Stephanos added. "How can we know that the experience of elder Ephraim or that of Saint Paisios is a direct communication with God Himself and not a form of delusion? It's the same concern that Kyriacos and Maria raised."

"Look. God Himself, through His words and those of the elders, offered us some criteria," Father Maximos replied. "Most important, we can verify authenticity on the basis of experience. If you are experienced you can easily detect delusion, just like an experienced jeweler can detect a real diamond from a fake." He paused, stroked his black beard, and thought for a while. Then he continued, "When the soul is accustomed to the presence and taste of Grace, it immediately then recognizes delusion, or what the elders call *plani*. On the surface something may look totally pure and innocent, giving you no reasons to doubt it or have any suspicions. The experienced soul, however, recognizes the deception. I mean the deception when it emerges as a manifestation of the spirit of deception. Do you understand?" We nodded as we understood that he meant Satan. "I do not mean a wrong idea. If the soul is ill and dominated by vanity, pride, and similar passions, then deception is likely. But if the soul is humble, then the spirit of deception can be easily detected."

"Is this what the elders mean," Stephanos asked, "when they say that it is humility that gives birth to discernment?"

"Correct," Father Maximos nodded. "By discernment they refer to the process by which one evaluates the origins of a spirit, whether it is from God or not from God. You see, without the soul's attainment of humility, discernment is impossible. Essentially discernment is none other than the sum total of experience, reason, and intuition. It is the capacity to recognize immediately that a particular spirit is one of deception. Both elder Ephraim and Saint Paisios were highly experienced warriors of the spiritual struggle and reached great depths of humility. They therefore reached discernment and could differentiate a real message or communication with God from one of illusion and deception."

"Isn't it possible that a saint may be deceived?" Maria wondered.

"On issues related to knowledge about worldly affairs, yes. But that's not delusion or *plani*. It is simply error, which is the product of human imperfection. It is an intellectual mistake, a mistake related to knowledge of this world. It is not a mistake based on discernment about good and evil spirits, or confusion as to whether a message comes from God or not from God. Do you understand? A saint may point to a tree, for example, and say, 'This is a pine tree' when in reality it is something else. A saint is not necessarily a scientist of the external world. After Pentecost, the disciples of Christ, being humble fishermen, did not all of a sudden become knowledgeable about this world. They were endowed with divine wisdom and gifts of the Holy Spirit like healing and prophecy. They were not endowed with specialized knowledge about the material world."

We ended our conversation, as many times before, when the *symandron* called us for vespers. Father Arsenios stood up first and we helped him carry the teacups to the kitchen. Stephanos and Erato walked to the chapel while Maria, after thanking Father Maximos and getting his blessings, went to her car for the two-hour drive back to Nicosia.

I reminded Father Maximos that we had not covered the issue of eldership and what one should do in cases of abuse, as was the case with elder Ephraim. "Remind me to take that up tomorrow," he said as we walked to the church with Father Nikodemos and Antonis.

It was eight-thirty in the evening when vespers were over and Stephanos and Erato returned to their mountain retreat, a twenty-minute drive. I headed for my cell and shut the door behind me as Father Maximos and the other monks withdrew to their own cells to continue their *askesis* before going to sleep. I, on the other hand, took notes and spent some time contemplating the issues that we discussed with Father Maximos.

Stories like the one of elder Ephraim and his struggle to free his own elder from the state of "eternal Hell" left a strong impression on my mind. In my estimation such experiences, which were part of the tradition of Athonite spirituality, went contrary to the hell-and-damnation theologies with which I'd been surrounded growing up. When I had once raised my concerns with Father Maximos, he reassured me by saying, "The only thing we can be totally certain about is that God will judge us with absolute love and absolute compassion."

Father Maximos's solutions, however, did not quench my interest in thinking about such issues. That evening as I began reading about the work of Saint Gregory of Nyssa,[6] one of the Cappadocian fathers who, along with his brother Saint Basil the Great, played a key role in the formulation of early Christian theology, I came across some material which, to my surprise, related directly to the issues that preoccupied us that very afternoon—and it was not the first time answers would somehow appear accidentally as I became obsessed with an idea or a question. It expounded Saint Gregory's position on the upward march of the soul toward God and contained his controversial teachings on the eventual redemption of all souls.

"The purpose of human life," wrote the author, referring to Saint Gregory's theology, "is the attainment of the absolute good, the attainment of perfection. This is achieved through a long, painful and arduous march which has as a starting point the cultivation of virtue and as an end point the attainment of *Theosis*. . . . This is the struggle of all human beings, particularly that of the ascetics, the true philosophers."

With great fascination I continued to read further on Saint Gregory's beliefs concerning Hell, which was perceived by him as a state for the therapy of the soul. I read on: "St. Gregory's thought is based on the conviction of the absolute goodness and love of God. . . . He believes that the torments of hell have as their sole purpose the healing of the soul which means that they are not eternal." Here is the answer I was looking for, I murmured to myself, and read further. "Therapy is accomplished through fire which is not the fire of the senses but one which is of a moral nature. . . . After their catharsis the souls then enter into eternity. Some of them manage to attain their purification during their earthly life while others achieve it during the life to come. Even those souls that have not tasted of the good and evil of this life will partake of God's love and goodness during the life to come. Resurrection for Gregory implies our restoration into our primordial natural state. Human beings, after catharsis and resurrection, will return back to God. The endpoint will be like the beginning."

The *Patristic* scholar of this book went on to state that according to Saint Gregory this restoration is attainable because of the desire of the soul to return to its angelic condition and because the goodness of God makes that possible and necessary. Upon its return, the soul gains a permanent state next to God, having first experienced this world. "At the end even the inventor of evil will be healed in a similar manner. And when everything is restored to its primordial condition, a hymn will be lifted up to God chanted by the entire Creation."[7]

Saint Gregory's unconventional notions about Hell and the restoration of the entire Creation did not prevent him from being recognized as a theological leader of the Eastern Church. During the Fifth Ecumenical Council he was declared "Father of the Fathers." Yet, the part of Saint Gregory's theology that referred specifically to the issue of Hell and restoration was put aside and did not become part of the official teachings of the Church, East or West. Instead the vision of the Apocalypse and that of Dante came to dominate the culture of Christendom.

My encounter that evening with the work of Saint Gregory, who provided me with answers to issues of great importance to me, was almost identical with a similar experience I had while struggling with such issues several years back. The answer came to me then in the form of a lecture by a leading, Harvard-trained Greek theologian and philosopher who made similar claims about the position of Christianity's founding elders concerning Hell. Dr. Constantine Cavarnos, unlike hell-and-damnation preachers, claimed that the great fathers of the *Ecclesia*, such as Saints Gregory of Nyssa, John Climakos, Simeon the New Theologian, Gregory of Sinai, and Nicholas Cavasilas, taught that the individual's spiritual evolution achieved here on earth does not stop with death. They taught that "in the afterlife there will be continuous progress, unending growth in perfection, in knowledge, and in love."[8]

Here it is, I thought to myself. Both in the experience of contemporary saints, like elder Ephraim, and in the teachings of the ancient Christian fathers, the notion of eternal Hell is absent. Yet, today that notion very much dominates the official doctrine of Christianity, leading many of its adherents to search for alternatives in other religions.

The next morning I went to the library to find Father Nikodemos to thank him for the book and share my thoughts with him. He was an archaeologist by training and had a reputation as an intellectual monk. He was standing on a stool shelving books when I raised the issues that had preoccupied me the previous night. Father Nikodemos turned toward me and said that just because someone is a great saint, it does not follow that all his theology is automatically incorporated into the dogmas and canons of the *Ecclesia*. Only those theological points that have been approved by ecumenical councils, he claimed, become official teachings.

Yet, I pointed out to Father Nikodemos, elder Ephraim's and Saint Paisios's experiences are not only plausible but also compatible with Saint Gregory's thesis on Hell and restoration. They are also in accordance with the teachings of many other leading early Christian fathers. And Saint Gregory's thesis as well as those of other Christian fathers are more compatible with the understanding of God as total compassion and unconditional, absolute love. "Don't you agree, Father?"

Young Father Nikodemos shook his head, smiled, and continued placing books back on the shelf without answering my question. "Don't you think, Father," I probed further, with a slight dose of irreverence in my voice, "that it is high time for a new ecumenical council to reexamine this issue as well as many, many others?" Father Nikodemos stopped shelving his books and turned toward me again. "Perhaps," he said cryptically, "it is Divine Providence that would not allow the formation of another ecumenical council, for the time being." He did not elaborate what his furtive response implied. When I later brought up this point with a leading Orthodox scholar and bishop of the church, I was led to understand that the level of education and saintliness of the majority of those that compose the clerical hierarchy at this point in time is so abysmally low that such a council might spell disaster for Christianity. It is best, therefore, that no such council be held for now, even though more than a thousand years have passed since the last one. The trouble is that in the meantime, critically thinking Christians are moving by the droves to Hinduism and Buddhism partly because of what they consider as the dominance of untenable hell-and-damnation doctrines and preachings. The irony is that such beliefs don't seem to be at par with the teachings of the founding holy elders of Christianity itself.

12

passion for justice

I t was already July, and the end of my sabbatical was fast approaching. The thermometer in the cities, particularly Nicosia, during noontime would routinely reach close to one hundred degrees Fahrenheit, making daily life not quite paradisiacal for those who lacked easy access to the sea or the mountains. Yet, when the sun set and the westerly sea breezes began to blow, no place in the Mediterranean could match the evenings on Cyprus, filled with the intense fragrances of jasmine and honeysuckle.

Surrounded by pine trees high up on the mountains, I felt singularly privileged. The Panagia monastery in the summertime was a real resting place for body and spirit. One day a group of about twenty black-clad nuns from Greece on a pilgrimage to the sacred sites of Cyprus rested for several hours at the Panagia monastery in an effort to escape the high temperatures in the plains. The real reason for their visit, however, seemed to be Father Maximos, whose reputation as a charismatic elder had reached their own monastic retreat in Greece.

I wished to explore several more issues on Athonite spirituality before my departure from the island. So when Father Maximos asked me in the afternoon of the nineteenth of July, after engaging the nuns in prolonged discussions about the spiritual life, to drive him to the Stavrovouni monastery very early the following morning, I was fully prepared.

We began our journey a little after four in the morning, apparently Father Maximos's favorite time of day. "The eldress of the nuns you met yesterday was very close to elder Porphyrios," he mentioned in passing as we began our journey. "She told me some really extraordinary experiences she had with him."

"Some time ago, Father Maxime, you asked me to remind you to tell me about experiences that you yourself have had with elder Porphyrios. Well? Perhaps this is as good a time as ever," I said in a light tone. Father Maximos stroked his beard and smiled, apparently anticipating my request, and then went on to narrate a few episodes from the life of this legendary elder.

"Old Porphyrios was completely open to the Holy Spirit.[1] I remember one time we hosted an Italian monk who spent several weeks with us on Mount Athos. He was from Calabria and spoke Greek so well that he passed for a Greek."

"Was he Orthodox?"

"No, Catholic. But nobody knew about it except myself and the abbot. We kept it a secret from the other monks. He was dressed like the rest of us and participated in the monastery just like everybody else. He heard about old Porphyrios, and when he was about to return to Italy he asked me if I would escort him to the elder. At this time old Porphyrios was in his eighties and lived in the outskirts of Athens. The moment we entered his house we welcomed us and, blind as he was, addressed the Italian monk by his first name. Nobody had told him that we were to visit him. The moment we entered his house he said, 'I have been waiting for you, Brother Augustine!' Then old Porphyrios began instructing him on what he had to do upon his return to Italy in order to avoid a disaster at their monastery. He told him that their source of drinking water was contaminated and gave him detailed instructions as to where they should dig to find good water. He spoke as if he knew the area thoroughly. He also warned the Italian monk that they faced another danger. A huge rock at the top of the hill under which their monastery was situated was loose. He suggested that they remove the rock or fortify it so that it would no longer pose a threat. The Italian monk was stunned and asked old Porphyrios to explain how he knew about all these details. His reply was simple. It was the Holy Spirit that enlightened his mind with such information."

"Did they find the water?"

"Yes. Brother Augustine called me several weeks later to let me know that they did exactly what old Porphyrios had instructed. They found the water and fixed the rock. The Catholic monks realized that had they done nothing the rock would have crushed their monastery, just as elder Porphyrios warned."

Father Maximos then went on to tell me that the *gerontissa* [eldress] from Greece that I met the previous day confided in him some experiences she had with elder Porphyrios that were much more dramatic and extraordinary than what he had experienced himself with the elder.

"Several years ago the eldress was to have a very difficult open-heart operation and was concerned that she may not survive it. She loved to chant but following her doctor's advice she refrained from doing so. During an *agrypnia*, however, the eldress was carried away and could not control herself. In her enthusiasm she joined the other nuns and chanted the *Trisagion*, the *Ayios O Theos, Ayios Ischyros, Ayios Athanatos Eleison Ymas* [Holy God, Holy Mighty, Holy Immortal, have mercy on us]. She chanted in a high-pitched voice with all her heart, but then became terrified that her heart might give out. She was offered communion and then went to her cell to rest, full of anxiety. As she lay down, the telephone rang. 'Who is it?' she asked. 'Father Porphyrios,' the voice replied. He was calling her from his home in Athens. 'How wonderfully you chanted,' he told her, 'the Holy God, Holy Mighty, Holy Immortal. . . . Then the Immortal One visited you and rescued you from death.' Soon after the phone call her condition improved drastically and she no longer needed surgery."

"Old Porphyrios," Father Maximos continued, "used to do these sorts of things all the time. He would get on the phone and talk to people he didn't even know and tell them exactly what was happening to them and offer them advice."

"I heard that someone, not knowing that elder Porphyrios had died, called him up and that the elder presumably answered the phone. Is there any truth in this?"

"Possibly so," Father Maximos nodded, and in a humorous tone he went on to say that it was something old Porphyrios was very capable of doing. "The fellow who called was from Sydney. He was not aware that old Porphyrios was gone and called him up a month after his death. Old Porphyrios answered the phone and told the Australian, 'Don't call me again because I am no longer in this world. I died and now I live in Heaven,' " Father Maximos said with a humorous tone.

"But the most dramatic story that I have ever heard was an incident that happened to an eldress and forty of her nuns after they visited elder Porphyrios."

There was a certain hesitation in the voice of Father Maximos. Sensing my eagerness to hear more, he went on to relate this time-warp yarn from the life of this contemporary wonder-worker.

"This experience was confided in me by the eldress herself. One day she and about forty of her nuns went on a pilgrimage to Arta, an all-day bus ride from their monastery. On their way back they decided to stop in Athens to pay a visit to elder Porphyrios. They reached his house in the early evening. Their monastery was another four and a half to five hours' drive by car. The bus ride would take even longer. The eldress was very emphatic as she warned her nuns, 'Sisters, it is already seven o'clock and we have been traveling for eight hours. We have five more hours yet to go and we are all tired. So we should stay at Father Porphyrios's no more than fifteen minutes. Let's get his blessings and move on.'

"So, with that understanding," Father Maximos continued, "they entered his house. But blind old Porphyrios so much enjoyed having the nuns around that he would not let them leave. The eldress was sitting on hot coals so-to-speak. She tried to interrupt him several times. 'Geronta [Elder], we must go.' 'Sit down, don't be in a hurry,' he would reply. It was already eight in the evening and they were still at his house. At some point she couldn't take it any longer. 'I am sorry, Geronta,' she snapped, 'but we must leave. We'll visit you some other time.' Old Porphyrios waved his hand dismissively and said, 'Don't be in such a hurry. Let me turn the radio on. There is a radio station in Piraeus that has some very good chants at this hour.'

"The eldress felt her blood boiling. It was ten after eight in the evening. She calculated that they wouldn't reach the monastery until about two in the morning. She was determined to leave at once. 'Please, Geronta, turn that radio off. We must get going.' As they boarded the bus he called her and signaled that he had something urgent to tell her privately. She stepped down from the bus and he began telling her all sorts of irrelevant things. She really became impatient and irritated and told the elder, 'I am sorry, it's way past eight o'clock and I am concerned that we will be very late when we reach the monastery.' 'Oh, don't worry, don't worry,' old Porphyrios reassured her, 'you will get there on time.'

"Finally the eldress was able to board the bus. But before they set off, old Porphyrios made another request that she could not refuse. He implored her to offer a lift to two young women who happened to be visiting him. Old Porphyrios asked that they be dropped off in downtown Athens.

"You can imagine the frustration of the poor eldress. Instead of bypassing Athens, as they had planned to do, they were stuck in the city traffic. They even ran out of gas. After hours of trials and tribulations they arrived at their monastery. It was way past two in the morning. The eldress hoped that with some luck a nun would be awake to open the door for them. To their amazement the monastery was still all lit up and the thirty nuns that had remained behind were still up and about. 'Strange,' the eldress thought. 'Why did they stay up until now? Have they been waiting for us?'

"The nuns that stayed behind were curious to learn about the journey and the encounter with Porphyrios. 'Please,' the eldress implored them with impatience. 'Let us have something to eat and don't ask such questions now.' But the other nuns were eager to hear about the journey. 'What did elder Porphyrios tell you?' they persisted. The eldress lost her patience. 'Is this the right time to ask such questions? And by the way, why are you still up at this late hour? Why aren't you in bed?' The other nuns looked at each other and burst into laughter. 'My dear Eldress,' one of them replied and pointed at the clock, 'is this late?' 'What do you mean? What kind of nonsense is this?' she reacted. 'It's past three in the morning and you wonder whether it is late?' The other nuns looked at each other and continued to laugh to their heart's content. 'Look at the clock, dear Eldress.' You can imagine how she felt when she turned towards the clock and realized that it was only eight-thirty in the evening. They had covered the distance from old Porphyrios's house in the outskirts of Athens to their monastery, a trip of more than five hours, in about fifteen minutes! And bear in mind that it was not one or two nuns. An entire busload of forty people were witnesses to that incident."

"How do you explain it?"

"How? There is no rational explanation. It's a mystery," Father Maximos replied.

"Perhaps they entered into a different time zone, a different dimension," I mused. "A skeptic would say that it was a phenomenon of mass hallucination or that their watches were not working properly." Father Maximos shrugged off my skeptical reasoning. "Such phenomena do happen in the lives of saints," he insisted. "Read about their lives and you will see it for yourself. Around old Porphyrios such happenings were routine." When a person attains sainthood, Father Maximos told me once, the ordinary laws of nature are on occasion transcended. This usually happens for higher purposes, such as healing or spiritual instruction.

I drove in silence for several minutes, thinking about the extraordinary tales that Father Maximos had narrated to me about elder Porphyrios. Then, "Father Maxime," I said breaking the silence, "yesterday you said something to the nuns that made me somewhat weary."

"What did I say?" he replied, showing surprise as he lowered his window to let in the coolness of the morning air.

"You mentioned that we should let go, surrender, that is, to the *Ecclesia* so that we may be spiritually nurtured, in the same way that little infants surrender with total trust and abandon into the arms of their mothers."

"To let go," Father Maximos explained, "means to live a spiritual life without angst and worries."

"But what does that mean?"

"It means not to be obsessed about the degree of your spiritual development. Just entrust yourself in the hands of your spiritual elder within the context of the mysteries of the *Ecclesia*."

"I have problems with this notion," I reacted. "Blind faith and un-questioned obedience toward an elder is totally at odds with my Western way of thinking."

"That's why you are not a monk," Father Maximos joked.

"Such an attitude," I went on, "can be constructive, assuming that the elder has reached high levels of saintliness. But isn't there a danger that someone considered to be an elder is neither saintly nor a possessor of gifts of the Spirit but could be someone who may create conditions of abuse, as was the case with elder Ephraim?"

"Unavoidably there are risks and dangers in everything we do. That's why we need to be very careful in choosing an elder. Of course what is needed is not necessarily someone who has reached great heights of spiri-tual development or someone who is charismatic, but someone who is truly humble. The tradition of the *Ecclesia* itself will do the nurturing, not the spiritual gifts of the elder."

"So the *Ecclesia*," I said as I kept my eyes on the road, "has its own in-ner dynamic, which is self-activating. Is the elder, therefore, simply a fa-cilitator?"

"That's one way of looking at it. Spiritual guides who may not have reached high levels of spiritual attainment but who faithfully follow the methodology as set down by the holy elders can effectively play that role. Under such circumstances, elders and disciples open themselves up to the energies of the Holy Spirit so that it may lead them to *Theosis*. It is also possible for the disciples to outflank their elders on the road to *Theosis*, as was the case with elder Ephraim."

"I can well understand that," I said. "It is similar in the case of students who may become better than their professors in their academic achieve-ment. My problem is the authority structure of the relationship, the su-perordinate/subordinate setup. It goes contrary to values of equality, freedom, democracy, and civil liberties."

An ironic smile dawned on Father Maximos's face. "We must first un-derstand what true freedom is before we are able to evaluate the wisdom of the elder/disciple relationship. Does freedom imply that persons are given the license to do whatever they wish? From the point of view of the holy elders, true freedom, in fact, presupposes liberation from one's ego-tistical passions and desires. In essence, freedom means subordination to Christ. It is Christ that truly liberates us."

"This is a radically different notion of freedom than the concept that we are familiar with," I commented.

"For us monks Christ is everything. He is our freedom, our peace, our success, our happiness. True freedom is not a matter of philosophical speculations about abstract notions of individual liberties. That is a different issue altogether. We leave that discussion to philosophers, politicians, and sociologists like yourself," Father Maximos said teasingly.

He went on to clarify that monastic obedience to a spiritual elder should not be confused with obedience to some worldly power. Such an objective would be contrary to the aims of monasticism. Worldly power, Father Maximos argued, is based on the domination of human beings by human beings. It is obedience to human will fueled by egotism.

"The late elder Sophrony taught, like all other elders before him, that obedience is a spiritual act that must be based totally on one's freedom of will.[2] Obedience to an elder is spiritually fruitful only when it is based on the free volition of the initiate. That means the surrender of one's own desires and personal judgment for the sake of seeking out, with the help of the elder, 'the avenues that lead to God,' as elder Sophrony put it. So, as you can see, the spiritual guide does not aim at subjugating the will of his subordinates by enslaving them to his own human will."

"This ideal, if it works," I pointed out, "is identical to the ideal that must govern the relationship between patients and doctors. They have an awesome power over our bodies. In fact they may literally cut us up with our full consent."

"And just because sometimes things may go wrong between patients and doctors, does it mean that we should be ready to dismantle medicine?" Father Maximos asked rhetorically.

"Obviously not."

Father Maximos further elaborated on the fact that a disciple is devoted to Christ, never to the elder as a person. If the latter did not fulfill that role then the subordinate had, according to monastic rules and tradition, the right to reject him and search for another suitable elder.

I drove in silence for a few seconds as I reflected on what we had just discussed. "Those who are truly free," I then went on to conclude, "must be only the saints who have managed to transcend their own desires."

"That's what the tradition of the *Ecclesia* demonstrates. The saints are the wisest and smartest people on earth because they have not been deceived by the temptations of this world and have set their goal in the right direction, union with God."

"For ordinary people," I mentioned, "freedom is often equated with the ability to satisfy one's desires and yearnings: to own property, to hold good jobs, to consume material goods, to succeed, to engage in sexual acts with other consenting adults, to travel, to democratically participate in decisions that affect their lives, and so on. In general it means to pursue happiness as one imagines it for oneself. Your notion of freedom, it seems to me, is radically different. It is to go beyond all these very desires."

"Exactly. It is these desires that keep us enslaved to this world of transience. So, what ordinary people consider freedom may be in reality a form of slavery, but unrecognized as such."

It was close to five-thirty in the morning when we arrived at the Stavrovouni monastery, one of the most ancient monasteries in the Eastern Mediterranean. Situated on the top of a conical peak 688 meters high, the monastery was built during the fourth century by Saint Helena, mother of Emperor Constantine. According to legend, on a return trip from the Holy Land, Saint Helena was led by a vision to set up Stavrovouni, where she left behind a piece of the Holy Cross. To this day the monks preserve the small piece of the Holy Cross, which is encased inside a silver cross. It is for this reason that the monastery is called Stavrovouni, literally meaning Mount of the Cross.

It was at Stavrovouni that Father Maximos first encountered the mystic tradition of Christianity. As a teenager he would take the bus from Limassol, disembark at the base of the mountain, and hike for several hours up to the summit to meet with elder Athanasios, the venerated abbot reputed for his saintliness and charisma. Stavrovouni, like the Panagia monastery, operated like an Athonite monastery, with an elder as the head of a community of monks.

"Without elder Athanasios there may not have been a trace of monasticism in Cyprus today," Father Maximos told me as I parked the car at the gate of the monastery after a thirty minute slow and careful drive, continually circumnavigating the mountain. "With his *komboschini* and with two other monks, elder Athanasios kept the spirit of true Christianity alive on Cyprus, when everybody thought that monasticism was a thing of the past."

We walked up the steps to the church as the rays of the sun rose out of the distant sea, giving us a panoramic view of the eastern part of the island. Seeing it thus, I realized it was no accident that Saint Helena had chosen that particular spot to set up her monastery. Far from the coast, on a precipitous mountaintop, the monastery was well protected from pirates and invading armies that chronically ransacked the coastline of Cyprus. It was also a place conducive to the practice of *Hesychasm* [quietude], the silent and ceaseless form of prayer meditation, the hallmark of Athonite spirituality.

We entered the small church as the monks were about to complete their morning services. They were delighted to see Father Maximos and welcomed him with the usual bows and hand-kissing. Then elder Athanasios made his appearance from a side door that seemed to serve as a confessional. For a second I froze in awe. With his long white hair and beard, elder Athanasios appeared like an Old Testament prophet, a figure that Renaissance painters could have used as a model had they wished to portray an image of God. Now about eighty-five years old, he had been a monk at the Stavrovouni monastery since the age of fifteen. Several years back, Stephanos told me about elder Athanasios, who became his first mentor in his search to rediscover his Christian roots after many years of involvement with Sufism and Hinduism. Utterly humble-looking, elder Athanasios, Stephanos once told me, could read one's soul like an open book. When Stephanos asked elder Athanasios how he could know things that Stephanos himself had told no one, the elder replied: "I just don't know, my son. There is some kind of a flame here, around my chest, that shows me things which I need to know."

The moment he saw us, elder Athanasios began making the sign of the cross in our direction while murmuring prayers of blessings. Then, after Father Maximos made a prostration in front of him and kissed his hand, they both entered the confessional. I realized at that moment the reason why Father Maximos had asked me to drive him to Stavrovouni. His turn had come to have his own confession. Elder Athanasios served as Father Maximos's elder in Cyprus.

After Father Maximos's confession we were treated to breakfast together with thirty or so monks. Then, after Father Maximos spent some private time with elder Athanasios, we headed back for the Panagia monastery. It was the twentieth of July, a day of mourning, anger, and unfinished business for Greek Cypriots. Twenty-three years before, Turkey had launched its invasion which created the de facto partition of Cyprus. It was a day for mass rallies in the central squares of the cities and towns, denouncing the invasion and demanding the withdrawal of all Turkish troops occupying the northern 40 percent of the island and the return of the refugees to their homes.

Fortunately the prophecies of a summer war had not materialized so far, and there were no imminent signs of further conflagration. Perhaps, I thought, the all-night vigils at the Panagia and Stavrovouni monaseries changed the spiritual landscape by canceling out those "negative *logismoi*" that prepared the way for war.

I brought up the issue of the invasion after we passed several villages where huge banners reminded us of the day's significance: "Justice for Cyprus," "I Shall Never Forget," "Turkey out of Cyprus." Father Maximos looked sad and lowered his head in deep thought as I reflected on the tragedy of the invasion and the role the higher clergy played in fueling the passions that paved the road to that catastrophe.

"It seems to me many clergymen around here speak and act in ways that undermine the very religion they profess," I muttered after a while as we passed the village of Kapedes and began on the winding, pine-covered road leading to the monastery. "They don't seem to be able to differentiate or to separate in their heads the idea of 'God' from the idea of the 'Nation.' We also have this problem in America with the religious fundamentalists.

They think of Christ and Americanism as synonymous. In Cyprus it is Christ and Hellenism. In Russia it is 'Holy Russia.' Just before I came to the monastery I heard a bishop delivering a sermon that interpreted Jesus' Beatitude on justice as if He were advocating a militant struggle against oppression."

Father Maximos did not respond to my casual comments for some time, and remaining sad-looking and thoughtful, he fiddled with his *komboschini*. "Look, Kyriaco," he finally spoke as he raised his eyes to the road ahead, "I am not a politician. My role is different. Do you see what I mean? People who get exposed to the words of God understand and interpret them in accordance to their level of spiritual maturity and receptivity. I know many who have heard only one word from God, one word from the Gospel, and that was enough to lead them to a total change of life. It was enough to start them on the path to sainthood.

"When it comes to Jesus' words," Father Maximos continued, "we must not interpret them using worldly criteria. This is totally unwise. Christ was not speaking of things of this world. This is what many people fail to understand, clergymen and laypeople alike. He was not trying to make this world better and more just. Whatever Christ offered us through the Gospel had a deeper meaning, the salvation of humanity, our eternal restoration within the Kingdom of God. Therefore, words like 'Blessed be those who are thirsty and hungry for justice for they shall be filled' have nothing to do with worldly concerns about justice." He paused for a second, then continued. "I am fully aware that what I am saying may sound very disagreeable to many."

"Some people look up to Christ because He spoke of great truths and taught us about justice and equality between people of all races and between men and women," I interjected. "Several scholars go as far as to claim that the Sermon on the Mount changed the world. It led to the abolition of slavery, the emergence of modern democracy, and the universal recognition of human rights."[3]

"Things are said about Christ that are just not accurate," Father Maximos scoffed. "People don't understand that Christ's focus and preoccupations were not with issues and concerns of this world. Many people want to see Christ as some kind of a social reformer doing good deeds and little else."

"Are you suggesting that Christ was not interested in doing good?"

"No, no, Kyriaco! Christ did go about doing good. Yes, of course. Who can question that? But, I repeat, that was not His chief mission for coming into the world."

"Oh, now I see what you mean. After all, others before Christ also preached love as a way of solving human problems," I said, having in mind the "Mohists" of ancient China.[4]

"Christ's primary concern was neither the abolition of slavery nor equality between races or between men and women," Father Maximos went on. "Please don't misunderstand me. These are very good developments that may have resulted from Christ's teachings. But His primary concern and His central preoccupation was with the very essence of human existence, the salvation of human beings in God's Kingdom. When He pronounced the Beatitude on justice, He did not mean that those who are active in the pursuit of worldly justice are necessarily the blessed ones.

"Just think for a moment," Father Maximos went on. "When we find ourselves in conflict with others we feel, as a rule, that it is the others who are at fault and who have been unjust to us. Have you ever met anyone who stops during a quarrel and tells the other: 'My friend, I am truly sorry. You are right, I have acted unjustly towards you?' "

"This is also true in our collective life," I added. "We enthusiastically go to war after we demonize those we consider our enemies. And we do so with the belief that God is on our side. Alas, Father Maxime, religious people have played a major role in this demonization of the other."

"Alas, indeed," Father Maximos muttered. Then he thought of something and his face lit up again. "I often ask people during confessions, 'Have you by any chance ever been unjust toward someone?' The standard answer is: 'Me? Never! On the contrary.' "

I smiled at the mischievous grimace on his face. "Where are all the unjust folks hiding themselves anyway? I have never met them. I only hear from those against whom an injustice has been committed."

"We have a tendency to believe," I pointed out, "that somehow a just God will intervene on our behalf and bestow justice as we see it, such as forcing Turkey out of Cyprus."

"Justice for us," Father Maximos added, "usually means seeing those we consider our enemies punished by God, preferably in front of our very eyes so that we can enjoy watching them fry in Hell."

"And when justice does not come," I interjected, "it appears to us as if God is absent from history, that things happen in ways that are beyond His control and concern. I once heard a refugee declare that there cannot be a God because the Turkish army took over his hometown."

"There you go. A person with human notions of justice can legitimately raise the question: 'Where was God when Turkey invaded Cyprus?' Yet we must not think that way," Father Maximos continued. "God is not absent from history. Nothing takes place without a Divine purpose behind it."

He paused for a few seconds and then continued. "One thing we have perhaps failed to learn in our religious education is that human ways are not necessarily God's ways. I remember in high school reading an argument in a religious textbook that stated that logic leads us to the conclusion that there must be a God so that justice may be dispensed. It saw God as some kind of supreme justice. Given that there are so many injustices in the world, sooner or later they must be dealt with by God, who will punish those who commit injustices."

"And reward us, the just," I blurted out.

"This goes to show," Father Maximos continued, "the kind of ethos that is being cultivated and how far removed it is from the spirit of God. Do you know what an old saint once said? 'Never call God just because God is not just,' according to human measures of justice, that is. The saint reasoned: 'How could God be just when He requests of us that when someone comes to grab our possessions, we do nothing but let him take them? And if he asks of us to go one mile with him, we go two? And if he gives us a slap on one cheek we turn the other also? Is this justice? He died for the sake of those who hated Him, who spat and kicked Him, for the sake of the entire World. When Christ was in human form and was about to die He did not pray for His apostles but for those who were crucifying Him. He did not tell the disciples, 'Just you wait and you shall see what I'll do to them once I get resurrected!' We have so many examples of martyrs and saints who demonstrated this form of Christian love. When the young martyr Stephanos was being stoned to death, he prayed for his assailants. He knelt down while his last words were, 'Please, Lord, do not hold this sin upon them.'

"So what's the meaning of all this?" Father Maximos asked. "That the justice of God is not the justice that we entertain in our minds. It is important for people to realize this so that they may not lose faith and become cynical when they are confronted with difficulties."

"There is so much injustice around us," I went on to say, "so much disease, so much death and destruction, so many tragedies of all sorts. Good people suffer, even saintly people, and then the question naturally comes to mind, 'Where is God? Where is His justice?' "

"God's justice," Father Maximos emphasized, "works in mysterious ways, beyond the reach of our intellects."

"It seems to me that notions like liberation theology are rather off the mark and outside the spirit of Christ," I pointed out.

Father Maximos had never heard of "liberation theology," so I explained that liberation theology views the doctrine of Christ as compatible with a violent insurrection to bring about social justice. "Of course," I went on, "the Pope repudiated this theology as heretical."

"I completely agree with the Pope on this issue," Father Maximos retorted.

"Critics may conclude that this is a recipe for passivity in the face of injustice. Are you suggesting that we must remain indifferent and inactive in the world, forget about making this world a better place and direct all our energies exclusively on the world beyond? Is this what the holy elders teach?"

"That's not the way to see it. By all means be active in the world and try to make it as good a place and as just a place as it can possibly be. But again don't live with illusions. Our notions of justice are different from God's. Do you see what I mean? Please, let us not turn Christ into a social revolutionary."

"So what is God's justice?"

"Real justice," Father Maximos responded, raising his voice after a deep breath, "is for God to help us through His Grace to rectify that which truly wronged us. And what is that? Our estrangement from our Divine nature. Real justice means the attainment of *Theosis*, the reunification with God who created us in His own image. We are endowed with the potential of becoming gods through Grace. Our ultimate goal is reunion with our Maker, our real homeland and final destination. It is exactly at the core of our being, ontologically speaking, that we have been wronged, through the Fall."

"If I understand you well," I repeated, "that means justice ultimately implies our reentrance into Paradise, the return of the Prodigal Son to the palace."

"Precisely. When that is done, everything within ourselves will begin to work in accordance to our essential nature. Then our minds and hearts will open up and be able to perceive the things of this world with radically different lenses and criteria, spiritual criteria. At that point, justice will be experienced and function, not as commonly understood, but as total, absolute, and unconditional Divine love. Paradoxically, what we notice is that whenever humans align themselves with Divine justice as unconditional love, then the laws of logic are transcended and God works within them in such a way as to vindicate them both on earth as well as in Heaven. That's why hermits who have attained saintliness are least judgmental with people. One would expect them to be austere and intolerant of human weakness. The opposite is true.

"Anyway," Father Maximos went on, "the meaning of Christ's words, 'Blessed be those who thirst for justice . . .' in reality implies 'Blessed be those who thirst for the Grace of God.' For God is justice, truth, peace, everything."

"Would you say then that the other Beatitudes also have the same underlying meaning, such as 'Blessed be those who are charitable'?"

"Absolutely. The Beatitudes have a single purpose, to help humans on their path to *Theosis*. They are not about humanly conceived morality or about behaving properly. They have a deeper, ontological meaning.

"It is for this purpose that the entire pedagogy of the *Ecclesia* is oriented to heal human beings so that they may begin to function naturally, the way they were originally intended by God. This spiritual work begins within the *Ecclesia*. People usually imagine this struggle as a legalistic way to save their souls. They think of saving their souls as something like jumping out of the boilers of Hell and onto the green pastures of Paradise.

"In reality the spiritual struggle that goes on within the *Ecclesia* aims at healing our existence, our personhood, and sealing our communion with the Divine which is our real destination and the justification of our being in the world. As long as this goal is not reached, we will continue to function in an imperfect, pathological way, experiencing one injustice after another."

"The social world we collectively create will naturally reflect this pathology that lies within ourselves," I added. "Speaking about the Beatitudes, how does the 'Blessed be those who are charitable,' relate to what you have just said?"

"If I remember correctly, we talked about this earlier. Anyway, the central characteristic of the movement of God toward humanity is exactly this charitable propensity. This is also the reason why during the liturgy we call God *Eleimon*, the Charitable One. According to the scriptures, God called Himself *Eleimon*. Right? Since we are called upon to become gods ourselves, we must by necessity also become charitable. We cannot be like God until we develop this quality within ourselves."

"Do you mean offering help to the needy?"

"By charity I don't mean only to offer alms to the poor and to donate money to various worthy causes. All these are external manifestations of charity. The charitable propensity, as the movement that characterizes God, is none other than absolute and unconditional Love."

Father Maximos reflected for a second before he continued. "As a form of spiritual practice we must learn not to allow the episodes in our lives to go by unnoticed. By that I don't mean that we should focus on the tragedies and difficulties that we encounter and make them appear more bleak than they already are, leading us to despair and depression. Rather, we must realize that whatever happens to us unfolds within the infinite ocean of God's mercy and compassion.

"When we learn to generate only good *logismoi* and develop right judgment and clear vision," he went on, "then we will realize that whatever comes our way is, in the final analysis, a blessing."

"It is very difficult for people who suffer from a tragedy to maintain such a frame of mind, let alone that we should suggest it to them," I complained.

"It is difficult, but true. We know this from the testimony of the saints and from our daily experience. Do you realize that those very things that are considered hurtful and which are causes of unhappiness by human standards may be transmuted into advantages within the Grace of God? I am totally convinced that human beings who have been traumatized in their lives either physically or psychologically have tremendous potential to become truly great. This is also why the holy elders have placed so much emphasis on how to confront temptations. They didn't mean by that the pseudotemptations related to the pleasures of the senses. They meant the temptations that accompany the difficult and seemingly hopeless circumstances that people find themselves in. They meant the temptations that torment human beings and which often lead to serious psychological traumas.

"When we find ourselves in such circumstances but approach God in the right way, allowing Grace to get energized within ourselves, then something paradoxical takes place. God, as the doctor of our body and soul, not only heals our traumas so that no trace of the trauma remains, but does something much more important. He transforms the old hurts into spiritual assets. The healed person has now become knowledgeable of the inner world of human beings and can therefore become a healer to others.

"That's why," Father Maximos continued, "God quite often permitted and even propelled saints to succumb under pressure to various temptations, great temptations, that caused them deep sorrow and psychic turmoil."

"Why?"

"Because a human being who has not been tempted, who has not experienced pain or shed bitter tears, is not able to understand others in their pain and sorrow."

"As a Cypriot proverb goes," I added, "if you have a full stomach it is not likely that you will think of those who are hungry."

"That's how it is," Father Maximos agreed. "A person who has not been tempted is like bread that has not been baked. All of life's temptations unfold within the Providence of God."

"Are you by any chance suggesting, Father Maxime, that God cooperates with evil?"

"No. God never cooperates with evil. He simply offers us the opportunity to transform the painful experiences in our lives into advantages and blessings. I'll never forget the words of elder Paisios, who used to tell us that the time will come when we will be grateful to God for all the hurts and pains that we underwent in our lives. Each one of us carries his or her own cross. If we persevere and face our trials in a spiritual way, we will realize at a certain point that these traumas and trials have been transmuted within us into great advantages, into real treasures. You see, Kyriaco, the saints knew about this mystery. That's why they would often intentionally not avoid trials and sorrows but rather allow them to get energized."

"I hope they were not pursuing pain and sorrow as a way to spiritual enlightenment," I interrupted in a wry tone.

"Oh, no. They were not masochists. But when they experienced a sorrowful incident they let it happen. They remained unmoved and unshaken within a prayerful state of mind. You may wonder what for? Because they knew that all these phenomena are not what they appear to be, but they unfold within the context of our spiritual life. In the final analysis the spiritual laws worked in such a way that instead of leading these saints to their destruction, they led them to their perfection. They led them to become true children of God. They accepted their trials and painful experiences quietly in the same way that Christ accepted His own trials and sorrows. Pontius Pilate implored Jesus to say something in his defense so that he could find a way to set Him free, but He remained silent."

"This is not the way Peter behaved in the Garden of Gethsemane," I interjected. "He drew his sword and cut the ear of the Roman soldier."

"But do you know why?" Father Maximos asked. "Because Peter at that time was still dominated by his worldly brains, by his worldly way of thinking. After he rejected Christ three times, without any real reason, he received a big lesson. Do you remember what that servant girl asked him? 'You were with Him, weren't you?' But Peter, out of cowardice, denied it. 'I don't know Him, I have never seen Him.' That was an incredible fall for Peter."

"Why do you suppose God allows something like that to happen to a great apostle like Peter?" I wondered.

"Precisely so that Peter may experientially learn what a human being is all about and develop a compassionate heart, become *Eleimon* rather than judgmental. Before that experience Peter was rough, moralistic, and intolerant. He was incapable of forgiveness and was impatient with human weaknesses. Peter was transformed through that experience. When people undergo such a humbling experience then their heart may develop an *Eleimon* predisposition. They become, first and foremost, compassionate with themselves. They learn how to have a proper relationship with themselves."

"Does that mean we must feel no guilt for our transgressions so that we may be compassionate with ourselves?" I asked.

"No. What I mean is that we must learn how to evaluate each situation properly. We should examine our actions without any masochistic intentions, without causing ourselves unnecessary depression and despair. We should proceed to cut off our transgressions but always within the context of self-compassion. Despair and depression are not of God.

"That reminds me of a story from the *Gerontikon* [compilation of biographical short stories about the lives of elders]," Father Maximos continued. "A young monk had intense sexual temptations and rushed to his elder for confession. 'Father,' he told him, 'I am plagued by the *logismoi* of debauchery and I don't know what to do.' The elder was a man of God but lacked experience. He had no understanding of what it means to be under the influence of intense sexual temptations. He reprimanded the young monk, telling him that having such *logismoi* went contrary to his monastic vows. Despondent, the monk decided to give up monasticism. He thought of himself as unworthy and left. On his way to the city he encountered another elder, a wise elder, who was also spiritually gifted. Through clairvoyance this elder realized immediately what had happened. 'Where are you going, brother?' he asked casually. The young monk related the incident that made him decide to give up his monastic life after being a monk for eight years. The elder's response was comforting. 'I have been a monk for seventy years and I still suffer from such *logismoi*. Go back to your hermitage, my son, and God will help you. I will pray for you.' The young monk returned to his monastery and was freed from the warfare of the *logismoi*. But that elder did something in addition. He looked up, raised his hands, and prayed: 'Please God, redirect these temptations toward the elder of this young monk.' According to the *Gerontikon*, the *logismoi* of sexual lust left the disciple and went straight into the mind of his elder. Soon after, the wise elder saw the inexperienced elder rushing off on his way to the city. 'Where are you going, Father?' he asked him in an innocuous-sounding tone. 'Oh, don't ask me, don't ask me,' the other replied. 'I am leaving for the city. I am pestered with sexual temptations. They are suffocating me. I am not worthy of being a monk.' 'Go back to your hermitage, Father,' the other replied. 'It is God that sent you these *logismoi* so that you may grow in humility and not say things to young monks that could lead them to despair.' " Father Maximos ended his story as I turned the last curve and parked the car under a shady oak tree just outside the gate of the Panagia monastery.

Before I went to sleep that night I spent some time reading about charity and came upon a quotation from the work of Saint Isaac the Syrian, a celebrated holy elder of early Christianity. Saint Issac in one of his homilies addressed the issue of the nature of the *Eleimon* heart. He wrote that a truly *Eleimon* heart is a heart which is on fire, consumed by love for the whole of creation, ". . . for human beings, birds, wild animals, demons, and every creature on earth. An extreme empathy towards the whole of Creation renders such a heart incapable of hearing of any hurt or even of a minor sorrow taking place within Creation. For this reason the *Eleimon* heart offers prayers for the beasts and for the birds of prey, for animals and demons, for serpents and for everything else within Creation, including the enemies of truth."[5]

I closed the book and dozed off, having Saint Isaac's homilies on compassion in my mind. I felt light-years behind, reaching such a state of being in the world. But Father Maximos's words were comforting. "Trust and don't be concerned about how far you are on the spiritual path."

13

SPIRITUAL LAWS

The conversation on justice that I had with Father Maximos during our trip to the Stavrovouni monastery left several unanswered questions in my mind, which I wrote down. At the next opportune moment I planned to raise them with him. As if he read my thoughts, a frequent happening during my stay at the monastery, Father Maximos asked me the very next day to join him for a walk to the *skete* [hermitage] of Saint John the Baptist.

On Mount Athos the *skete* was built as a possible residence for a hermit or as a retreat for periodic and more intense spiritual work by individual monks. An integral part of Athonite spiritual practices and methods, Father Maximos introduced it to the Panagia monastery as part of his intention to transfer that tradition to the island in its entirety. By building *sketes* around the Panagia monastery, Father Maximos's long-term vision became apparent. It was a clear signal that his goal was to create the institutional structures that could produce saints in a similar manner that universities produced great scientists and Nobel laureates.

Most of the Athonite elders and saints of the twentieth century, such as the Russian Saint Silouan and elder Paisios, lived a large portion of their lives in such hermitages where they engaged in continuous and undistracted prayer. So far the three *sketes* that Father Maximos had created around the Panagia monastery remained unoccupied and were used only on special occasions as temporary retreats.

We set off during the late afternoon for the hour-long hike. Father Maximos handed me one of the two walking sticks he kept in his office. After we passed through a field of rosebushes that the monastery cultivated for producing and selling rose water, I raised my first question.

"Father Maxime," I began, "there is much talk in the teachings of the elders about temptations and how to confront them. In the minds of many people such language sounds quite outdated and pretty archaic. In fact, it is this very language that often triggers negative feelings toward religion. If I understood well from everything you told me yesterday, the popular understanding of the word *temptation* seems to be very different from that of the elders."

"That's right," Father Maximos replied as we began our walk at a vigorous pace.

"What we usually mean by that word," I went on to add, "is the pull toward some sinful act such as stealing, lying, fornicating, and so on. It is something that we assume will give us pleasure or satisfy some forbidden desire."

"This is only a small part of what the elders mean," Father Maximos responded. "As I explained yesterday, by temptation the elders implied anything that causes difficulty or sorrow. A temptation could be a failure in some pursuit or a disappointment of some kind, anything that causes us to feel less than content or uncertain that we are on the right path toward God." Father Maximos stopped for a second and, turning toward me, he asked: "Do you remember what Christ offered us as a prayer? 'Lead us not into temptation. . . .'"

"On the other hand," I responded as we resumed our pace, "I heard elders claim that temptations are good for us. That if all temptations were to be eliminated no one would be saved. Isn't that a contradiction?"

"No. It's a misconception. Christ refers to those temptations that have power over us and can damage our souls. He was not talking about all the unavoidable temptations that come our way. When properly handled, such temptations are spiritually beneficial."

"How is that?"

"The elders taught that no one is immune from temptations. Both the saintly and the sinful suffer from all sorts of trials and tribulations. Suffering is an integral part of the human condition. In fact, the pain and sorrow of the great saints can be much more intense than that of the rest of us.

"You see," Father Maximos continued after taking a deep breath that sounded like a sigh, "most of us are unaware of the ways spiritual laws work in our lives. Consequently we complain and become impatient with the slightest provocation or difficulty that we encounter along our way. We become bitter and resentful, wondering why we and not others are stricken by this or that misfortune."

"It is an old question," I pointed out. "Why do tragedies happen to good people?"

"The reason why we raise such questions is because we are ignorant of the real purpose of our existence. Had we known, as the saints do, we would welcome such temptations as opportunities for spiritual advancement," Father Maximos claimed. We remained quiet for a few seconds as we focused on our walk through a rugged turn of the footpath.

"It is very difficult to maintain such a perspective in the face of extreme grief," I suggested. "But, how do the elders explain the causes of human suffering?"

"They identify a variety of causes," Father Maximos replied as we entered a wooded area covered with pine needles along our path. "One cause may be our past actions. This is part of the spiritual law through which God rules the Universe. It is the law of cause and effect."

"If you live by the sword you shall die by the sword," I muttered.

"No one is immune to this law," Father Maximos declared. "We are free agents. When we think and act in ways that cut us off from God, this very estrangement prepares a fertile ground for painful episodes to happen. The powers of evil will be mobilized against us. Do you know why? Because we have given the green light for such sorrowful episodes to come our way. If we steal, for example, the police will come after us and we will end up in jail. It is not God that punishes us but the natural outcome of our own actions."

"This is simple to understand," I pointed out. "But what about painful experiences coming to us for no apparent reason. Skeptics would claim that such arguments are often used as a way to blame innocent victims for their suffering. If you have cancer for example, you must have done something bad of which you have no memory. You are now paying for past sins."

"The spiritual law of cause and effect is only one possible source of such temptations. It is not the only one."

"Are there any other spiritual laws besides the law of cause and effect?" I asked somewhat surprised.

"Of course there are. Quite often terrible things happen to good people, even to saints, for the sake of their spiritual growth or for other reasons."

Noticing an inquiring look on my face, Father Maximos went on to elaborate. "Let us assume that we are deeply spiritual and we pray to God day and night to save our souls. At the same time we may not exert sufficient effort for the attainment of what we most crave for, to unite with God. We may simply lack sufficient momentum to reach such a state. It is also possible that we may not be aware that some of what we do or don't do may be harmful, as far as our goal of union with God is concerned. So we deprive ourselves of the progress that we should have made, given our strengths and the level of our spiritual development at that point."

"I suppose it would be similar to the case of promising students who do not exert enough effort to attain their full potential," I commented.

"Well said. Good teachers who have only the well-being of their students in mind may on occasion employ punishment in order to stimulate them to work harder so they may actualize their inherent talents. The students have great potential, but perhaps out of ignorance or out of laziness they may not exert enough effort. Likewise we often fail to realize that we need to be more focused and serious with our spiritual life. Our hearts 'get stolen,' as the elders say, by the circumstances of our everyday life, and we don't seem to progress as much as we should. But at the same time we fervently seek God's Grace. In doing so, however, we give the right to God to help us advance on our spiritual path. This is not done through some kind of magic but through the events around us. Do you remember the story I told you about elder Paisios?"

"Which one?"

"When he prayed to God to make his heart humble in order to be able to see Him. God obliged him and created that episode with the priest who humiliated him in church as he was about to receive Holy Communion. Do you remember?"

"Oh yes, I do recall the story."

"So if we ask for humility, then God allows an episode to unfold in our life which can help us reach that goal. God will never intervene unless we give Him permission to do so."

"I'd better be careful about what I ask for," I joked. Then Father Maximos elaborated further by saying that what is needed under such circumstances is to perceive that event as a spiritual gift. "For if we react negatively and conclude that God has forgotten us or has not listened to our prayers, we may lose the chance of benefiting from the very thing we have prayed for."

"What you are telling me is somewhat different from the oriental notion of *karma*, which means that what happens to us is the inevitable result of our past actions."

"I don't know what that means. What I do know is that according to the teachings of the holy elders there may be a variety of reasons why bad things happen to people. In addition to the law of cause and effect and the law related to spiritual growth, people may suffer for the sake of others through the law and power of love. This applies particularly to advanced spiritual masters. In some mysterious way they often take upon themselves the burdens of those under their guidance, relieving them from the heaviness of their debt. The sorrows and temptations of the disciples are transferred onto the spiritual teacher. It is called the law of *anadoché*."

"I suppose it must be analogous to Christ's taking upon Himself the sins of the world?"

"Exactly. Christ is our archetype. Therefore, spiritual masters imitating Christ may, through *anadoché*, lighten the burden of their people by taking much of it upon themselves. This may often lead to serious physical harm, even death."

"Well," I pointed out, "most of Christ's apostles had terrible deaths, by crucifixion, beheading, and the like. I have also heard of contemporary saints dying from cancer, like elder Paisios."

"In the history of the *Ecclesia* there are thousands of examples. Saint Athanasios of the Holy Mountain, the founder of the Great Lavra [the first monastery on Mount Athos, built during the tenth century], fell to his death from the top of the church while working during its construction. One may legitimately wonder why such a misfortune happened to such a great saint."

"Couldn't one just as easily explain it as a tragic accident?" I snapped as Father Maximos's statement awakened the skeptic in me.

"There are no accidents," he rushed to remind me, hitting the earth with his stick for emphasis. "Nothing, absolutely nothing happens in the Universe without a deeper meaning to it. That great saint followed Christ's example. He accepted upon himself the burdens of his disciples for the spiritual progress of the monastery which he was busy setting up."

We stopped talking for a while, as if Father Maximos was deliberately giving me time to ponder the significance of what he had just said. Then he resumed our conversation. "And do you want to know something else? The law of *anadoché* can also work in a negative way."

"In a negative way?"

"Yes, this is part of the mystery of how spiritual laws operate in life. Just as the holy elders can assume the burdens of others in a positive, altruistic way, the rest of us, without even realizing it, we may assume the burdens of those we mistreat. If, for example, we slander or tell lies about people and they do not respond in kind, then part of their own burdens, sorrows, and temptations may be transferred on to us as the culprits who caused them harm. In such cases there is *anadoché* in a negative way."

"But if this is the case," I reasoned, "then those who harm us are, in reality, our benefactors. One could argue that this is pretty bizarre, at least from the point of view of ordinary common sense."

"Bizarre or not bizarre, that is exactly what the elders teach. There are spiritual laws at work that most people know nothing about. So when others hurt us, our tendency is to strike back because we assume that we must defend ourselves, defend our name, our honor, our career, and so on. In reality we strike back at ourselves."

"But isn't it normal to react in such a manner?" I asked. "Psychologists and counselors never cease to remind us that if we let others step all over us, then we have a problem. We lack assertiveness, we become a 'doormat' to our tormentors. Isn't it only natural that we should strive to protect ourselves and defend our rights?"

"Striking back may be normal but it is not necessarily always the proper response. I do realize that this is not an easy principle to accept but that is the way spiritual laws work. What we consider as justifiable defense of our rights may in reality plunge us into a vicious cycle that can undermine our very spiritual foundation. By reacting to aggression with aggression we lose the opportunity to spiritually benefit from the experience. This law also explains why saints, when hit, often would literally turn the other cheek."

As Father Maximos spoke of the law of *anadoché*, it became clear to me why he had refused to defend himself against an avalanche of accusations hurled relentlessly at him by a local bishop since the father's arrival on the island. The bishop repeatedly stated in public that Father Maximos was part of a conspiracy engineered by Athonite monks to take over the *autocephalous* Cypriot Church. When these tactics failed to convince anybody, the bishop began to spread rumors that Father Maximos engaged in sexual improprieties. Disgusted with the bishop, a group of Father Maximos's followers set up a committee that included several lawyers to defend him against what they considered to be blatantly false accusations and malicious lies. When Father Maximos found out about this initiative he asked the lawyers to immediately stop all such activities and allow the bishop to say whatever he wished. Father Maximos explained to them that he preferred to totally put his trust in God's Providence. He therefore needed no defenders. It so turned out that the bishop was thoroughly discredited by his own actions while Father Maximos's popularity as a charismatic spiritual leader skyrocketed. Apparently the law of *anadoché* worked.

Father Maximos went on to say that in addition to the law of cause and effect, the law of spiritual progress, and the law of *anadoché*, bad things can happen to people because of the malevolence of evil spirits. A classic example of this possibility, he elaborated, is the case of Job in the Old Testament.

"His children were killed, his property was destroyed, and he was turned into the lowest of the low. He was rejected by everybody, including his wife. This once-happy, prosperous, and just man, who hurt no one in his life, who was a benefactor to anyone who sought his help, was forced to live on piles of garbage while his body was filled with leprosy. Job reached the ultimate of despair beyond human endurance, so much so that he cursed the day he was born.

"Worst of all," Father Maximos continued, "Job experienced the silence of God."

"The silence of God?"

"Yes, the feeling that somehow God is absent from our lives, that He does not exist, that God mercilessly allows evil to hit human beings."

"That's how people must have felt when the Nazis marched them into the gas chambers," I pointed out.

"Yes. Human beings under such circumstances can reach the ultimate point of despair, beyond which no further endurance is possible, while God remains silent as in Job's case. Remember his former friends teasing and provoking him, asking him, 'Where, then, is your God?'

"Suddenly, at that ultimate state of despair, God spoke to him and revealed His true nature. Then Job spoke those unforgettable words: 'I had heard of thee by the hearing of the ear, but now my eye sees thee; therefore I despise myself, and repent in dust and ashes.' At that ultimate point of despair Job began to experience an immediate and clear vision of God.

"One of our elders," Father Maximos went on as we came out of the wooded area, "used to tell us that God becomes manifest at the end stage of an excruciating patience. At that ultimate point when the person has no more capacity for endurance, God may make His appearance."

"I suppose this is what happened to elder Ephraim," I commented.

"Exactly so. It is the same God that revealed Himself to both of them," Father Maximos pointed out. Once again we walked in silence until we reached the *skete* of Saint John, a small, stone structure with a tile roof that blended nicely with the mountainous surroundings. It stood at the edge of a cliff with a narrow balcony facing east. Next to the building a tall and wide pine tree offered shade to the hermitage during the hot hours of the day. The *skete* seemed to be ideal for a life of prayer, contemplation, and total silence.

The first thing that Father Maximos did when he opened the door was enter the tiny chapel. After crossing himself followed by several prostrations, he kissed the icons of Christ, then the Holy Virgin, and then John the Baptist. After this he poured oil into the lamps that hung in front of the three icons and lit them. He then burned some incense while I stood on the side, watching his every move.

"They like it, you know," he said with a smile just after a thought crossed my mind wondering why he was lighting the lamps, since we would be gone soon.

When he completed the ritual we sat on a bench outside on the balcony for some rest. After a few minutes of gazing at the open expanse of land in front of us, I resumed the conversation. "Since the cause of temptations that come our way can be varied, how can we know whether they are the result of past actions or caused by something else? If someone becomes seriously ill, with cancer, how can we know that such a temptation is the result of the law of cause and effect or, say the law of *anadoché?*"

"You cannot know. It is a mystery that can never be cracked open by the human intellect. The only certainty we can have is that there are spiritual laws at work, as outlined by the holy elders, those human beings who have a knowledge of God. How these laws work in specific situations, only God Himself knows."

"So," I concluded, "it is futile to search for causes."

"Not only is it futile but it can potentially undermine our spiritual life."

"Oh, I see what you mean. Our ego unavoidably gets entangled in such a search. Therefore, it could become a distraction in our effort to overcome our passions and weaknesses."

Father Maximos agreed and advised that we focus on how to confront a given temptation regardless of its cause. "The holy elders teach that anything that comes our way can be transformed into a temptation."

"For example?"

"Poverty, prosperity, happiness, unhappiness, health, illness, success, failure. Any such conditions that we may face can become temptations."

"I can see temptation in poverty, illness, unhappiness, failure. But it is hard to see it in happiness, prosperity, success."

"The elders instruct that wealth and worldly success can also become great temptations if they imprison your heart and mind to this world, or make you arrogant and vain," Father Maximos replied. "The same principle applies to happiness, health, and so on. For every conceivable situation, therefore, we must remind ourselves that at this point in time we are confronted with this particular temptation. What should we do and how should we handle such a temptation? Let us say, I am rich. How should I confront my richness spiritually? Or, I am poor. How should I confront my poverty spiritually? I am happy. How should I confront my happiness spiritually? I have difficulties in my family. How should I confront my difficulties spiritually? Do you follow me? Notice that as a rule the holy elders, as the valiant souls that they are, place the cause of any problem they face squarely on themselves."

"Not so easy for ordinary mortals like myself," I reacted.

"Just think of it this way," Father Maximos continued as he stood up and spread his arms around. "Christ reminded us that God looks after the birds of the sky and attends to every single blade of grass. Isn't He going to look after us? And if it is true that every single hair on our head is within God's Providence, how much more true is this about serious matters in our life? If we bear this in mind as our deepest conviction and faith, then why despair? Even if the sorrows we experience are the result of our transgressions, assuming that we are patient we can transform them into spiritual advantages. God has the power to vaccinate, to transmute the evil we committed and turn it into good. Why, you may ask? Because it is not possible for God to reach dead ends, to become checkmated. Nor it is possible for the evilness of human beings to have victory over God's infinite wisdom. Even the evil committed by the most terrible of murderers cannot possibly win over the love of God."

There was passion in Father Maximos's words. His absolute and unadulterated faith in God's Providence was like a soothing medicine to wavering minds like mine, schooled and nurtured for years in the virtues of doubt.

Father Maximos locked the *skete* and we set off for our return walk. "What you just said, Father Maxime," I said, "reminded me of David."

"Oh, David. David!" Father Maximos reacted and shook his head. "That's a good example of what we have been talking about, alright."

Two years earlier I had received a letter from David, a death row inmate who had read my books. David wrote that since his death sentence he had developed an intense interest in spirituality. He asked whether I could suggest a teacher he could write to. I gave him Father Maximos's address. Three months later he wrote back to update me on what had happened. David wrote that he had begun a regular correspondence with Father Maximos. Never before, he claimed, had he experienced so much love coming to him from another human being. In addition to the letters, Father Maximos sent him books on the teachings of the elders such as the *Philokalia*[1] and the Russian classic *The Way of the Pilgrim*.[2] Apparently this material and the contact with Father Maximos had a profound impact on David. The best thing that ever happened to him, he wrote, was his arrest. It opened him up to spiritual realities and rescued him from further damaging his soul.

Coincidentally, or perhaps providentially, not far from the maximum security prison where he was held an Athonite monastery had been created a few years earlier with the financial assistance of a Texas millionaire who was miraculously healed by an Athonite hermit. Father Maximos called up the abbot, an American monk he knew from Mount Athos, and asked him to visit David. It took nine months before permission was granted, as the prison authorities had no precedent on how to deal with monks. Until then the only categories of religious functionaries they had recognized were ministers, priests, and rabbis. The bearded, black-robed monks began visiting David regularly. They assigned him a strict regimen of spiritual practices including systematic and continuous prayer, all-night vigils, reading the works of holy elders, fasting, and prostrating in front of the icon of Christ and the Holy Virgin. Under such an ascetic, rigorous regime, David had undergone a deep *metanoia*, a radical shift in his heart and mind.

"He has certainly changed," Father Maximos lamented, "but his sentence hasn't changed!"

For Father Maximos, David's case was in no way different than that of the robber who was crucified next to Jesus and was spiritually rescued thanks to his repentance. The holy elders have taught, he would say, that human beings can attain the Kingdom of Heaven even at the last moment, before their last breath, assuming that they genuinely undergo true *metanoia*. Whatever happened to David, or to any human being for that matter, must be seen as unfolding within God's Providential Will. Therefore one must never despair, no matter what.

We accelerated our pace as dusk began to set in. Vespers would start soon and after that a light dinner. A quarter of a mile before reaching the monastery we met Father Christodoulos mounted on a tractor. In his sixties, he was the oldest of the monks at the Panagia monastery. I learned from Stephanos that Father Christodoulos had become a monk only a few years ago, after his wife had passed away and his four children got married. Having been a farmer most of his life, he was assigned the *diakonia* [assignment for service] to be in charge of the monastery's fields. He had just plowed some fresh ground on the side of the mountain and, with the help of two Russian novices and a Romanian migrant worker, he was busy planting. Father Maximos chatted with them for a few minutes about the state of the potato crop. Then, as they were themselves in a hurry to get ready and return to the monastery, we moved on.

"I have one last question for today, Father Maxime," I said as we approached the monastery's outer gate. "What do the holy elders understand exactly by God's Providential Will?"

"That's what we have been talking about all along," Father Maximos mused. "But let me be brief since we are running out of time. The holy elders teach that God's Will manifests itself in four different ways." He paused for a few seconds to collect his thoughts. "The first is the Will of God as *Evdokia*, or Favor. This is what God really wishes."

"I am not sure that I follow you."

"The Will of God as *Evdokia* was to have the first humans be in continuous union with Him. That is what the heart of God really wished. But God's Will as *Evdokia* was set aside as a consequence of the Fall. Then God, the holy elders claim, replaced *Evdokia* with *Economia*."

Father Maximos noticed that I made a grimace upon hearing the word *Economia* as the second stage of God's Will. He hastened to explain that the elders meant something else than what is commonly understood by that word. "First, God sent his Son. Then He created the *Ecclesia*, set up the mysteries, and so on. In other words, God offered to fallen humanity a methodology on how to attain their deification, their *Theosis*. He created an *Economia* for spiritual salvation.

"But once again human beings failed to live up to this second stage of God's Will. They failed to take advantage of the tools available to them to reestablish their lost connection with God. Then God's Will was manifested as *Concession*. God allowed for seemingly painful experiences to happen to people in order to help them awaken to their real situation so they could propel themselves toward their eventual deification. This was not what God's heart really wished. Nevertheless, God allowed painful episodes and various temptations to unfold in people's lives in order to help them reach the ultimate goal, which is restoration within their real Divine state."

"I suppose," I added, "it would be like a bitter medicine that a sick person needs to take in order to get well. It must be at this point that the law of cause and effect begins to operate."

"Good," Father Maximos nodded before he continued. "According to the elders there is also a fourth manifestation of God's Will. This is what they call the *Abandonment* of a person by God."

"Is it possible for God to abandon anyone?" I reacted.

"This *Abandonment* is only ephemeral and phenomenal, or external. Of course, in reality God never abandons anyone. It is actually we humans who abandon God and cut off all relationship with Him. Yet even within this fourth manifestation of God's Will, of this seeming *Abandonment*, it is possible for men and women to attain their salvation provided they undergo a genuine *metanoia*, as was the case with David.

"Do you see how simple it really is, Kyriaco?" Father Maximos asked in earnest as we entered the monastery's yard. "Once we recognize that everything that happens in our lives moves within God's Providence, within these four stages of His Will, then we no longer allow ourselves to be suffocated by the difficulties or tragedies that may come our way."

"You can only be in such a frame of mind if your primary goal is union with God," I pointed out.

"But this is the fundamental issue of our existence, our relationship with God," Father Maximos reacted with intensity in his voice. "Just think, parents come and complain about all sorts of problems they face with their sons and daughters. I remind them that whatever they consider to be their child's problem is really not the primary issue. The primary issue is whether their son or daughter has an authentic relationship with the living God. If not, then this vacuum will unavoidably be filled by vices such as drugs, promiscuity, drinking, sloth, you name it. But when they establish a right relationship with God, then all other problems will eventually find their resolution. That's how things work."

The *Ecclesia*, Father Maximos repeated time and again, must be seen as the spiritual hospital that can heal the split between humans and God. When that occurs, all other worldly problems will reach a resolution. Such a notion was grossly at odds with secular ways of thinking, the way I was trained to think.

We entered the monastery's chapel while vespers were in progress. Father Maximos, after crossing himself and kissing the icon of the Holy Virgin, walked to the *stasidi* that was customarily reserved for him as the abbot. I stood in a dark corner at the back of the church, listening to the chanting, an art that Father Maximos considered central to the spiritual life. In fact, he hired a teacher who specializes in phonetics and Byzantine music to train his monks on how to chant well.

Just before vespers were over, the monks began chanting the "*Fos Ilaron Ayias Doxes . . .* ," one of my favorite melodies of Byzantine music chanted during vespers. I hummed along.

> *Radiant light of the holy glory*
> *of the immortal, heavenly, holy, and blessed Father:*
> *O Christ Jesus!*
> *Now, as we come to sunset, as we see the evening lights,*
> *we sing to God, the Father, Son, and Holy Spirit!*
> *At all times are you worthy to be praised by undefiled*
> *tongue,*
> *O Son of God, who give life to the world:*
> *For this, the whole world praises you!*[3]

ceaseless prayer

any people who come here or visit Mount Athos assume that we monks are possessors of magical formulas and apocryphal secrets. They expect that when these esoteric formulas are passed on to them they will be on the road to spiritual perfection. I am not aware of such secrets," Father Maximos declared as we took a short afternoon walk and sat on a bench under a shady oak tree overlooking the Panagia monastery.

Fondling his *komboschini*, he explained that according to the teachings of the elders, the path to spiritual perfection is none other than full participation in the methodology of the *Ecclesia*. That presupposes prayer, fasting, obedience to an elder, confession, repentance, communion, study of the word of God and the writings of enlightened elders, and so on. "We have no occult secrets and formulas on how to reach God," he scoffed. "Once you seriously begin to participate in the prescribed methods of the *Ecclesia*, you are invigorated and spiritually uplifted. You are offered the kind of spiritual nourishment that is uniquely appropriate for you."

"Will this happen automatically?" I wondered.

"Look at it this way. The *Ecclesia* is like the *manna* with which God fed the starving Hebrews. *Manna* food was the same for everybody. Yet, through God's Grace it was transmuted in such a way as to fulfill the specific nutritional needs of every individual. Let us say someone needed vitamin B, then *manna* gave that person more of that vitamin. Somebody else needed vitamin D, once again the *manna* was transformed in a miraculous way into that vitamin. God nourished His people in a personal, individualized way.

"The same principle applies to the *Ecclesia*," Father Maximos continued while stroking his beard. "During Divine Liturgy the Holy Spirit is activated differently for each individual. In one person it may generate a deep sense of sweetness, in another a profound sense of reverence. Every person is given what is needed for spiritual growth. This is the reason why, as I mentioned the other day, we must not be concerned about how far we have progressed."

Father Maximos went on to point out that human beings vary greatly in their level of understanding and spiritual maturity. They are not all of the same spiritual age. Yet, all of them can be accommodated within the *Ecclesia* precisely because the Holy Spirit works in this mysterious way, offering each person a correct and specific amount of nourishment.

"Contrary to what some people believe, no one has ever been taught any hidden lessons that led to their spiritual development, absolutely no one. All of us start in a very simple way and proceed on the basis of our receptivity and level of development. Most of the teachings of the elders are really forms of practical exercises to overcome pride and develop true humility and compassion. There is no spirituality without genuine humility. That is an axiom."

Father Maximos smiled as he remembered an episode from his own apprenticeship. "The first assignment that I received from my elder was to go and wash the floor of the church. I had expected him to instruct me on the secrets of mental prayer and so on. Instead he handed me a broom, a sponge, and a bucket of water. . . ."

"The experience you just described is similar to that of another novice who went to Mount Athos to become a master of spiritual secrets," I interrupted while taking out of my handbag a book I was reading. I began flipping through the pages. I then translated a relevant passage into Greek, sentence by sentence.

"Not too many years ago," I read, "a young monastic aspirant went to Mount Athos. In talking with the venerable abbot of the monastery where he wished to stay, he told him, 'Holy Father! My heart burns for the spiritual life, for asceticism, for unceasing communion with God, for obedience to an elder. Instruct me, please, Holy Father, that I may attain spiritual advancement.' Going to the bookshelf, the abbot pulled down a copy of *David Copperfield* by Charles Dickens. 'Read this, son,' he said. 'But, Father!' objected the disturbed aspirant. 'This is heterodox Victorian sentimentality, a product of the Western captivity! This isn't spiritual; it's not even Orthodox! I need writings which will teach me *spirituality*!' The abbot smiled, saying, 'Unless you first develop normal, human, Christian feelings and learn to view life as little Davey did—with simplicity, kindness, warmth, and forgiveness—then all the Orthodox spirituality and Patristic writings will not only be of no help to you—they will turn you into a spiritual monster and destroy your soul.' "[1]

"Nice!" reacted Father Maximos. "This is what the elders warn us time and again. Spiritual knowledge by itself does not lead us to God. It may in fact push us in the opposite direction. We may succumb to the temptation and fantasize that because we are knowledgeable we are especially favored by God. It could stimulate our pride and vanity," Father Maximos pointed out as I returned the paperback to my handbag.

"Father Maxime," I interrupted him abruptly with urgency in my voice, "in a few days I'll be leaving the monastery and I still have some questions I would like clarified."

"Well, what are you waiting for?" he prompted me as he gazed at Morphou Bay stretched out in the distance through the ravine below the monastery's grounds.

"You constantly emphasize the centrality of ceaseless prayer for the spiritual life. The question that many people would raise is the following: why engage in prayer and not in something else, meditation, for example? First, what is the purpose of prayer? Second, how does one engage in ceaseless prayer?"

Father Maximos fiddled with his *komboschini* for a few seconds to collect his thoughts. Then, after filling his lungs with a deep breath, he replied. "The *Ecclesia*, as we have discussed many times, has as its primary objective the restoration of human beings to their natural state, unity with God. We said that prior to the Fall, human beings lived in a state of continued contemplation of God. After the Fall, our minds and hearts were scattered and focused on the objects of this world and we were therefore cut off from this sacred unity and connection.

"Do you know the real meaning of sin?" Father Maximos asked abruptly, as if changing the subject.

"Well," I replied, "people think of sin as a violation of some moral code. But I know this is not what you have in mind. The ancient understanding of *amartia*, of sin, is to be 'off your mark,' which means being cut off from God."

"Good. When we say, for example, that such and such an act is sinful, somebody may wonder why this is so? Why is lust a sin, since it brings pleasure to a person and doesn't hurt anyone? Why is avarice a sin, or gluttony for that matter?

"The elders teach," Father Maximos continued, "that when your mind and heart, your *nous*, gets stuck on the objects of this world, whether these objects are called money or pleasures of the body, or egotism or opinions or ideologies or whatever else, then you are committing an *amartia*, a sin. You become enslaved by these distractions that keep your heart and mind away from God."

"Are you implying then that we should all abandon the world and join a monastery?" I reacted with a dose of protest in my voice.

"Nothing of the sort. Simply be aware not to enslave your mind and heart to the objects of this world that keep you cut off from God. Do you know what else the elders say? That it is possible for a person to be extremely rich, yet not be considered rich in the eyes of God. Someone else may own only a single needle and be rich in the eyes of God. On the other hand a wealthy person may be freed of avarice and psychologically completely liberated from his wealth and be close to God, while a person who owns only a single needle may have his mind and heart stuck on that needle."

"So Jesus' statement that it is easier for a camel to go through the eye of a needle than a rich man to enter the Kingdom of Heaven should be interpreted in this light."

"Of course. The 'rich' person who cannot enter Heaven is the person who is obsessed about things of this world, whether it is his millions or his needle. Entering the Kingdom of Heaven means liberation from the objects of this world, what the elders call *kenosis*, or emptiness."

"What about prayer?"

"I am getting there. The methodology of the *Ecclesia* is to help us reach that freedom, that *kenosis* from passions. Prayer is the force that propels a human being in the direction of reconnecting with God. Prayer necessitates shutting all doors to thoughts, ideas, and obsessions, and directing all of one's energies towards this personal God. It is not a movement toward some abstract impersonal intelligence out there beyond the manifest world or beyond the clouds. Rather, the moment I begin to invoke the name of God, I begin to establish a personal relationship with Him. It is toward that Person that my soul begins to move as I pray."

"In practical terms, how should one pray?" I interjected.

"As you know, there are many ways and forms of prayer," Father Maximos replied. "One way is to pray along with others. We are not isolated atoms in the universe. We are persons in relationships. Communal prayer reaffirms our connection to each other and to God.

"There is also personal prayer. The *Ecclesia*, based always on the experience of the holy elders, has offered us a plethora of prayers that we can resort to when we pray by ourselves. There are prayers for all occasions that we can utilize, depending on the problems we face."

"And these prayers are charged with spiritual energy," I pointed out.

"Always! They were written by God-conscious holy elders who were filled with the Grace of the Holy Spirit. Their love for God was overflowing as they composed their poems, in the same way that lovers write poetry to express their love for each other."

"Saints are the lovers of God," I reiterated as I remembered a previous conversation with Father Maximos. During that discussion he claimed that the so-called "fear of God" is a gross distortion of Christianity based on an infantile understanding of God. The "fear of God" of the saints, he claimed, refers to the fear of *losing their connection* with God, the Divine Lover, and not the fear of a patriarchal despot that rules over the universe with an iron fist.

"It was in that spirit that the hymns of the *Ecclesia* were written," Father Maximos repeated. "By getting into the habit of reading prayers written by saints, we become connected with the spirit of holiness that prompted the writing of these prayers. The energy of divine love as it is embedded in this poetry is then transferred onto our own souls. That is the reason why it is important to learn how to pray using these well-established prayers. Let us suppose, for example, that you experience something which causes you deep sorrow. You could then read either the *paraklesis*, or supplication canon, to the Holy Virgin or the *paraklesis* to the Christ. By focusing on the words of the hymns, the Psalms, or the Gospel, you link up with the divine energy that was the very source of inspiration which led to the writing of these verses."

"But sometimes, Father Maxime, people don't understand their meaning."

"It doesn't matter. You can still get the benefit. The spiritual energy emanating from these words can still affect you in ways that you may not be aware of."

Father Maximos then talked about the *Efche*, the "Lord Jesus Christ, Son of God, have mercy upon me, a sinner," a subject that we had discussed earlier. This special form of prayer has been considered by the holy elders as central to the spiritual life. He reminded me that the Prayer is to be recited continuously by the serious pilgrim and full-time practitioner of the spiritual arts. It is, he claimed, the most potent medicine for the cure of the soul, the "science of the sciences," precisely because it is the method which, once mastered, can lead to the opening of the doors toward God. Repeating these simple words, Father Maximos said, by virtue of their power, can lead us into realms beyond the words and into the great mystery of *Theosis*.

"Perhaps these are the spiritual secrets that people are looking for," I suggested.

"Wait a minute. Whatever secrets are revealed are not the result of intellectual knowledge of some occult formula. They are revelations that come from above as a result of the purification of the heart through deep *metanoia* and humility. As elder Sophrony writes, it is when the Prayer is energized like a soothing flame within the individual that divine insights and inspirations are offered. It is, in his words, 'the sweet feeling of God's love which snatches the mind and exposes it to spiritual visions, which is occasionally accompanied by visions of the Divine Light.'[2] They are the gifts that are offered to the struggling soul for union with God."

"They are secrets that cannot be unlocked by pure reason," I added as I thought of the Kantian idea of the impossibility of reason to know the nature of ultimate reality. I kept these thoughts to myself as Father Maximos continued.

"When you practice the Jesus Prayer systematically, it is as if you move about within a polluted city wearing an oxygen mask over your face. Nothing can touch you."

"It sounds simple," I said, "I mean, to repeat over and over the 'Lord Jesus Christ, have mercy on me.' "

"It's simple in its expression but rich in its energy. It is also simple in its implementation, at least in its initial stages. I first thought that learning about the *Efche*, the Prayer, was some sort of a complex initiation that I had to go through, but when I first met my elder he just handed me a *komboschini* and asked me to begin reciting the Prayer with humility and without fantasies, nothing else. 'Go and do it,' he urged me, 'and then we'll talk again.' "

"How long should those of us who live in the world devote to the Prayer?" I asked.

"You can start with as little as five minutes each day. But it is important to be consistent. After a few weeks you can devote more time, like ten minutes in the morning and ten at night, but always at the same hour of the day and in a quiet place. At first it may be difficult to concentrate. Your mind may wander away but you must persist. Expect that the moment you begin the Prayer, you will start remembering all the work that you needed to do, all the things that you forgot to do during the day and so on. Do not give up under any circumstances."

Father Maximos went on to say that before starting with the Jesus Prayer it is helpful to "warm up the heart" with a few minutes of regular prayer. After that, one can begin to recite and focus on the Jesus Prayer, chasing all other thoughts away.

"The moment you realize that your mind is wandering here and there, you should make an effort to bring it back and keep it focused on the words of the Prayer. This is the first step on how to pray ceaselessly."

Father Maximos laughed as he recalled an incident with a fellow monk at Mount Athos. "He was always very forgetful, he claimed, but fortunately for him the moment he began to pray, the devil would always remind him of all the things he forgot to do during the day."

Father Maximos claimed the Jesus Prayer can become a habit that can generate the kind of energy that may "crack our hearts open." A human being, then, begins to manifest a radically different sensitivity. "Grace visits the heart, leading to the resurrection of dormant powers, and the person begins to function within the energies of God. You know," he went on to say with a serious tone in his voice, "for the saints, the Jesus Prayer was more important than their very breathing."

"So the mysteries and secrets of God are revealed through Grace as the natural outcome of the Jesus Prayer," I concluded.

"It is a key factor. But this stage cannot be reached so easily. In order for the Prayer to reach the deepest recesses of the soul it requires constant and persistent spiritual struggle. Once that is achieved, the person becomes enlightened and endowed with wisdom. At that stage a different instrument of understanding, beyond logic and the rational mind, gets activated. In fact, it guides logic as it is superior to it. A person who reaches that state of mind judges everything only after it passes through the test of the Prayer. If a message comes during prayer that goes contrary to logic, then such a person will obey the message that comes while in prayer, no matter what conventional logic dictates. Really, Kyriaco, when the spirit of the Jesus Prayer takes over the heart, only then do people get healed within the depths of their being. The flame of God has now been ignited in the heart."

"Father Maxime, the other day someone who was waiting for confession mentioned to me that whenever she is in a plane ready to take off, she begins to recite the Prayer. But she feels as if she is not honest. That somehow she has an ulterior motive, to keep herself safe. When that idea enters her head she loses the urge to pray."

"It does not matter what your motives are when you concentrate on the Prayer. Even if your intentions are not perfect, with time the systematic practice of praying will also perfect your motives. What happens, you see, is that the Jesus Prayer teaches you how to pray. Do the Prayer and then God will take care of the rest. He will lead you to Him through the Prayer."

Father Maximos's eyes beamed as he uttered those words. I had a feeling that he was speaking from personal experience, but he would never attest to it. I suspected that it might be so because of an episode I had with him during the early stages of our relationship. At that time in our friendship I had faced some difficulties with Father Maximos. He had apparently misunderstood the content of my previous books and, not knowing English, assumed to my great chagrin that I was somehow writing and dealing with magic, therefore endangering my spiritual well-being. One day in my frustration I blurted out that our problem of miscommunication stemmed from our radically different backgrounds. "Had I spent ten years on Mount Athos and had you spent ten years in an American university," I told him in a state of friendly exasperation, "we would have had a perfect understanding of each other." After expressing my frustration so forthrightly I feared that I may have burned my bridges with my Athonite friend. He looked distressed and sad. But something quite wondrous happened shortly thereafter. The following day his attitude changed completely. He showed no concern that I was dealing with magic and therefore tampering with the destiny of my immortal soul. I learned what had transpired, not from Father Maximos himself, who I felt began to trust me completely after our honest encounter, but from my friend Stephanos, who was both Father Maximos's confidant as well as mine. Stephanos related to me that Father Maximos went into his cell and began praying, seeking to find an answer to the difficulty we faced in our relationship. It was after that prayer that he received "enlightenment from above" in the form of a message, that "Kyriacos did not come to you to become a disciple. His task is different. He is to conduct scholarly work in order to bring the Athonite spiritual wisdom to a wider audience." My relationship with Father Maximos was restored and from that moment on he became willing to patiently share with me his deepest insights. I was finally able to continue my investigation of the Athonite spiritual tradition with his full cooperation.

"Must you hold a *komboschini* in order to recite the Jesus Prayer?" I asked, pointing at the one he was holding.

"This," he said, raising it up, "can only help you focus on the Prayer. Each time you say 'Lord Jesus Christ, Son of God, have mercy on me,' you move your thumb to the next knot. This particular *komboschini* has one hundred knots. When I come around to the point where I started from, I know that I have recited the Prayer one hundred times. If my elder assigns the recitation of the Prayer four hundred times before going to bed, then the *komboschini* can help me keep track without being mentally distracted. It is not, of course, necessary to have a *komboschini*. You can pray without it."

"Someone not familiar with Athonite ways would wonder what the purpose might be of endlessly repeating Christ's name." I mentioned that the Jesus Prayer reminded me of *mantra yoga*, the form of meditation that I had practiced for several years. Father Maximos rejected the comparison.

Invoking the name of Christ is not the same as other forms of spiritual practice, he insisted. The purpose of the Jesus Prayer and its results are completely different from those of meditation as a form of deep relaxation of the mind. He claimed that a mysterious, divine process is at work with the Jesus Prayer. Christ, he went on to say, is a living God, a living Person. Repeating the sacred name therefore is an invocation of that holiness, which has an immediate effect within the deepest recesses of the psyche. The soul gradually begins to experience a sense of divine sweetness.

"This is one of the early experiences that happen to a person who begins to pray," he went on to say. "It's what the saints do, keeping the name of God ceaselessly in their minds."

"Considering that most of us laypeople are neither monks nor saints, how could this repetitive prayer be of any use? We don't have the time."

"Look! The first thing you need to do is to be convinced of the power of prayer, that it is real and that it can affect not only you personally but also those for whom you pray."

I mentioned that some scientists today claim that there may in fact be experimental evidence on the efficacy of prayer.[3] Father Maximos made a dismissive grimace indicating that he was not impressed or concerned about the verdict of science on the power of prayer. He knew it from direct experience.

"You will be surprised to realize the incredible power of the Jesus Prayer on ordinary people," he went on to say. "It may have been invented by saints but it is for use by everybody—monks, hermits, and ordinary people. This is particularly true today when people feel isolated and cut off from each other. I have realized, based on my experiences with confessions, that people somehow have difficulty relating and communicating with their children, their spouses, their neighbors, their fellow human beings. They feel psychologically abandoned, deprived of personal intimacy. It is really very sad."

"These are the problems of industrial civilization," I suggested. "Here in Cyprus the sense of community is still fairly strong."

"Not as much as you may think. In any event, the Prayer is the best antidote to this sense of disconnectedness, whether you live in Cyprus or in the middle of New York City."

"Are you suggesting, then, that this is a form of therapy for the lonely and alienated?"

"Not only for them, but yes, you are right, there is no better therapy," Father Maximos emphasized. "The Jesus Prayer offers people a tremendous sense of empowerment. I know for a fact that this modern sense of alienation and loneliness simply evaporates with systematic prayer. I remember years ago I met a hermit on Mount Athos who lived by himself in the wilderness. I asked him, 'Father, aren't you afraid to live here all alone?' His reply was that he could never feel alone since he continuously prayed. He was filled with the living presence of God's love.

"Ceaseless prayer does offer you this deep sense of sociability," Father Maximos stressed as he tried to chase any doubts from my mind. "It offers you such a sense of connectedness that it is immaterial whether anyone speaks to you or whether you live in the midst of a hostile world. Believe me, all sense of isolation, of being unloved, of being disliked, of being envied, disappears with the power of ceaseless prayer. There is no medicine more powerful than this. Through the Prayer you begin to commune with the living Christ, who is at the very depths of your being. This is in fact one of the early phenomena that begin to manifest in a person who prays continuously."

"It sounds so simple," I said and shook my head, betraying some residue of doubt in my mind. "I mean, to pray nonstop. It is difficult for people who live in the world to fathom something like that."

"But as I told you before, it is simple," Father Maximos insisted. "Just fill up your idle time with the Prayer."

"I don't have idle time," I reacted half-humorously.

"Look. You drive a car, don't you? While you do that, you can neither read nor solve mathematical puzzles. Use that time to recite the Prayer. Or, while you cook, wash the floor, wait at a bus stop, recite the Prayer. If you get into the habit of filling up these empty time slots with the Jesus Prayer you will experience extraordinary benefits in your heart, truly extraordinary, believe me."

"I suppose it is a way to keep the *logismoi* in check," I commented.

"That also," Father Maximos replied. "But it is more than that. The name of Christ itself has power. It brings tranquillity to the soul."

"Is this what you call Grace?"

"No, tranquillity is reached only at the very early stages, when one begins to practice the Prayer, and a feeling of inner peace, joy, and sweetness takes over the heart. The Jesus Prayer becomes even more effective when, in addition to filling up idle time, one takes a few minutes regularly every day to exclusively focus on it."

"When I first met you on Mount Athos you had mentioned that there are other ways also of reciting the Jesus Prayer, but you did not give me any more details."

"Well, there are several ways that can help the mind focus. However, because these methods require continuous supervision by an experienced spiritual guide, we don't recommend them for laypeople. Those who live in the world may lack discernment, overindulge in these practices, and as a result damage their psychic and even physical well-being."

"How is that possible?"

"There are some breathing exercises that a monk can practice while reciting the Prayer. But such exercises may be inappropriate for unsupervised people.

"So," Father Maximos went on, "the best way for someone to practice the Prayer, the *Efche*, is to focus on the words with humility. This is a safe approach that protects the layperson from possible pseudospiritual experiences and delusions. What's important, you see," he expanded, "is to get into the habit of praying. And if one has access to a spiritual guide, so much the better."

Our conversation was interrupted by the roar of vans carrying German tourists. They passed us by and parked outside the outer gate. The monastery was also an archaeological attraction, a tradition that Father Maximos had to adapt to, and that afternoon was the designated time for such visits. We stopped our conversation for a while and watched from a distance of a hundred meters as the tourist guide began her routine. When they entered the monastery's yard we resumed our conversation

"Here is another point that I meant to ask you," I said as I looked at my notebook. "You mentioned that we should engage in the Prayer as much as possible, even when we are preoccupied with something else. But at the same time you pointed out that when we pray, we should intend it and focus on the prayer. I wonder, how is it possible to do that when our mind concentrates on something else?"

"You can do that only if you carry on with activities that do not require concentration, such as waiting at a bus stop, taking a walk, or peeling potatoes. At the beginning stages of your practice you cannot pray while lecturing to a classroom of students. There is something paradoxical, however, about the Prayer," Father Maximos added. "When we get into the habit of continuous prayer, we can then get involved with several other activities simultaneously. While the Prayer is recited within us, it offers no interference with whatever else we might be doing. It is self-activating. And as we reach a more advanced state, we can even solve mathematical problems while the Prayer goes on ceaselessly, in the heart."

"In the heart?"

."As I explained to you before, the holy elders differentiate the functions of the mind from those of the heart. This point is stressed time and again in our practices. Experienced elders continue to pray even while asleep. As the chant goes '*Ego kathevdo kai e kardia mou xagrypna*,' 'I am asleep but my heart is awake.' "

"Who prays and who is asleep? How can one be asleep and continue to pray?"

"Look. You start by reciting the name of Christ. This is imperative. The aim is not to manufacture some kind of abstract feeling of well-being and joy that takes place in your heart. The aim is a concrete movement towards Christ. Prayer evokes the very energy that springs directly from Christ and is directed back to Christ."

"I am still not clear about this. Does it mean that during prayer a person listens to the heart reciting the words of the Prayer?"

"Let's say that with the habitual recitation of the Jesus Prayer, the Holy Spirit takes up residence in the heart and gets activated there. It is beyond words and meanings. We need not get stuck on words."

"So we use words in order to go beyond words."

"You can say that." Then Father Maximos emphasized once more that the Prayer must be recited with "utter humility and *metanoia*" and not be treated like a technique for the attainment of spiritual experiences lest it lead to delusion.

"As paradoxical and strange as it may sound," he hastened to add, "it is possible to reach the point where people pray ceaselessly but are still in a state of delusion."

"But given what you have been telling us about prayer, how is that possible?" I asked with a puzzled look on my face.

"By reciting the Prayer in a mechanical way and without humility. The Grace of the Holy Spirit cannot be present under such conditions. Old Paisios never tired of reminding us of this. He said that we can reach authentic spirituality only by having deep repentance or *metanoia*, which means the radical transformation of our hearts and minds at their very foundation. We must never seek from God to offer us charismatic gifts like the ability to prophesy, or have visions, or to manifest miracles. It is *metanoia* that will bring humility and it is humility that will pave the way for the acquisition of spiritual gifts, by necessity. That's how the Holy Spirit works.

"Even saints had to face such obstacles in their spiritual struggle. We are the beneficiaries of their mistakes and triumphs. This is what happened to Saint Silouan while he was a novice at the Russian monastery of Saint Panteleimon on Mount Athos. Saint Silouan reached a state of complete despair when he thought that the Prayer was having no practical effect on his life.[4] In fact," Father Maximos went on, "I've noticed that a lot of people who pray ceaselessly suffer from the same shortcomings. The Prayer has no effect on them. In the case of Saint Silouan we see a young monk who was patient, obedient, and loved by everybody in the monastery. As a result he was assaulted by the *logismos* of self-praise, that he was living like a saint. Such a *logismos* springs from worldly vanity. He was doing all the external things that one is supposed to do and yet the *logismos* of vanity was still haunting his mind. Since he lacked spiritual experience he assumed he was right on target heading toward sainthood."

"He was not quite off the mark," I pointed out. "After all, the Church did canonize him as a saint."

206 Kyriacos C. Markides

"But at that time he was young and still under the influence of worldly vanity. His experiences are very instructive. Even though he prayed ceaselessly, the Holy Spirit did not as yet take residence in his heart and that eventually led him to despair and doubt."

"I suppose," I pointed out, "that in this case there is an interesting convergence of delusion mixed in with virtue. After all, he struggled for God and dedicated his life to God."

"This is absolutely so. It was extremely difficult for him as a young monk to discern whether his experience was from God or not from God. One night while praying," Father Maximos continued, "his cell became permeated by an unusual light. It penetrated his entire body. Then a *logismos* suggested to him, 'This is Grace, accept it!' But his heart was full of tension and confusion, a sure sign that the light was not from God. The Prayer continued inside him but the spirit of *metanoia* receded to such an extent that while praying he suddenly started laughing uncontrollably. In reality Silouan had a demonic experience of light. It entered his mind as a *logismos* pretending to be Grace. And because in his heart there was still the seed of vanity, the spirit of *metanoia* left him. When he realized what had happened he banged his head against the wall in despair."

"But if a saint can be so deceived, what does it say about ordinary mortals like most of us?" I complained.

"Again, don't forget that Silouan underwent these experiences when he was quite young, a novice who was in a great hurry. From his experience we learn the lesson that ceaseless prayer, without utter humility and *metanoia*, as old Paisios used to tell us, can lead to all sorts of delusions. It can lead to worldly vanity and even to pathological symptoms. In the case of young Silouan, demons began manifesting in front of him. He would have conversations with them, something forbidden in spiritual life. In his testament he talks about the various discussions he held with them. Sometimes they would raise his pride to the sky, at other times they would lead him to states of euphoria, products of vanity, and yet at other times they would lead him into an abyss of despair and disillusionment. These sentiments of exaggerated euphoria and exaltation followed by utter despair," Father Maximos claimed, "are the typical attributes of the vain personality. They are the two poles between which such a personality oscillates."

"Yet, did he not get out of that state and did he not attain sainthood?"

"Of course. He was able to do that through mercurial spiritual struggles that lasted for years. You see, Kyriaco, Divine Grace eventually does come to the aid of the struggling soul."

"That's very comforting."

"Anyway," Father Maximos continued, "Silouan was in a state of deep despair because he became conscious of the gulf that separated him from

God. He truly experienced this absence of God in his heart. This is an extraordinary martyrdom for a person who is aware. Do you know what I mean?" My facial expression gave Father Maximos the message that I had no clue of what he was talking about.

"There is really nothing worse in life. This experience was decisive in the subsequent life of Silouan. When he reached a state of complete exhaustion, a *logismos* entered his mind telling him that God is distant, unreachable, aloof, and that it is impossible for a human being to have a relationship with God. Of course, it was Silouan's darkness in his own heart that led him to that desperate conclusion," Father Maximos said. He remained pensive for a few seconds as he continued fiddling with his *komboschini*.

"I believe that all of us will experience such a state of spiritual despair sooner or later, but always in accordance to our capacities and strengths. May God provide that we may pass through such a trial only once. I don't think it is humanly possible to withstand it twice. But from what my elders told me, all of us will have to go through this trial, through this state of utter exhaustion and despair, before our union with God."

"I am really not looking forward to such a prospect," I muttered.

"That's why we need great faith and patience because it is exactly at that stage of despair when God may reveal Himself to us."

"How did Saint Silouan come out of his despair?" I asked. "How did he find his way to God?"

"Silouan's agony was really not that different from Jesus' agony in the garden of Gethsemane. It was the agony that led Christ to perspire blood. Can you imagine that? Of course, no human being can withstand that kind of agony."

"But Silouan's experience seems to be archetypal," I suggested. "It is what is called 'the dark night of the soul,' a stage before one ascends towards God."

"Yes, he did reach a state of darkness, alright. While in that state, he went for vespers to the church of prophet Elias. Then while standing there in front of the icon of Christ, in total despair and agony, feeling abandoned by Grace, Silouan saw the living Christ materializing in front of him. At that moment his entire existence of body and soul was filled with the fire of Grace, the kind of fire that Christ brings along with His descent on Earth. It is exactly at that moment that the person becomes a repository of the Holy Spirit."

"It appears as if Saint Silouan had his own Pentecost," I noted.

"Yes, exactly. At that moment Saint Silouan experienced the mystery of Pentecost, identical to that of Christ's apostles two thousand years earlier. All human beings have the potential to experience such an epiphany.

It is the experience of the saints throughout all the generations, from the time of Adam to our days. The experience of God felt by Saint Silouan and all the other great saints was no different from that of Paul, of Moses, of Abraham, of Isaac, or of Jacob. The context of the experience was different each time, but it was the same God that spoke and revealed Himself to all of them."

"From my readings on the life of Saint Silouan," I pointed out, "one gets the impression that Grace would manifest in his consciousness, leading him to ecstatic states of euphoria and joy, but sometimes it would recede, plunging him into feelings of utter despair."

"You see, living saints who have attained Grace always run the risk of losing it. They could fall from Grace and they would have to struggle hard to regain it. That is also why venerated saints like Saint Silouan and elder Paisios were extremely vigilant until their last breath.

"Really, the feeling of being abandoned by Grace is insufferable," Father Maximos said somberly. "That is also the reason why Saint Silouan, in order to regain and maintain the presence of Grace, would do things that were unduly harsh and would even be considered by others a distortion of Christianity.

"It is not of course right to see it that way. A soul that was lifted up to the vision of God and the eternal light and then lost it is in such a state of despair that is inconceivable to those who have not had such an experience. In fact, Saint Silouan claims that only those who have lost the most dear person in their life, a wife, a husband, a daughter, a son, can have but a feeble taste of the pain of those who, after having had the experience of God, lose it. Persons who find themselves in this most painful of situations can act in ways that to the rest of us appear incomprehensible. Ordinary people cannot understand why a hermit would lock himself in a cave for years or even a lifetime. Those who approach the spiritual life through their logic would find such behavior bizarre, a form of mental aberration."

"To reacquire God's Grace, therefore," I concluded, "would require even greater *askesis*, more intense ascetical practices."

"Not necessarily so," Father Maximos responded. "It is not up to the individual's efforts to bring back the Grace of God. An ascetic may literally melt away with *askesis* without any results. And someone else who hardly engages in *askesis* may be flooded by divine Grace."

"I don't understand."

"Look. There are no practical methods, no specific exercises that will guarantee that the Grace of God will automatically be bestowed upon you. There is no formula involved here. A layperson with little or no *askesis*, but who may have already reached the depths of humility, may be visited by Grace. You cannot buy God's Grace through practical exercises. A lot of people today claim that they pray to have spiritual experiences and they see lights, have visions, or witness various phenomena that they assume to be manifestations of the energy of the Holy Spirit. Such experiences are often nothing more than delusions, products of their narcissistic imagination. Let me repeat once again. Persons who are not utterly humbled, who are plagued by pride, will experience not even a trace of Grace.

"It is really a great mystery as to when God becomes manifest in the life and consciousness of a human being," Father Maximos continued. "We must therefore not agonize or be anxious about people who, no matter how often they are exposed to God's word, are simply not receptive to it. It is not up to us to decide when a person is ready to receive God's message. That possibility is totally up to Providence."

Hardly did Father Maximos finish his sentence when we heard the *symandron* calling monks and pilgrims to vespers. We stood up and began walking toward the monastery.

"Father Maxime," I said as we approached the gate, "I notice that monks and many of the pilgrims carry their *komboschini* to church during services. Should one practice the Prayer during services? Shouldn't one instead focus on what is being said and chanted?"

"What is important, Kyriaco, is to keep the mind preoccupied with God. Whether you focus on the words of the liturgy or whether you focus on God by reciting the Jesus Prayer, the end result is always the same."

"So it's a matter of what suits you best."

"Yes. Just keep alive the memory of God in your mind. With practice, God willing, it may become a receptacle of the Grace of the Holy Spirit. Then at some point the Prayer will enter your heart and become self-activating. During my life I have known not only monks and hermits but also quite a few laypeople who were overwhelmed by Grace. I know of a man who was taken over by Grace to such an intense degree that he was unable to sleep. We had to advise him to stop praying for a while."

"Conventional psychiatrists would consider such behavior pathological."

"Then they would also have to assume that when a man and a woman are deeply in love with each other, that is also pathological," Father Maximos snapped.

"On the other hand," I pointed out, "some contemporary psychologists who take spirituality seriously may consider cases like these as 'spiritual emergencies' that require an altogether different approach to treatment."[5]

"What is needed here is an experienced spiritual guide who knows what is really happening and what is best for the person," Father Maximos argued as we stood outside the gate and refreshed ourselves with cool water gushing out of the side of the mountain.

"I also remember the case of a university professor from Thessaloniki.

He came to Mount Athos to tell us about his experiences with the Prayer," Father Maximos said as he knelt down to wash his face. " 'Father, I cannot stop praying,' he complained to our elder. 'There is a fire in my soul that burns continuously.' Whenever he stepped into his classroom to lecture, he would experience great difficulty. The moment he would open his mouth, instead of delivering the lecture, he would experience a strong urge to recite the Prayer. 'When that happens to me,' he told the elder, 'I feel like crying in front of my students and telling them how much I love them. Inside me I feel the flame of God's love burning my soul and everything else becomes irrelevant.' "

"So what do you do in such a case?" I wondered.

"Our elder simply instructed him to stop praying for a while so that he could focus on his lectures. Unlike monks and hermits, he lived in the world. He had to function in the world."

Father Maximos thought for a second and then continued. "Do you know what Saint Ephraim (not the elder Ephraim mentioned earlier) used to do? He would implore God to withdraw His Grace for a while from his heart because he could not take it anymore. He felt as if he were going to burst from too much Grace. Can you imagine? God's Grace can be like an ocean that can overwhelm you. As I told you before, it happened also to elder Paisios."

Then as if he had a flash of insight, Father Maximos added, "Christ declared that He had come to this world to put fire to the Earth. Did he really come to burn our planet? It would be foolish to assume anything of the sort. He came to this world to bring fire to the hearts of human beings. This is the kind of fire that no fire engine can extinguish and no human being can start. Only the Christ can ignite it in the human heart and only human beings can put it out."

"How do they put it out?"

"Through their *logismoi* and sinful actions, of course," Father Maximos replied. "You see, *amartia*, or sin, is like a light switch. You push it off and the light is gone, instantly."

We stepped into the yard as the tourists crowded around their guide who was speaking to them in German while the monks hurried to church for vespers. Father Maximos asked me to follow him to his office because he had something to give me. "Tonight, read this section" he instructed as he handed me a hardcover text. "It will help you understand why saints who have tasted God's Grace feel so humbled." I thanked him, placed the book in my handbag, and joined him for vespers.

That night, following his suggestion, I perused the work of Abba Dorotheos, an early Christian elder whose work has been spiritual nourishment for monks and hermits for centuries.[6] The section that Father

Maximos asked me to read was on humility, the sine qua non of the spiritual life and the foundation of "perfect prayer."

"Humility," I began reading, "is the highest of virtues encompassing all others. Only humility has the power to attract God's Grace to the human soul." I turned the pages and read further. "Humility renders the person immune to anger and incapable of making anyone else angry." According to Abba Dorotheos, if something unpleasant happens to the humble person he always takes full responsibility. "He criticizes no one and refuses to blame others as the cause of whatever problems he may face. For this reason his mind is perfectly at peace." As I went on reading, I lamented the vast gulf that separated my state of mind from Abba Dorotheos's ideal of humility. Perhaps, I thought, Father Maximos wanted me to reach my own conclusions.

There are two types of humility, Abba Dorotheos taught. First, you must always consider others wiser and better than yourself, and second, you must never take credit for whatever achievements you may attain but attribute everything to the Grace of God. This is the perfect form of humility that characterizes the saints throughout all the generations. "The closer the saints come toward God, the more they see themselves as unworthy and sinful." I went on reading and came across a passage where Abba Dorotheos clarified this paradoxical claim with an example.

"I remember one time," Abba Dorotheos wrote, "as we were talking about humility, a nobleman from Gaza overheard us saying that the closer one comes to God, the more sinful he sees himself. 'How is this possible?' he asked with puzzlement. 'Your Lordship,' I responded, 'just tell me, how do you consider yourself within your own town?' 'I see myself as the most important nobleman,' he replied. Then I asked him: 'If you leave your town and go to Caesarea, how would you see yourself?' 'I will consider myself as the lowest of the local noblemen,' he answered. 'If you leave and go to Antioch, how would you then see yourself?' I asked him again. 'I will see myself like a worthless peasant,' he replied. I then asked him further: 'Suppose you move to Constantinople, living next to the king, how would you see yourself?' 'I would feel like an absolute pauper,' he said. 'That's exactly how the saints feel,' I told him. 'The closer they come to God, the more sinful and worthless they consider themselves to be.' "

I placed the book about Abba Dorotheos next to my bed and held my arms behind my head as I reflected on the extraordinary difficulty of being truly humble, particularly in our ego-absorbed, individualistic age. Yet, the saints warn us that neither worldly achievements nor philosophical virtuosity nor psychic powers can lead us back to God, but only *metanoia* and humility. "Very, very difficult, very difficult," I sighed, and turned the light off.

the threefold way

I left Cyprus during the last part of August, shortly after the Assumption, a major celebration at the Panagia monastery. My intention was to return next Christmas and the following summer for additional encounters with Father Maximos. It was clear to me that I would need further contacts to deepen my understanding of the Athonite spiritual tradition.

Welcome to Maine, the way life should be, I read as I got off the plane at the Bangor International Airport and passed under the sizable banner with the provocative motto. I felt tired but elated. As much as I cherished my spiritual adventures with Father Maximos and the monks of the Panagia monastery, it felt good to be home and to reconnect with Emily and our two grown-up children, Vasia and Constantine. I was able to quickly overcome the unavoidable culture shock, acclimatize myself to my new surroundings, and readjust to the radically different calendar around which I ordinarily organized my daily life. No longer did I have to wake up at three-thirty in the morning in order to attend four-hour services until daybreak. Nor did I have to stay all by myself in a cell after seven-thirty in the evening for reading, prayer meditations, and contemplation. Instead my familiar old routines automatically took over, including the resumption of long walks in the woods while Emily updated me about her work with the "eco-peace village" project and helped me process the information and experiences I had brought back from Cyprus. I also resumed my frequent walks with my friend Mike Lewis, whose input, coming from the perspective of someone who was neither a Christian nor a Greek, was invaluable. These peripatetic exchanges played a catalytic role in structuring my thoughts on the mystical tradition I had been exposed to and in figuring out how to proceed with the writing. It was during one of those invigorating walks with Emily that I recognized more clearly what all the monks and hermits of Mount Athos have taken for granted—that there are in Christianity three identifiable stages in the search for God. They are so obvious, Western scholars had simply failed to notice. At that moment of realization, all the teachings that Father Maximos had passed on to me came together in a coherent whole.

The soul's journey toward God, I explained to Emily that day, must go through three identifiable and distinct stages. At first there is the stage of **Catharsis,** or the purification of the soul from egotistical passions. It is then followed by the stage of **Fotisis,** or the enlightenment of the soul, a gift of the Holy Spirit once the soul has undergone its purification. Finally comes the stage of **Theosis,** union with God, as the final destination and ultimate home of the human soul. The last two stages are impossible to attain without having the soul first pass through the fires of catharsis from egotistical passions.

In addition to sharing these ideas with Emily and Mike, I also had the opportunity to develop and present them at a conference held the following May in Montreal. The theme of the yearly conference was the interface between the wisdom traditions of the world and modern science. Preparing for my presentation helped me summarize the importance of this *Threefold Way,* as I came to understand it through my exploration of Athonite spirituality and my apprenticeship with Father Maximos.

According to the wisdom tradition of the holy elders, I told the audience, Catharsis is essential in helping us overcome two basic obstacles that keep us cut off from the knowledge and vision of God. The most fundamental barrier is first and foremost the sum total of our worldly passions and desires. These passions are products of the enchantment and enslavement of our hearts and minds to the gross and transient material universe with its myriads of temptations and seductions.

The second fundamental barrier preventing us from knowing God is our exclusive reliance on our senses and rational intellect for understanding reality, which we have come to equate with gross matter. Most of Western philosophy and theology has fallen victim to this rationalistic and sensate fallacy.

By focusing primarily on the material world, we lose our connection to Heaven. We lose the relationship with God that Adam and Eve enjoyed prior to the Fall, or that the Prodigal Son had prior to his decision to leave the heavenly Palace. This split is at the core of our existential predicament and is the cause of all subsequent psychic turmoil and suffering.

How can humans heal the split and how can Catharsis be achieved? The Athonite response is through *askesis*, or spiritual exercise. The full-time practitioner of *askesis* is the "ascetic" who, contrary to popular negative notions about the meaning of that word, is someone who engages exclusively in spiritual exercises to gain the ultimate prize of *Theosis*. Like the marathon runner whose body is subjected to rigorous and often painful training, so must the "ascetic" be subject to similar systematic and strenuous training. Such acts may appear incomprehensible and even masochistic to an outsider.

According to the Athonite elders, *askesis* implies the overcoming of the allurement of the senses that keep the mind and the heart enslaved to this world of gross matter. Monks and nuns as well as committed layper-sons must replace culinary pleasures with periodic and systematic fasting as a form of spiritual exercise, in order to master the passion of gluttony. Monks and nuns must also replace sexual life with abstinence in order to free their energy and redirect it exclusively towards the higher goal of es-tablishing an "erotic" relationship with the Divine. Ownership of material objects must give way to total propertylessness and poverty. Furthermore, aspiring novices must empty themselves of all worldly desires and ambi-tions and give up whatever social positions of power and prestige they may have held in society.[1]

Eastern Christianity offers some dramatic cases from history of indi-viduals rejecting great wealth and power for the sake of a full-time con-templative existence. One such case was that of Saint Savva, the greatest of Serbian saints who was once king of Serbia. He relinquished his throne, joined Chilandari, the Serbian monastery on Mount Athos, and later re-turned to Serbia to serve his former subjects as a spiritual teacher and healer.

Laypeople must develop a sense of inner freedom from external pos-sessions, positions, and feelings of self-importance. They are asked to use the objects of this world, but not to become emotionally attached and en-slaved by them. Ordinary people living in the world can also engage in *askesis*, for, according to the holy elders, life itself is a form of *askesis*. When this is practiced, whatever event comes along must be seen as a "temptation" that can be "exploited" spiritually for the attainment of hu-mility, the real and only pathway to God. Humility, or the overcoming of egotistical passions, can be attained either within the context of monasti-

cism or within life in the wider world with its myriad of positive and negative "temptations." Marriage, for example, is considered by the *Ecclesia*
as a form of *askesis*, an arena for transcending one's ego absorption for the
sake of the other. It is a mistake, Father Maximos argued, to consider marriage, as many traditional Christians do, as first and foremost a means for
procreation. The primary aim of marriage is *askesis* engaged in by two people who are asked to overcome their separateness in their common ascent
towards God.

When one is emptied of worldly attachments and concerns and attains *kenosis*, the mind may then be filled with the reality of God. Ceaseless prayer replaces the exclusive reliance on reason and the intellect to
apprehend the nature of reality. Whether one lives in the world or in a
monastery, the practice of prayer remains at the center of one's spiritual
life.

When undertaking serious spiritual work one ideally needs an experienced guide, an elder who is divinely gifted. Such an elder would take the
sacred responsibility of monitoring the novice's spiritual development and
helping the novice navigate through the myriad of obstacles likely to be
encountered in this kind of work. The Athonite tradition has preserved this
system of "eldership," but it seems to have disappeared everywhere else
within the Christian movement. In the absence of an elder, the layperson
may still be spiritually nurtured by the tradition of the *Ecclesia*. It is also
possible to study sacred books like the Bible as well as the lives and teachings of the saints. The saints, Father Maximos said repeatedly, can serve as
beacons for navigating the spiritual path. They can teach us how to live
and how to develop the type of discernment needed so we may distinguish
the authentic from the unauthentic, the master or saint from the false
prophet and impostor, angels from demons.

I told my audience in Montreal that the notion of Catharsis is seriously lacking, that it is almost completely overlooked in the West. Even
within the New Age human potential spiritual movement that has been
flourishing in recent times, little attention has been given to Catharsis as
the defocusing of the mind from egotistical preoccupations and refocusing
on the Divine. Most attention has been on personal empowerment, transformation, and on the attainment of ecstatic states and psychic powers.
Therefore one of the spiritual gifts that the Christian East can bring to the
contemporary West, I argued, is the methodology of Catharsis for overcoming the cult of narcissism.

Fotisis, the enlightenment of the soul, I went on to argue, cannot be
attained by human effort. Fotisis is the natural consequence of the work
carried out during the previous stage of Catharsis and is offered to the
heart as a gift by the Holy Spirit. It is only at the stage of Catharsis that hu-

man will can and ought to be actively engaged. Fotisis as a gift of Grace is, among other things, Holy Wisdom itself. In this state the purified soul, the saint, becomes a channel through which God reveals His Wisdom, which is the true meaning of Enlightenment, or Fotisis.[2]

The Christian holy elders teach that a soul that has been cleansed of egotistical passions and reached the stage of Fotisis is usually endowed with gifts of the spirit such as prophetic vision, healing, clairvoyance, and other so-called "paranormal" abilities that seem to violate the known laws of physics. Most important, however, Fotisis means the vision and the experience of the *Uncreated Light*, God's Divine light. It is the mystical experience of Moses on Mount Sinai, of Jesus on Mount Tabor, of the apostles at Pentecost, and of all the saints throughout the ages.

Before his death in 1994, elder Paisios confided to a hieromonk who was a close acquaintance of his about an extraordinary experience he had with the *Uncreated Light* that was typical of other accounts. "One night while I was in my cell reciting the *Efche*, the Jesus Prayer," he reported, "I began to feel overwhelmed by a heavenly joy. My dark cell, lit by only one candle, began gradually to fill up with a most beautiful white-blue light. At first the light was very intense. But then my eyes got accustomed to its brilliance. It was the *Uncreated Light* manifesting Itself! I stayed in that condition for several hours and lost every sensation of worldly matters. I lived in a different, spiritual world, much different from this world of carnality.

"While in that state I was exposed to heavenly visions and extraordinary experiences. Without noticing, many hours passed by. Then the *Uncreated Light* began to recede and I returned to my previous condition. I was hungry and I ate a piece of dried bread. I was thirsty and drank some water. I was tired and sat down to rest. I felt like an animal and deplored myself for being no different than the beasts. This natural humility was born inside me as a consequence of the change in my situation. From the spiritual condition I was in, I had entered into this one and, perceiving the difference, there was little left for me but to condemn and loathe myself. When I walked outside I thought it was still night with a full moon. Not far from me there lived another brother in his hermitage. I walked there and asked him for the time. It was ten in the morning. The *Uncreated Light* was so intense that I thought the light of day was like the night and the Sun was like the Moon!"[3]

The experience of the *Uncreated Light* may also take other forms. It may bring about dramatic healing phenomena and serve as a shield against external dangers. An extraordinary case is that of the famous Russian art critic Peter Andreyevich Streltzov, who joined the monastery at Optina and became a hieromonk by the name of Father Arseny. During the Stalinist terror, Father Arseny was exiled to Siberia in a *gulag*, one of the notorious prison camps. For nineteen years, between 1939 and 1958, while under extreme conditions, the charismatic Father Arseny brought healing and solace to many prisoners, including communists and hardened criminals. Many of these prisoners, touched by his acts of kindness and altruism, were transformed and became his disciples. The most dramatic episode took place when Father Arseny and a young prisoner named Alexei were locked up in an unheated isolation barracks made of nothing other than sheet iron. Their sentence was to stay locked in there for forty-eight hours in temperatures below minus thirty degrees Fahrenheit. In reality, they were sentenced to a cruel death. The guards expected to find two frozen corpses when they opened the door two days later.

According to his biographer, the moment the guards shut the door, Father Arseny calmly advised his companion to take the opportunity they were offered and to pray openly and without fear. He then put himself immediately into a state of intense prayer. Alexei, who was not religious, thought that Father Arseny had lost his mind. He was beginning to feel his body freezing up and prepared himself to die. The space was filled with Father Arseny's voice praying. Suddenly everything changed. The darkness, the cold, the numbness, the pain, and the fear disappeared. Alexei looked at him and could not believe his eyes. The isolation chamber had become spacious and very bright and the interior resembled a church. Father Arseny was now wearing brilliant vestments as he prayed loudly with his hands stretched upwards. On each side of Father Arseny stood a very handsome young man wearing a brilliant costume. Alexei stood up. His body felt warm, he was able to breathe freely, and his heart was filled with joy. He then began to follow Father Arseny with the prayer, feeling God's presence with them. Twice the thought crossed Alexei's mind that they were dying and that they were in a state of delirium. But everything felt otherwise. Everything felt totally real. Father Arseny then asked him to lie down and get some sleep while he continued with the prayer. At some point they heard shouts and knocks at the door. Alexei opened his eyes and saw that Father Arseny was still praying. The two young men blessed them and disappeared instantly. The light gradually receded and they found themselves once again inside the narrow and frozen shack. When the guards opened the door they were stunned. Instead of two frozen corpses they found them both standing with guarded smiles and serene faces. We are alive, Father Arseny simply announced to the speechless guards, refusing to offer any further explanations.[4]

It is important to note here that the experience of the *Uncreated Light* can unexpectedly befall any human being, regardless of their station in life. Alexei was not a believer yet he had the experience of the *Uncreated Light*, which not only saved his life but also transformed him as a person.

Saul was a persecutor of Christians until he fell off his horse on the road
to Damascus and was temporarily blinded by the brilliance of the *Uncreated Light*. That experience catapulted him to fulfill his extraordinary historic mission as Saint Paul, apostle of the nations.

Once the gifts of Grace are bestowed upon a person through Fotisis,
then Theosis is the next and final destination of the soul's journey. This
stage is beyond all stages and defies all human understanding. According
to the tradition of the holy elders and Christianity in general, the individual soul does not lose its uniqueness upon its return to God. It does not
merge with God in such a way that its autonomy is compromised or destroyed. The Prodigal Son does not lose his identity upon his return to the
Palace. On the contrary, he carries along with him into his new deified
state the accumulated experiences of his worldly sojourn.

This particular point may be one of the key differences between the
spirituality of the Christian elders and some Buddhist beliefs concerning
the final destination of the human soul. From the perspective of the Christian elders, what is annihilated through Catharsis is not the inner, self-
aware "I-ness" but the sum-total of egotistical passions that obstruct our
vision of God. Saint Seraphim of Sarov may be in a state of oneness with
God, but he still remains autonomous within that oneness as a self-aware
soul, as Saint Seraphim serving God's plan. In saying that, one needs to be
reminded that the best of all the wisdom traditions warn that the nature of
the final destination of our spiritual journey is beyond all humanly constructed notions, all dogmas and beliefs. Therefore, whatever we say about
God and Theosis must be a priori insufficient, if not false.

In spite of these inherent limitations in understanding Theosis, spiritual adepts, great saints, and contemporary theologians tried to convey to
us a most feeble glimpse of this ultimate mystery of human destiny. "The
divinization of the individual is the supreme gift of the Grace of the Holy
Spirit," wrote a contemporary Greek theologian who based his work on the
experiential testimonies of the leading elders of the *Ecclesia*.[5] *Theosized*
human beings undergo changes not only in mind and soul but also in
body. Such individuals become forgetful of ordinary bodily needs such as
food and sleep since they do not have the physical urges and needs of ordinary humans. Such persons are no longer as subject to and confined by
physical laws as ordinary humans. "Their soul has tasted the depth of divine Eros and the sweetness of mental gifts and, therefore, it cannot rest
on what it has so far achieved but proceeds to further heavenly realms."

Finally, the teaching of the holy elders about *Theosis* has its social dimension. "*Theosis* must not be seen within the context of a personal, ego-
centric joy. It is often stressed by the holy elders that the *theosized*
individual, even though he (or she) has attained perfection within a per-

fect God and is united with the highest archangelic powers of Cherubim and Seraphim does not rest within this joyful condition. Instead, he becomes an emissary of the Holy Spirit, choosing to live among fellow humans and serving them through word and deed like the apostles. Such a *theosized* person, being in continuous contemplation of God, is capable of guiding others towards their own salvation and *Theosis*."[6]

After my presentation at the Montreal conference on the *Threefold Way*, Professor John Rossner,[7] whom I referred to earlier, took the floor and added his own comments in reference to the life and practices of monks and hermits:

"Such practices are based on the belief that it is important to get away from the world and its attractions for the acquisition of the Holy Spirit. This is the path of the hermit throughout history. Keep in mind that the aim of these people is not to become members of monastic communities, a brotherhood, or a sisterhood. Monasteries in the West have been focused on communal life itself. In eastern monasteries, on the other hand, the focus has been elsewhere. They are communal only in a very secondary sense. It's the bonding between the individual and Heaven that is of central focus, not the bonding of the members of the monastery with each other. The early hermits originally came together in monasteries only to celebrate the liturgy but continued living separately in their caves. They created monasteries where they could eventually eat together because it was simpler. They were struggling for knowledge and wisdom that comes not from logical processes but from superconscious levels and that happens when the mind stops, as it is in yoga and in Buddhism. Lamas and monks and nuns live separately from each other in these non-Christian traditions and they can't go into each other's monasteries for similar reasons as in Christian monasteries. But if we don't understand that, if we impose our twentieth century, North American concepts into what went on then and dismiss the whole thing, we will be the losers. We can't accept that lifestyle because we are in a different situation. We live in the modern world. But we still have from time to time to go apart from it and dwell in this inner relationship with Heaven. It is as a result of that relationship that the great miracles of the saints occur."

Why have Western intellectuals, historians of religion, and theologians been unaware of the teaching of the Christian elders about the *Threefold Way*, I wondered? Why has the influential and controversial Anglican bishop of Newark, Dr. John Spong, for example, stated in utter frustration that "if the Anglican Commission can turn this far to the right, then it joins a strident fundamentalist Protestantism, an antiquated Roman Catholicism, and an *irrelevant Orthodox tradition* [italics added] as the major expressions of Christianity at the dawn of the twenty-first century . . .

I see no hope for a Christian future in any of them. There is very little in any of these conservative traditions with which I could identify."[8]

Bishop Spong seems to be a rationalist, radical theologian who shows neither an interest in nor awareness of the mystical and miracle tradition of the holy elders. He judges Christianity on the basis of how it is represented by the churches, not the mystical *Ecclesia* as embodied in the lives of saints. He is not alone among critically thinking Western theologians, historians, and philosophers in offering this kind of assessment in regard to the external aspects of the Christian tradition. Their interest is in ethics, social justice, and reform. Salutary pursuits as these may be, they are not as I understand it paths to mystical illumination. The question that I tried to explore is, why are these scholars unaware of or willing to disregard an entire Christian mystical tradition? These were questions I raised with my students during a seminar on the sociology of religion that I offered the following academic year.

The sociological answer, I explained to my students, lies in the way Christianity developed within the historical parameters of the Roman Empire. Constantine, the fourth-century Roman emperor, made some crucial decisions that had a lasting impact on both Western civilization and Christianity. During the middle of the fourth century he elevated Christianity from a persecuted sect to the official religion of the Roman Empire. Since then Christianity, and the Judaism out of which it emerged, along with Greek philosophy and Roman law, became the third cultural pillar that sustained what we understand as Western civilization. The polytheism of the ancients was replaced by the One and only God of Israel, and the Ten Commandments became the ethical foundation of the West. Constantine then shifted the capital of his empire from Rome to Constantinople after he realized that the former had become vulnerable to the barbarian tribes from the north. Changing the capital to "the New Rome" was a crucial strategic decision that affected the course of Western history. It allowed the empire to last another thousand years. There was, perhaps, an additional reason for relocating his capital to the east. The old Rome was too stained with its pagan past. Constantinople was a fresh start, a city without a history, founded exclusively on the new religion.

Whereas the eastern part of the empire known as Byzantium thrived and prospered, the social and political infrastructure of the Western part of the empire eventually collapsed under the weight of the Germanic invasions. This development left the Roman Church as the sole organized institution keeping a politically fragmented and barbarized Western European society together. The Dark Ages descended upon Europe, a development that did not take place in Byzantium, and this is an important point that Western historians have often overlooked. It is interesting to note that during the Dark Ages, Constantinople was a leading center of culture with over a million inhabitants whereas Paris had only a few thousand. Here is how a medieval historian described the prevailing conditions in the West.

> The leadership which was so badly needed by the disorganized Western society of the sixth century could come initially only from the church, which had in its ranks almost all the literate men in Europe and the strongest institutions of the age. The church, however, had also suffered severely from the Germanic invasions. The bishops identified their interests with those of the lay nobility and in fact were often relatives of kings and the more powerful aristocrats; the secular clergy in general was ignorant, corrupt, and unable to deal with the problem of Christianizing a society which remained intensely heathen in spite of formal conversion of masses of Germanic warriors to Christianity. The grossest heathen superstitions were grafted onto Latin Christianity. . . . By the beginning of the 7th century church discipline in Gaul was in a state of chaos, and the problem was the most basic one of preserving the sufficient rudiments of literacy to perpetuate the liturgy at doctrines of Latin Christianity. . . . The Latin church was preserved from extinction, and European civilization with it, by the two ecclesiastical institutions which alone had the strength and efficiency to withstand the impress of the surrounding barbarism: the regular clergy (that is, the monks) and the Papacy.[9]

These historical developments signaled the beginning of the preoccupation of the Western Church with the management of this world, so much so that in some cases the Pope himself participated in military expeditions and used the sword with the same ease as the Gospel. It was a ghastly development for the Eastern monks and hermits, who objected to any form of violence. "The reluctance of the Byzantine church to accept that ends could justify means (even to the point of insisting that killing enemy soldiers in battle was sinful) led to a feeling that no one could engage in politics, war, or commerce without some moral taint. This put the Byzantines at a certain disadvantage against western merchants or Crusaders, or Muslim Holy Warriors."[10]

While the political and military institutions of the western part of the empire collapsed, the overall social and political infrastructure of the eastern part of the Roman Empire remained relatively intact. The various emperors still handled the affairs of this world, often committing atrocious crimes against their enemies, while the Church remained otherworldly both in its praxis and in theological orientation, fulfilling its role as the conscience of the empire and often serving as a countervailing power against the arbitrariness of imperial power. Its focus and legitimate domain were not the affairs of state but the realms beyond this world. The mystical element in Eastern Christianity (the *Threefold Way*) which has survived to this day in some ancient monastic communities may therefore be attributed to the fact that in Byzantium, the Church, unlike its Western counterpart, did not exercise direct political power and authority over society. There were clear and definitive boundaries between the ecclesiastical, religious sphere on one hand and the imperial state on the other. The emperor as the "vicegerent of Christ" on earth perceived as his primary role the safeguarding and protection of Orthodox Christianity. With full economic and political support from the state, the monks were left in peace in their monasteries to focus all their energy and attention on the systematic exploration of inner spiritual life and otherworldly goals. While Western Christianity became more oriented toward this world, Eastern Christianity remained monastic and eremitic in character.

> The essential function of both monks and nuns was seen as the pursuit of holiness. Byzantine monasteries may have devoted less time to study, scholarship and education than their western counterparts, but they took seriously the obligation of hospitality and sponsored works of charity, establishing hospitals, orphanages and houses for the poor. Yet the greatest stress was placed on abnegation of the world, as was fully demonstrated by the citing of the monasteries of the Meteora clinging to the perpendicular rocks of the Thessalian mountains or by the extraordinary monastic republic of the Holy Mountain of Athos.[11]

The different historical developments of the western and the eastern parts of the Roman Empire paralleled and perhaps were responsible for the rise of two distinct orientations in Christian theology. The type which developed in the West was based on the thought of Aristotle, the philosophical precursor to the scientific revolution and the philosopher whose primary focus was the study of this world. God as the "Unmoved Mover," Aristotle taught, can be known and proven by studying nature and through philosophical, logical deductions. Saint Thomas Aquinas, who introduced Aristotle to the West, was the catalyst for the Roman Catholic Church to embrace Aristotelian philosophy and establish it as the central orientation in Catholic theology. Western theology, by adhering to such an orientation, did in fact plant the seeds for the scientific revolution and the rise of rationalism that paved the way for the modern secular world as we know it. This "scholastic" perspective, however, was at odds with that of Eastern

Christianity, which believed that God can only be known through spiritual practice and direct mystical illumination.

Christianity eventually split formally into the Roman and the Eastern Orthodox churches during the Great Schism of A.D. 1054. Since then the "two Christianities" followed their radically different and separate ways.

Western Christianity underwent further radical convulsions that led to increasing secularization. In the middle of the sixteenth century Martin Luther nailed to the door of his church his "Ninety-five Theses" that launched the revolution against the Pope. With Protestantism, monasticism as an institution was abolished altogether as well as the practice of honoring the saints, who traditionally had served as spiritual beacons on the path towards *Theosis*. In the words of Father Maximos, it was as if "the heart was taken out of Christianity."

In addition to a cultural repudiation of cloistered life, Protestantism redirected believers to express their faith through a "this-worldly asceticism," an orientation of disciplined, rational action *within* the world. As the great German sociologist Max Weber showed,[12] this reorientation of Western culture had as an unintended consequence the development of a "Protestant work ethic" that has played a major role in revolutionizing the world by opening the gates to modern capitalism and the Industrial Revolution.

By means of a primarily rational, scholastic approach to God, and by marginalizing the *Threefold Way*, Western Christianity waged a losing battle with science, which eventually came to be viewed by many leading Western thinkers as an alternative to religion. The Western intellectual tradition since the Middle Ages has therefore been galvanized by an unrelenting adversarial spirit against religion, which was identified and equated with social backwardness and reactionary politics.

Eastern Christianity on the other hand remained until recently cut off and insulated from these secularizing influences, primarily because of the fall of Constantinople to the Turks in 1453 and the fall of Orthodox Russia to the communists in 1917. A consequence perhaps of this cultural hibernation and isolation from Western historical developments was the preservation of the Eastern Christian monastic tradition, which has safeguarded to date the *Threefold Way* and the institution of "eldership." They were products of the millennial existence of the historically defunct and forgotten Byzantium.

Given the social and cultural characteristics of Byzantine state and society, it was possible for the nurturing of an "enchanted" and otherwordly orientation to the world, a state that Max Weber assumed existed only in Asiatic societies. It is this mystical version of Christianity that Byzantium may offer to the present, postmodern, secular age, namely the restoration of the "eye of intuition" as a pathway to knowledge as legitimate as that of science, or the "eye of the senses" and of philosophy, or the "eye of the mind." I suggested to my students that Byzantium's legacy and its gift to the modern age may be the *Threefold Way* in a parallel way that the gift of Western Christianity to the world has been the growth of science, critical social thought, and modern democracy.

16

DOXOLOGY of peace

I returned to Cyprus at Christmas and again during the following two summers. Each time I flew there I spent several days at the Panagia monastery for further conversations with Father Maximos. Besides the imperatives of my research that required further contacts with the Athonite elder, periodic retreats at the monastery had become a psychological and spiritual necessity for me. Somehow, spending a few days in its tranquil setting made me feel spiritually renewed and invigorated. I felt as if I had a second home and was grateful to the monks and nuns who devoted their lives to God and in so doing preserved monasticism. They rescued the Christian spiritual tradition and maintained this vital institution for the rest of us living at the dawn of the twenty-first century. "Everybody should have access to a monastery for periodic spiritual renewal and as an antidote to modern alienation and meaninglessness," I wrote in my journal on the flight from Amsterdam to Larnaka.

The Christmas period of 1999 was different. I arrived on the island on December 29 with the world in the midst of high anxieties about the coming millennium. In many minds there were fears about the "Y2K bug." Will computers recognize the year 2000? Will the world plunge into chaos? Will there be a world as we have known it? Airlines canceled flights for the first of January as a precautionary safety measure. Rational friends back in Maine advised us to stay put and stockpile food, gasoline, and water for an undefined number of days. A former colleague who was knowledgeable about computers gloomily predicted that there was bound to be global confusion and advised making prompt preparations, expecting the worst. She handed me a score of articles written by experts to convince me of the seriousness of the situation. "By December," she predicted, "there won't be any batteries in the stores."

Emily on the other hand, ever an optimist and a peace activist, had spent several months the previous year in Cyprus as a consultant setting up the "eco-peace village" which, in spite of local political tensions, was becoming a reality. Brushing aside concerns about Y2K, she flew to Nepal for a tree-planting project and to be with Vasia, who was there on a junior semester study-abroad program studying Tibetan culture. They looked forward to a "mother/daughter bonding" and planned to welcome the new millennium by trekking the Himalayas. I kept my fingers crossed, said my prayers for their safety, and made certain that I arrived on Cyprus before the end of the century. In the meantime the mass media were saturated with the prophecies of Nostradamus and astrological forecasts about massive catastrophes. Some of the more religiously zealous discovered John's Apocalypse and the number 666. They obsessed about the Antichrist, Armageddon, and, with heightened anticipation, even joy, looked forward to a Christ who after defeating the forces of darkness would descend from the clouds with trumpets blowing. As far as they were concerned, the sooner this scenario unfolded the better.

I planned to spend the fateful New Year's Eve in Nicosia with my sister Maroulla, a self-taught artist, and Vasos, my brother-in-law, a retired telecommunications engineer. Their home was a hub of human activity. Relatives, friends, and acquaintances would routinely come and go at any hour of the day, a situation that led my late father to declare that "this is not a home but an embassy." Cyprus could not be more different than Maine and I loved the contrast. My sister's open house had been a point of reference and a pillar of stability and continuity in my life, helping me maintain my ties to the island regardless of how many years I spent living in a far-off land. I was part of a fortunate generation of immigrants that came of age during the jet age. My uncles, who had migrated to the U.S. before jets began crisscrossing the skies, hardly ever traveled back to pay a visit to their ancestral homeland.

Mercifully the lack of any serious concern on the island about the change to the new century lowered my own anxieties. Cypriots were too preoccupied with the Greek-Turkish dispute to worry about Y2K. Besides, computers had not as yet penetrated Cypriot society to the same degree as in America. I looked forward to an anxiety-free New Year's celebration.

There was going to be a gathering of friends and relatives, including my sister's three children and four grandchildren, to celebrate the coming of the new year. Thomas and Niki were to be present and I was looking forward to reconnecting with them. By this time both of them had become regular patrons at the Panagia monastery and developed into enthusiastic supporters of Father Maximos. We had much to talk about since that riveting encounter that Thomas had with Father Maximos three years earlier, during the beginning of my exploration.

I planned to travel to the monastery sometime during the first week in January and be there for a few days before heading back to Maine for the winter semester. But my plans changed abruptly when I talked to Stephanos over the phone. There was going to be an *agrypnia* in the central cathedral of Limassol starting at eight-thirty on the evening of December 31 and lasting until the early hours the next morning. A special liturgy was going to take place to welcome the new millennium and Father Maximos had been asked to preside over the service. "I wouldn't miss it if I were you," he advised.

As much as I looked forward to spending the festive night with my sister and the extended networks of friends and relatives, I felt I could not miss such a unique opportunity. After overcoming my initial hesitation, I got into the car and drove off to Limassol. Fortunately my sister was fully understanding and supported my decision.

While driving to Limassol during the early evening of the last day of the millennium, my mind returned to the concerns of Y2K and possible pending global disasters. I did not need to resort to Nostradamus for a scenario that could spell the end of life on Earth as we have known it. For a number of years rational social scientists, philosophers, and environmentalists have been warning us about possible massive dislocations and upheavals brought forward by modernity. Alas, as a species we have unlocked the secrets of nature but without developing the appropriate wisdom to handle the genie that we set loose. Consequently, during our most progressive twentieth century, the bloodiest of all centuries, over one hundred million people have died in global and regional wars, a figure fifteen times bloodier than the nineteenth century.[1] I remembered what the late Arthur Koestler once wrote, that ever since Hiroshima, humanity has lived on borrowed time. He suggested that in order to drive home this awesome truth we ought to begin measuring time starting with 1945, the year of that fateful event.[2] Will the Russians and Americans keep their missiles in their silos or will they set them off accidentally and trigger Apocalypse now? That was a major fear of nuclear scientists and computer experts as they pondered the changeover to the new century. It was this type of reflection that made me decide to give up worldly celebrations about the coming of the new millennium and join the *agrypnia* with Father Maximos for a doxology of peace.

It was exactly eight-thirty in the evening when I met Stephanos and Erato, who waited for me at the steps of the Katholike cathedral in the center of Limassol. Father Maximos, I was told, was counseling pilgrims at the confessional, a small room adjacent to the church. Stephanos told me that Father Maximos was not very happy about this since it was not part of his program to do confessions that night. But when several people had appeared at the church to have a face to face audience with him for confession, he felt it was his duty to see them. It was part of the Athonite tradition that he tried to maintain in Cyprus, an increasingly impossible task given his growing popularity. He was to join the long service after all the confessees had unburdened themselves of their sins.

I was surprised to see so many people at the *agrypnia*. The church was filled. Given the importance of secular New Year's celebrations, such a phenomenon was most unusual and a sign of Father Maximos's increasing reputation on the island.

We sat in the middle of the large cathedral with its tall Byzantine dome. There was no other light except that from candles the pilgrims had lit in front of the icons. I could barely recognize people's faces in the dark. I looked around to see if there was an electric light on that I could use as a way to check whether we would still have electricity after midnight. I noticed one at the sanctuary and decided that this light would be a signal for me. If it stayed on, then everything would be fine.

Three hundred meters beyond the church at the central square, preparations were being made for rapturous celebrations to welcome the new millennium. It was a great contrast to the silence and solemnity of the service going on inside the cathedral. As the chanters began with the customary long recitation of the Psalms of David, the presiding priest rhythmically swung his censer back and forth, filling the church with the familiar, intense smell of incense.

The hours passed one after another with chants and hymns that have stirred the spiritual and aesthetic sensitivities of believers for hundreds of years. Many thoughts crossed my mind as I listened, sometimes standing, sometimes sitting, to the ongoing service. I never experienced any fatigue or boredom thanks to the masterful alternate singing of the two groups of chanters, one on the left side of the church and the other on the right.

Father Maximos maintained that the lyrics and music of the Eastern Church were created by holy elders while in states of divine inspiration. That is the reason why one feels so rejuvenated by such chants rather than bored no matter how many times one hears them, assuming that the chanters know how to chant. When someone questioned the need for prolonged *agrypnias* and endless chanting, Father Maximos's response was: "It takes time to bake bread," implying that it takes time before a person may enter into a mystical frame of mind in order to become spiritually receptive. This is the function of long services that people of a rational predilection find hard to understand or endure. It is no wonder that in the West, where rationalism has become triumphant, the liturgy is considerably shortened and replaced by sermons.

Indeed, it may very well have been the aesthetic experience of the services and the liturgy of the Eastern Church that helped it survive over the centuries, for it was this very aesthetic aspect of the liturgy that, it is said, converted the Russians, Ukrainians, and other Eastern Europeans to Orthodox Christianity. During the tenth century Prince Vladimir of Kiev, a fun-loving womanizer, wished to give his empire a common religion primarily for purposes of political unification. Before making the final decision about which religion to adopt for his fragmented empire of unruly tribes, he dispatched a delegation to visit various countries and places of worship where different religions were practiced in order to find out which one would be the most suitable for his empire. The delegation included in its itinerary a visit to Constantinople, at the great church of *Aghia Sophia* [Holy Wisdom] built by Justinian a few centuries earlier. Upon their return they presented their findings to the prince in a memorable report. Among many others, they described their experiences when they visited *Aghia Sophia*: "Then we went to Greece, and the Greeks led us to the edifices where they worship their God, and we knew not whether we were in heaven or on earth. For on earth there is no such splendor or such beauty, and we are at a loss how to describe it. We know only that God dwells there among men, and their service is fairer than the ceremonies of other nations. For we cannot forget that beauty."[3]

The report allegedly convinced Prince Vladimir to convert to Eastern Christianity, and along with him eventually all the millions of his subjects. A more pragmatic reason for his conversion may have been his intention to maintain his independence from outside political control, specifically from the Germans. Furthermore, the ground for mass conversions to Eastern Christianity had been prepared by Byzantine missionaries, particularly Cyril and Methodios, the two monks from Thessaloniki credited with converting the Slavs to Eastern Christianity. Regardless of the reasons for his conversion, Prince Vladimir eventually became Saint Vladimir thanks to the historical consequences of that decision and his apparently genuine personal transformation into a just prince.[4]

These ideas were swirling in my mind when Father Maximos, dressed in his full liturgical regalia, finally made his appearance. I looked at my watch. It was ten-thirty in the evening. In an hour and a half a new century would begin. He stood in front of the altar flanked by Father Nikodemos and Father Isaac, who had accompanied him. They both held white candles throughout the service. Then at exactly five minutes before midnight the two choirs began to chant the *doxology*. Father Maximos raised his hands upward and focused his gaze at the dome of the cathedral on which a large portrait of Christ *Pantokrator*, Ruler of the Universe, was painted holding the Gospel with one hand and with the other blessing the congregation. The two choirs alternated as they chanted the different stanzas, a practice that enhanced its dramatic effect. "Glory to God in the highest and Peace on earth, good will to humanity. . . ."

At exactly midnight the chant of the *doxology* ended and Father Maximos, his hands stretched upward and his eyes fixed on the Christ *Pantokrator*, started the liturgy in a strong voice uttering the ancient prayer: *"Evlogimene e Vasilia tou Patros kai tou Yiou kai tou Agiou Pneumatos nyn kai ai kai es tous aeonas ton aeonon Amen"* [Blessed be the Kingdom of the Father and of the Son and of the Holy Spirit, now and forever and unto the ages of ages. Amen].

The moment Father Maximos uttered the word *"Evlogimene . . ."* a pandemonium of fireworks broke loose, coming from the central square and other parts of the city. The thunderous celebrations for the coming of the new millennium had begun. Father Maximos remained transfixed, not the least disturbed by the deafening explosions. I looked at the altar. The electric light was still on. Civilization might survive after all, I thought. I leaned towards Erato and Stephanos and wished them a happy new millennium. The *agrypnia* continued uninterrupted until 2:30 in the morning.

Before going home we spent some time with Father Maximos at a house next to the cathedral where we were all invited. After exchanging good wishes for the new year, we caught up with the news while enjoying an early morning breakfast of pastries traditional for the new year. It was four-thirty in the morning when I finally went to bed at Stephanos and Erato's apartment in Limassol. The streets around the central square and the promenade by the waterfront were all filled with jubilant Limassolians celebrating the millennial changeover. I felt fortunate that I had followed Stephanos's suggestion to join them for the *agrypnia*. Before sleeping we checked Euro News. The global village was celebrating and the missiles remained silent in their silos. At least this time the aficionados of John's Apocalypse and the prophecies of Nostradamus were off the mark.

I looked forward to the afternoon when I was to drive Father Maximos back to the Panagia monastery. Just like old times he had accepted my request to be his driver for a few days. During this drive I decided, with Father Maximos's active encouragement, that I should pay another visit to Mount Athos as the last stage of my exploration of the mystical tradition of Eastern Christianity.

To my delight, Lavros, a mutual friend of Stephanos and myself who lived in Limassol, was to join me in that venture. A former professor of environmental economics in Iowa and an enthusiastic follower of Father Maximos, Lavros was a man of good humor and easygoing disposition. Having spent more than ten years in America and with a similar academic background as myself, Lavros would be an ideal companion. Thanks to repeated and prolonged visits, he knew Mount Athos well and had good connections with various elders, abbots, monks, and hermits. He was therefore going to be a promising scout and informant for me as we trekked the Holy Mountain and hiked from monastery to monastery in search of remarkable elders.

Before I left Cyprus, Lavros and I met with Father Maximos to discuss our upcoming pilgrimage, get his blessings, and hear his suggestions as to where we should go and whom we should contact during our two-week exploration of the Holy Mountain. We planned our journey for the upcoming March, during the University of Maine's spring recess.

the mountain of silence

It was eleven-thirty in the evening when I arrived in Thessaloniki via Milan on an Alitalia flight out of Boston. I looked forward to meeting Lavros at the airport, who was supposed to arrive two hours earlier on a flight from Cyprus. We would stay in Thessaloniki for the night and begin our journey to the Holy Mountain the following morning on Sunday, March 12.

As soon as I cleared customs I began to look for him. Our agreed-upon meeting place was outside the gate, but he was nowhere to be seen. I was despondent. After wandering aimlessly for forty minutes around the virtually deserted airport and learning that there was no other flight coming from Cyprus at that late hour, I took a taxi to the City Hotel in downtown Thessaloniki. There I found Lavros's fax waiting for me: "Sorry I couldn't reach you before you left the States but I have some bad news. I was informed at the last moment that we chose the wrong time to visit Mount Athos for the purpose of meeting and talking to elders. After sunset on Sunday, March 12th the first week of Lent begins and the entire Mountain is under a very strict regimen of fasting and praying. But more than anything else everybody is under a strict vow of silence. We did not realize, my friend, that we were headed for the Mountain of Silence! If we have the good luck of meeting someone, he will only look at us speechless like a fish. This is true for the first three days, until Wednesday the fifteenth. I realize the complications, as far as your plans are concerned, but I am assured that we shall be able to accomplish a lot in the days before you will have to fly back. So, Kyriaco, instead of both of us wandering around Thessaloniki, very reluctantly I decided to ask for your mercy and to approve my change of plans. I can meet you at the airport in Thessaloniki on Tuesday at three in the afternoon. Please confirm and God Bless, Lavros." I faxed him back that he was forgiven and that I would see him on Tuesday. Then I went to sleep.

I had three days to spend in the city and I intended to take full advantage of this temporary inconvenience. Thessaloniki is the second largest city in Greece and during the Byzantine era it was regarded the second most important center of Eastern Christianity after Constantinople. Thessaloniki, the city which inspired poets, writers, and singers for generations, is replete with archaeological sights dating back to the time of Alexander and his mentor Aristotle, both native sons of the area. Most important for my work, the city is filled with ancient churches built during the time of Byzantium. Its history, like that of Constantinople, marked the history of Christianity itself.

The Thessalonians received a number of Paul's epistles; it was from Thessaloniki that the two scholar monks, Cyril and his brother Methodios, embarked on their ninth-century mission to spread Christianity to the Slavs. In fact, I realized that Thessaloniki was the city of the founders of two major theological orientations that defined the development of Christianity since the time of the Great Schism in 1054, Aristotle and Saint Gregory Palamas. This thought jolted me while having tea in Aristotle Square next to a large, imposing statue of the ancient sage after I realized that only a few blocks away lay the church of Saint Gregory Palamas. This fourteenth-century archbishop of Thessaloniki played the decisive role in blocking Western scholastic theology, founded on Aristotelian thought, from becoming the dominant theological orientation of Eastern Christianity.

During the declining years of Byzantium an influential group of Byzantine theologians and churchmen, affected by developments in the Western Church, advocated the adoption of scholasticism as the primary approach to theology and denounced the spiritual practices of the hermits and monks of Mount Athos as heretical. The Athonite monks' way was known at the time as *Hesychasm*, or the way of quietude. Their goal was the direct experience of the *Uncreated Light* and Theosis.[1]

The leader of the anti-*Hesychast* campaign was Barlaam, an erudite,

Western-trained Greek monk from Calabria, Italy. As a humanist theologian and scholar he advocated intellectual contemplation, Aristotelian metaphysics, and *Thomist* theology as the appropriate ways to contemplate and search for God. He mocked the methods of the Athonite ascetics as the product of ignorance and superstition and considered reports of holy elders having experiences of the *Uncreated Light* as pure nonsense and delusion. Barlaam and his group taught that God's essence is beyond reach and beyond all human knowledge. The *Uncreated Light* as experienced by Athonite elders, therefore, is not of God but purely the product of the elders' distorted imaginations.

The leading proponent of the *Hesychast* school of thought was the archbishop of Thessaloniki, Gregory Palamas, who as a monk on Mount Athos for many years is said to have had a firsthand experience of the *Uncreated Light*. An erudite scholar, Palamas vigorously opposed the arguments of the scholastic philosophers and theologians and skillfully defended *Hesychasm* as the primary pathway toward God-realization, toward *Theosis*. He agreed with his opponents that the essence of God is absolutely unknowable and beyond all human understanding. Palamas, however, based his theology on the teachings of the early holy elders of the *Ecclesia* and stressed the fact that human beings can have a real experience of God through His *Energies* which are emanations of His Divine Essence. The experience of the *Uncreated Light* as the energies of God are therefore real and not delusions. By making that argument Palamas tried to rescue the belief that *Theosis* is humanly possible. He claimed that a purely philosophical approach to knowing God may prevent human beings from really knowing God.[2]

The theological confrontation between Gregory Palamas and the *Hesychasts* on one hand and Barlaam and his supporters on the other went on for some time during the middle of the fourteenth century. It unfolded in the form of public letters, books, and debates that created much dissension within the Eastern Church. Eventually Palamas's position won the day, and the Church in Constantinople, during the two subsequent Councils of 1341 and 1351, declared his teachings as the true teachings of the Orthodox Church. At the same time Barlaam's teachings were rejected and anathematized as heretical. "The struggle of St Gregory," wrote a contemporary Athonite abbot and former professor of theology at the University of Thessaloniki, "did not aim at justifying some philosophical position, but had as its target *Theosis* as an achievable goal for human beings."[3] According to Saint Gregory and the *Hesychasts*, a philosophical approach is insufficient as a method to know God. "A theology that is based on intellectual constructs and not on the direct experience of God is philosophy and not theology. It is a human creation that offers neither real knowledge of God nor peace to the heart."[4]

With Palamas's victory over Barlaam, and by implication over Aristotle, the *Hesychasts'* beliefs of the path of the *Threefold Way* survived and were preserved for posterity in ancient monasteries like those of Mount Athos. Interestingly, leading transpersonal theorist Ken Wilber in his masterful critique of Western thought claims that Western civilization lacks a "yoga," or a method of acquiring knowledge beyond the senses and the intellect. Western thought remains therefore trapped within its intellectual and scientific constructs. Wilber, like most transpersonal theorists today, finds this "yoga" in Eastern philosophy and religion, particularly Zen. Nowhere in his work is there any mention or awareness of the *Hesychast* tradition or the concepts behind the *Threefold Way*.[5]

Sipping tea and contemplating these issues in Aristotle Square, I could not avoid the temptation of thinking that perhaps behind this theological dispute there lay the invisible hand of Providence at work. That in fact both the *Hesychast* approach to God on one hand and the philosophical approach to God on the other may be two sides of the same Christian coin, one dominant in the East and the other dominant in the West. Christianity, a Catholic bishop in Maine once told me, has two lungs. One is Western, meaning rational and philosophical, and the other Eastern, meaning mystical and otherworldly. Both, he claimed, are needed for proper breathing. Being a product of the Western intellectual, Enlightenment tradition, yet strongly drawn to my cultural roots in mystical Eastern Orthodoxy, I was most sympathetic to that metaphor. I could not imagine breathing with only one lung. Having studied to some extent the works of Saint Thomas Aquinas, I could not but marvel at his genius and the breadth of his knowledge. But even he had to declare, after being catapulted into an ecstatic state during a religious service, that what he had written up to that point was trivial compared to what he had experienced in that state of inner illumination. After that episode and until his death a year later, Saint Thomas never wrote another page. Aquinas's own experience provided fodder for the position advocated by Saint Gregory Palamas in his dispute with Monk Barlaam the Calabrian.[6] However, the words of Aristotle resonated in my mind, that if you claim that you should not philosophize then you are in fact philosophizing. Therefore, you cannot avoid philosophizing. Gregory Palamas was himself thoroughly versed in Aristotle and had to use philosophical arguments and logic invented by the great ancient master in order to defend *Hesychasm* and confront the points raised by Barlaam. So who was right in the final analysis, Saint Gregory Palamas or Aristotle? I never raised such issues with Father Maximos and I wasn't certain what his response would be. What was clear to me was that his great hero was Saint Gregory Palamas, in whose honor he built the impressive chapel next to the Panagia monastery.

I wondered how Christianity would have developed had the western part of the Roman Empire not collapsed under the Germanic invasions and had Byzantium not fallen to the Turks. Would Western civilization have maintained a more balanced approach between mysticism and rationality, between faith and science? After all, the early fathers of the church like Saint Basil the Great and Saint Gregory of Nyssa were erudite scholars thoroughly steeped in classical learning. They honored the ancient philosophers and incorporated much of their teachings into their own mystical and experiential understanding of God. In other words both the mystical and the rational approaches to God were part of the early Church. They were only set asunder by subsequent historical developments.

Perhaps these developments had to unfold in that manner for reasons beyond our grasp. Perhaps we needed to develop our rationality. But now that our scientific, rational faculties have developed to the point that they may threaten our very existence, we need perhaps to bring to the forefront the forgotten mystical tradition as it is preserved in places like Mount Athos. At this stage in history, no matter what our personal religious preference may be, we need to reintegrate the rational with the intuitive, the scientific with the mystical, for the sake of our collective physical and spiritual salvation.[7]

With these unanswerable questions turning in my head, I took the bus to the airport. I was greatly relieved to welcome Lavros, who walked through customs with a disarming smile on his face. We hurriedly took a taxi to the bus station to catch the last bus leaving for Ouranoupolis, which lies three and a half hours away at the southern part of the Chalkidike Peninsula.

It was about nine in the evening when we arrived at Ouranoupolis. We were to stay there for the night and get the ferry for the Holy Mountain the following morning. Lavros, who like Stephanos had become a confidant of Father Maximos, brought with him plenty of news on the latest developments in Cyprus. Knowing that upon entering Mount Athos we would be under a strict regimen of fasting, we gave ourselves license and indulged in a memorable feast of fresh octopus and *retsina* wine at a local taverna by the sea.

A vigorous man of average height, slightly on the heavy side, with a trimmed white beard covering his round face, Lavros had natural wit and earthy wisdom. He had just retired and was devoting his time to environmental advocacy and to helping Father Maximos in his social and spiritual mission. The son of a prominent priest from Limassol, Lavros as a young man during the fifties took part in the underground guerrilla campaign against the colonial government, a campaign the British called terrorist. His task was to carry secret messages from one part of the island to another.

But a particular episode during those dark years drastically changed his life. One day on his way to a village at the eastern part of the island on a special mission, he got lost and stopped his motor scooter near an open field. He suddenly noticed an unusual sight. In the middle of that field he saw a shepherd sitting on a rock reading a book. He walked toward him to ask for directions when he realized that the shepherd was reading the Bible. "Before I give you directions," the man replied, lowering his glasses to get a clearer look at Lavros, "please answer this question for me. Had Jesus been the archbishop of Cyprus, do you think he would have taken a machine gun to fight the British?"

"The shepherd's question changed my life one hundred and eighty degrees," Lavros declared emphatically. "Right there and then I became a pacifist and renounced violence as a means of solving human problems. That shepherd was either an angel or someone the angels had sent to help me see more clearly."

At ten-thirty the following morning we boarded the ferry *Axion Esti*, named after a venerated icon of Mount Athos, and headed deep into the Athonite promontory. The day was brilliant and the sea was calm as we passed one monastery after another, dropping off pilgrims and monks and getting others on board. Beyond the monasteries to the south, snow-covered Mount Athos rose to over six thousand feet from sea level. Visiting the Holy Mountain, I felt once again as if I were going back in time to the only surviving remnant of Byzantium.[8]

Our first destination was the monastery of Vatopedi, where both Lavros and I had connections and from where we could plan our itinerary. Once we disembarked at Daphne, we had a choice to either walk to Vatopedi, a six-hour hike through a scenic trail, or to hire a truck together with other pilgrims that would take us there in an hour. We chose the latter option in order to reserve our strength for the long hikes that awaited us later.

Notwithstanding the pristine beauty of the Athonite countryside, the journey was certainly not a joyride. The roughness of the terrain and the less than ideal conditions of our travel made it feel more like a strenuous physical exercise, a sort of *askesis*. The lack of any paved roads or conditions of comfort was a deliberate choice on the part of the Athonite monks. They wanted nothing to undermine the purpose for which they were drawn to the Holy Mountain.

"Kyriaco, what do you think of the Pope's latest statement?" Lavros asked me as we rode along in the back of the truck, holding tightly to the railings as it moved ahead like a boat in a storm.

"It is extraordinary, to put it mildly. Don't you think? I would say it is historic. Perhaps this may be the beginning of a reconciliation between East and West."

"I hope you are right but don't raise your hopes too high. There are still feelings of animosity that go a long time back in history," Lavros, who knew well the culture of Mount Athos, responded. "Let's see what the monks have to say."

I had indeed been astounded to hear that after the Pontiff had asked forgiveness from Muslims and Jews for sins committed by his Church in the past, he had proceeded to ask forgiveness from fellow Orthodox Christians. It was major news all over the world. Before I left Maine I had discussed the topic with my students. I explained that the primary historical causes of the animosity between East and West date back to the division of the Roman Empire; this eventually led to the Great Schism of the Church in 1054. After that turning point, relations only deteriorated, with sporadic and ineffective attempts at reconciliation. The events that traumatized the Byzantines and generated deep suspicions were the effects of the Crusades on their society. The holy warriors, on their way to Palestine to fight the "infidels" during the Fourth Crusade, turned their weapons against the Byzantines and instead of the Holy Land they conquered much of Byzantium, including Thessaloniki and Constantinople, where they indulged in unparalleled savagery and violence. In Thessaloniki women and children were raped, houses were pillaged and burned, and churches were desecrated and destroyed. According to a contemporary chronicler:

These barbarians carried their violence to the very foot of the altars. It was thought strange that they should wish to destroy our icons, using them as fuel for the fires on which they cooked. More criminal still, they would dance upon the altars, before which the angels trembled, and sing profane songs. Then they would piss all over the church, flooding the floors with their urine.[9]

A similar fate awaited Constantinople and many of the monasteries on Mount Athos, inflicting deep wounds that severed the bonds between Eastern and Western Christianity. By the time Byzantium was restored, it was too exhausted to defend itself against the Ottoman Turks. Historian John Norwich had this to say about that tragic episode in Western history:

The Fourth Crusade . . . surpassed even its predecessors in faithlessness and duplicity, in brutality and greed. By the sack of Constantinople, Western civilization suffered a loss greater than the sack of Rome in the fifth century or the burning of the library of Alexandria in the seventh—perhaps the most catastrophic single loss in all history. Politically, too, the damage done was incalculable. Byzantium never recovered any considerable part of its lost dominion. Instead, the Empire was left powerless to defend itself against the Ottoman tide. There are few greater ironies in history than the fact that the fate of Eastern Christendom should have been sealed by men who fought under the banner of the Cross . . . [they] must accept the major responsibility for the havoc that they wrought upon the world.[10]

While reading in the library of the Panagia monastery, Sir Steven Runciman's graphic and riveting description of the day by day events that followed the fall of Constantinople to the Ottomans,[11] I could hardly control my tears. I was not just vicariously experiencing the pain of the collapse of Constantinople during three days of looting, destruction, and massacre, nor was I also reliving memories of the 1974 invasion of Cyprus. What I was most riveted by was the devastating significance of the destruction of an entire civilization, the eastern "lung" of the Occident, and what that implied for the fate of the world.

This history remains pretty much unknown in the West for a variety of reasons. One may be the fact that after the fall of Constantinople there were no longer any Byzantines to focus on that period. Those who did survive fled to Venice and Florence carrying along their books and their knowledge of classical civilization, thus playing a catalytic role in boosting the social forces that started the Renaissance. Another reason may be the fact that the great eighteenth-century historian Edward Gibbon in his monumental classic work on the decline and fall of the Roman Empire[12] dismissed Byzantium as irrelevant and painted its millennial history in the most negative of stereotypes. Such attitudes were inherited by other Western medieval historians who focused primarily on Western history and judged Byzantium with Gibbon's lenses. "The history of Byzantium," wrote a contemporary medieval historian,

> is a study in disappointment. The empire centering on Constantinople had begun with all the advantages obtained from its inheritance of the political, economic, and intellectual life of the fourth-century Roman empire. Except in the realm of art, in which the Greeks excelled, Byzantium added scarcely anything to this superb foundation. The east Roman empire of the middle ages made no important contributions to philosophy, theology, science, or literature. . . . Modern historians of the medieval eastern Roman empire have strongly criticized the tendency of nineteenth-century scholars to write off Byzantium as the example of an atrophied civilization. Yet it is hard to find, outside the field of art, any contributions by way of either original ideas or institutions which the medieval Greek-speaking peoples made to civilization.[13]

These negative stereotypes seem to have crystallized in the collective consciousness of the West, affecting its attitude toward the Byzantine civilization which the West's holy warriors played such a central role in destroying. These taken-for-granted biases towards Byzantium kept scholars, until recently, more or less uninterested and misinformed about its history. They also kept Western theologians unaware of the reality and significance of Mount Athos and the spiritual legacy preserved there.

We were warmly welcomed at Vatopedi by the monks, particularly those we knew from previous visits. Although they looked totally exhausted after completing the three-day regimen of total fasting, which meant no food, no water, and no talking, they were eager to hear news from Cyprus, particularly about Father Maximos, as half of the one hundred or so monks at Vatopedi were Cypriots. It was at Vatopedi that Father Maximos had spent many of his years on Mount Athos, just like his hero Saint Gregory Palamas.

We felt comfortable at Vatopedi and, given the informal setting, tried to test their reaction to the Pope's declarations. We were taken aback to discover that there were still strong feelings of suspicion and misgivings about the Western church. They expressed concern that perhaps there were ulterior motives on the part of the Pope in making those declarations in order to take control of the Orthodox Church. From their responses I realized, alas, that it was not only the *Threefold Way* that was being preserved on Mount Athos but the memories and traumas that marked the troubled history of Christianity. "The Pope," one young monk said, "must give up the notion that he is infallible and that the Vatican is the center of Christianity. Don't get me wrong. We love the Pope." He then handed me a booklet written by the abbot of another monastery who, after criticizing the Vatican for its policies in Eastern Europe, traditional territory of Orthodoxy, had expressed the hope that a miracle may happen one day and that ". . . the Holy Orthodox Church of the Old Rome will return to its Apostolic Faith. Then we or our descendants will welcome the Pope on Mount Athos with open arms as the Primary Bishop of the One Catholic and Apostolic Church and our joy will be eternal."

When I suggested to the young monk that perhaps the Pope's declaration was an indirect admission that the Papacy is not infallible and that there is room for reconciliation, his response was: "We will have to wait and see. We want actions, not just words." Elder Dionysios, however, an almost blind, ninety-two-year-old Romanian hermit, considered to be a living saint on the level of elder Ephraim and Paisios, reacted differently to the news when we met him in his hermitage, two hours on foot from Vatopedi. The long-bearded and frail-looking hermit made the sign of the cross, raised his arms toward the sky, and with delight pronounced that this was the best news he had heard in a long time. When Father Seraphim, one of the two monks who accompanied us there, reacted with skepticism, elder Dionysios counseled that "when someone asks us for forgiveness we have no choice but to forgive, without any reservations or second thoughts. This is what Christ asks of us." The old hermit, in his soft, accented Greek, went on to instruct us on the virtues of patience, forgiveness, humility, and love, central values of the culture of the Holy Mountain.

We stayed at Vatopedi for four nights. The monks including the abbot made us feel so welcome, their hospitality was so disarming, that it was difficult for us to leave and move on to other destinations. But our days were limited and there were more elders that we wished to meet, other monasteries that we needed to visit. We promised our friends that we shall return in the near future.

For the next seven days we visited monastery after monastery on the thirty-mile-long by ten-mile-wide promontory. We covered considerable distances, mostly on foot and sometimes by ferry, until we exhausted the recommended list that Father Maximos had given us. It was a unique and unforgettable exposure to the Holy Mountain and its culture that no words can ever do justice to or capture. In addition to talking to elders and hermits we paid homage to several ancient icons reputed to be miraculous. We were also shown extraordinary relics such as portions from the remains of Christianity's greatest saints like a foot from John the Baptist, a hand from Maria Magdalene, the skull of John Chrysostom, pieces from the Holy Cross, the miraculous Girdle of the Holy Virgin, and similar other sacred objects that the monks deeply venerate without ever having a trace of doubt in their minds about their historical authenticity. We, on the other hand, having come from the secular, skeptical world, had no way of knowing whether there was any empirical evidence that the silver-encased hand that we were shown was in fact that of Maria Magdalene. As I had learned by then, such questions are really not relevant on the Holy Mountain. If, however, there were to be a place in the world where such extraordinary relics might have been collected and preserved since the beginning of Christian times, it would be the twenty or so monasteries of Mount Athos.

Our pilgrimage was coming to an end when we began walking down the mountain towards the sea after spending two nights at Simonopetra, a monastery on the western part of the promontory built nine stories high at the top of a precipitous rock. A marvel of Byzantine architecture, Simonopetra looked like an unconquerable citadel housing about forty monks from fifteen different nationalities. The uniqueness of Simonopetra was not only the ethnic diversity of the monks but also their high level of educational and professional achievements in the world prior to their becoming members of that monastic community. The monk responsible for the *archondariki* was a forty-five-year-old former professor of microbiology at an American university. He was cleaning the floors when we met him. Another one was a former professor of subatomic physics at an English university. He was the cook. Yet another was a former NASA scientist. We were stunned. They had abandoned their scientific careers and high status in the world in order to join the cloistered life for the pursuit of the knowledge of God.

The monks of Simonopetra were the first to point out to us that their achievements in the world had nothing to do with what they attempted to accomplish on Mount Athos. These very scientists would sit at the feet of an elder like Paisios for spiritual counseling, a hermit who had only six years of formal schooling.

"We call the Holy Mountain," an elder from Simonopetra told us, "the Garden of the Holy Virgin. In a garden you have great variety of flowers, trees, bushes, weeds, and all kinds of fruits and vegetables. Similarly on the Holy Mountain you will find a great variety of people with different educational backgrounds, personalities, opinions, spiritual development, and understanding of the world outside."

What they do share is a common objective, overcoming egotistical passions through Catharsis. Regardless of their level of educational and spiritual development, regardless of how open or closed their minds are, they all practice the same methodology of *askesis*, of ceaseless prayer, of fasting, confession, communion, and so on. They all chant the same chants and follow the same *typikon*, the clearly delineated program for daily communal prayer and spiritual practices. This is what I found most notable: the commonality of purpose and method of spiritual work, irrespective of whatever intellectual and cultural capital each one brought along when they entered the monastery to become full-time practitioners of the art and science of the search for God.

"Think of it this way," Lavros proposed as we hiked down the mountain to catch the ferry back to Ouranoupolis. "Suppose you are a Nobel laureate and you want to learn Chinese. You will have to start from the ABC of that language like children do in the first year of elementary school. It makes no difference how educated or how developed you are in your scientific field."

"But imagine if some of these monks reach, in twenty or thirty years, the spiritual level of someone like Paisios," I marveled.

"Then you will have elders who have not only mastered worldly knowledge but who have also acquired the knowledge of God," Lavros hypothesized as he walked ahead of me, leaning heavily for support on his walking stick.

"And when that happens," I added, "the future of the *Ecclesia* may be greatly affected."

Fifteen minutes into our downward hike we came across a group of farmworkers hired by the abbot of Simonopetra to help in the fields. They had discovered a large hive of honeybees at the root of an olive tree and, following instructions from the abbot, they were getting ready to retrieve it and place it in a special beehive container. None of them had any training for such a delicate task. They looked confused and hapless. It so happened that Lavros was a seasoned and experienced beekeeper. Encountering the workers at that critical juncture was one of those uncanny synchronicities that routinely unfold in our lives, but we usually fail to take note of it. The workers, however, considered the episode nothing short of a little miracle and thanked the Holy Virgin for sending Lavros to them. Had he not appeared there on that spot to help them they would have certainly destroyed the nest and possibly even suffered the severe punishment of multiple bee stings.

For the next forty minutes I sat on a rock and from a safe distance watched Lavros and the farmworkers successfully retrieve the nest with the honeybees. The moment Lavros placed the last piece of the buzzing nest into the beehive, the words of Saint Basil the Great flashed through my mind, who urged his disciples to become like honeybees collecting the nectar from wherever they could find it. What a fitting metaphor, I mused, to end our pilgrimage to the *Agion Oros*, the Mountain of Silence.

Notes

1. PROLEGOMENA

1. Kyriacos C. Markides, *The Magus of Strovolos: The Extraordinary World of a Spiritual Healer* (New York: Penguin Arkana, 1985); *Homage to the Sun: The Wisdom of the Magus of Strovolos* (New York: Penguin Arkana, 1987); *Fire in the Heart: Healers, Sages, and Mystics* (New York: Penguin Arkana, 1991).
2. Michael Harner, *The Way of the Shaman* (New York: Bantam, 1982).
3. Robert W. Funk, *Honest to Jesus* (San Francisco: HarperSanFrancisco, 1996), p. 305.
4. Robin Amis, *A Different Christianity: Early Christian Esotericism and Modern Thought* (Albany: State University of New York Press, 1995).
5. Kyriacos C. Markides, *Riding with the Lion. In Search of Mystical Christianity* (New York: Penguin Arkana, 1996).
6. Ken Wilber, *Eye to Eye: The Quest for the New Paradigm* (Garden City, NY: Anchor, 1983).
7. Robert Thurman, *Inner Revolution: Life, Liberty, and the Pursuit of Real Happiness* (New York: Riverhead Books, 1998).

2. ELDERS AND SAINTS

1. Kyriacos C. Markides, *The Rise and Fall of the Cyprus Republic* (New Haven: Yale University Press, 1977).

2. Thomas Cahill, *How the Irish Saved Civilization: The Untold Story of Ireland's Heroic Role from the Fall of Rome to the Rise of Medieval Europe* (New York: Doubleday, 1995).

3. Dimitri Obolensky, *The Byzantine Commonwealth* (New York: Praeger, 1971).

3. TRANSFORMATIONS

1. See Kallistos Ware, *The Orthodox Way* (London and Oxford: Mowbray, 1979); Archimandrite Sophrony (Sakharov), *The Monk of Mount Athos; Staretz Silouan, 1866–1938* (Crestwood, NY: St. Vladimir's Press, 1975).

2. Archimandrite Sophrony (Sakharov), *We Shall See Him As He Is* (Essex, England: Stavropegic Monastery of St. John the Baptist, 1988).

3. An excellent spiritual text translated into English is *The Ascetical Homilies of Saint Isaac the Syrian*, trans. from the Greek by the monks of the Holy Transfiguration Monastery (Boston, MA: The Holy Transfiguration Monastery Press, 1984).

4. KNOWLEDGE OF GOD

1. Monk Joseph, *Geron Iosef Oh Hesychastes* [*Elder Joseph the Hesychast*] (Daphne, Mount Athos, 1984).

2. Sophrony, *The Monk of Mount Athos*.

3. Nun Gabrielia, *E Asketike tes Agapes: Gerontissa Gabrielia, 1897–1992* [*The Ascetic of Love: Eldress Gabrielia, 1897–1992*] (Athens: Eptalofos Abee, 1997)—published in English as: Nun Gabrilia, *Mother Gavrilia: The Ascetic of Love* (Thessaloniki: Series Talanton, 1999).

5. ILLNESSES OF THE HEART

1. See Archimandrite Sophrony (Sakharov), *On Prayer* (Crestwood, NY: St. Vladimir's Press, 1998).

2. Timothy Ware, *The Orthodox Church* (London: Penguin Books, 1993), p. 305.

3. Quoted in Ibid, p. 306.

4. Viktor Frankl, *Man's Search for Meaning* (New York: Pocket Books, 1985).

6. ICONS AND IDOLS

1. See Henri J. M. Nouwen, *Behold the Beauty of the Lord: Praying with Icons* (Notre Dame, IN: Ave Maria Press, 1987); Richard Temple, *Icons and the Mystical Origins of Christianity* (Rockport, MA: Element, 1992).

2. In the Eastern Orthodox tradition the priest who conducts confession usually sits face to face with the person who comes for help, just like in an encounter of counseling. At the end of the session the priest is empowered by the *Ecclesia* to place his stole over the head of the person and read the *Synchoritike Efche* (Forgiveness Prayer).

7. SIGNS AND WONDERS

1. See Larry Dossey, *Healing Words: The Power of Prayer and the Practice of Medicine* (New York: HarperCollins, 1993).
2. Michael Murphy, *The Future of the Body: Explorations into the Further Evolution of Human Nature* (New York: Jeremy P. Tarcher, 1993), p. 466.
3. Patrick Glynn, *God: The Evidence. The Reconciliation of Faith and Reason in a Post-secular World* (Rocklin, CA: Forum, 1997), p. 123.
4. Elder Paisios, *Epistoles* [*Epistles*] (Thessaloniki: Sourote Monastery Press, 1994); *Me Pono kai Agape yia ton Synchrono Anthropo* [*With Sorrow and Love for the Modern Individual*] (Thessaloniki: Sourote Monastery Press, 1998); *Pneumatike Afypnise* [Spiritual Awakening] (Thessaloniki: Sourote Monastery Press, 1999).
5. Markides, *Riding with the Lion*, p. 301.

8. ANGELS AND DEMONS

1. "Candlesticks Fly, So French Call Exorcist," *New York Times*, October 22, 1998.
2. Sophrony, *The Monk of Mount Athos.*
3. Holy Transfiguration Monastery, *The Ascetical Homilies of Saint Isaac the Syrian.*

9. INVISIBLE INTRUDERS

1. Markides, *Riding with the Lion*, pp. 47–60.
2. Georg Feuerstein, *Lucid Waking: Mindfulness and the Spiritual Potential of Humanity* (Rochester, VT: Inner Traditions International, 1997), p. 84.
3. Nun Gabrielia, *E Asketike tes Agapes.*

10. STRATEGIES

1. Nun Gabrielia, *E Asketike tes Agapes.*
2. I. M. Kontzevitch, *The Acquisition of the Holy Spirit* (Platina, CA: St. Herman of Alaska Brotherhood, 1996).
3. Leo Tolstoy, "The Three Hermits" in Ann Charters, ed., *The Story and Its Writer: An Introduction to Short Fiction* (New York: St. Martin's Press, 1987), pp. 169–73.

11. ESCAPE FROM HELL

1. See Olivier Clement, *La Verite vous rendra libre* (Paris: Editions Jean-Claude Lattes, 1996). Trans in Greek as *E Alethia Eleutherosi Ymas* [*The Truth Shall Set You Free: Conversations with the Ecumenical Patriarch Bartholomew I*] (Athens: Akritas, 1997).
2. Abbot George Burke, *An Eagle's Flight* (Geneva, NV: Saint George Press, 1994), p. 37.
3. *O Megas Synaxaristis tes Orthodoxou Ecclesias.* [*The Greek Synaxaristis of the Orthodox Church*], vol. 5 (Athens: E. M. Langi Publishers, 1989), pp. 255–58 [compiled during the nineteenth century by Saint Nikodemos of Mount Athos. It is used in the Eastern Orthodox Church as a resource for spiritual instruction for novices, monks, and spiritual seekers]. See also Hieromonk Makarios of Simonos Petra, *The*

Synaxarion: The Lives of the Saints of the Orthodox Church, English text trans. from the French by Christopher Hookway (Ormylia, Chalkidike, Greece: Holy Convent of the Annunciation of Our Lady Press, 1999); Archimandrite Cherubim, *Contemporary Ascetics of Mount Athos*, vols. 1 & 2 (Platina, CA: St. Herman of Alaska Brotherhood Press, 1992).

4. Reported by the Associated Press, *Bangor Daily News*, January 19, 1996.
5. Sophrony, *The Monk of Mount Athos*.
6. Panayiotes Christou, *Ellenike Patrologia* [*Greek Patrology*], vol. 4 (Thessaloniki: Kyromanos Publishers, 1989).
7. Ibid., pp. 159–200 [my translation]. For an important discussion of this issue see also Bishop Kallistos Ware, "Dare we hope for the salvation of all? Origen, Gregory of Nyssa, Isaac of Nineveh," *Theology Digest* (winter 1998), pp. 303–17.
8. *Hellenic Chronicle*, August 12, 1993. Quoted in Markides, *Riding with the Lion*, p. 296.

12. PASSION FOR JUSTICE

1. Constantinos Yiannitsiotes, *Konta Sto Geronta Porfyrio* [*Near Elder Porphyrios*] (Athens: The Women's Monastery of the Transfiguration of the Savior Press, 1995).
2. Archimandrite Sophrony (Sakharov), *Askesis kai Theoria* [*Ascetics and Theory*, trans. from Russian] (Essex, England: Stavropegic Monastery of St. John the Baptist Press, 1996), pp. 53–54.
3. Page Smith, *Rediscovering Christianity: A Search for the Roots of Modern Democracy* (New York: St. Martin's Press, 1994).
4. Huston Smith, *The World's Religions* (San Francisco: HarperSanFrancisco, 1991), pp. 166–67.
5. Kallistos Ware, *E Endos Emon Vasilia* [*The Kingdom Within Us*] (Athens: Akritas Press, 1997), p. 133.

13. SPIRITUAL LAWS

1. St. Nikodemos of the Holy Mountain and St. Makarios of Corinth, *The Philokalia* (translated from the Greek and edited by G. E. H. Palmer, Philip Sherrard, Kallistos Ware), vol. 1 (London: Faber and Faber, 1990).
2. Anonymous, *The Way of the Pilgrim and the Pilgrim Continues His Way* (New York: Ballantine Books, 1974); Anonymous, *A Night in the Desert of the Holy Mountain* (Crestwood, NY: St. Vladimir's Press, 1991).
3. The Monks of New Skete, *In the Spirit of Happiness* (New York: Little, Brown and Company, 1999), p. 234.

14. CEASELESS PRAYER

1. Monk Damascene Christensen, *Not of This World: The Life and Teaching of Father Seraphim Rose, Pathfinder to the Heart of Ancient Christianity*. (Forestville, CA: Father Seraphim Rose Foundation, 1993), pp. 894–95.
2. Sophrony, *On Prayer*.
3. Dossey, *Healing Words*.
4. Sophrony, *The Monk of Mount Athos*.

5. Stanislav Grof and Christina Grof (eds.), *Spiritual Emergency: When Personal Transformation Becomes a Crisis* (Los Angeles: Tarcher Putnam, 1989).
6. Abba Dorotheos, *Erga Asketika* [*Ascetical Works*] (Athens: Etimasia Publishers, 1981), pp. 111–31.

15. THE THREEFOLD WAY

1. For a comparative study of the phenomenon of eremitism, see Peter France, *Hermits: The Insights of Solitude* (New York: St. Martin's Press, 1996).
2. Kontzevitch, *The Acquisition of the Holy Spirit.*
3. Dionysios Tatses, *O Asketes Tes Panagoudas* [*The Ascetic of Panagouda*] (Konitsa, Greece: Melissa Press, 1998), pp. 39–41. Reference on the experience of elder Paisios appeared in English in Hieromonk Damascene's *Christ the Eternal Tao* (Platina, CA: Valaam Books, 1999). A similar experience has been reported in the life of nineteenth-century Russian *starets* Saint Seraphim of Sarov. See Timothy Ware, *The Orthodox Church* (New York: Viking Penguin, 1964), pp. 130–32.
4. Holy Monastery of Parakletou, *O Pater Arsenios* [trans. from Russian, *Father Arsenios*] (Oropos, Greece: Holy Monastery of Parakletou Press, 1998), pp. 85–95, published in English as *Father Arseny* (Crestwood, NY: Saint Vladimir's Press, 2000).
5. Demetrios Tsames, *Ayiologia* [*Agiology*, the study of sainthood] (Thessaloniki: Pournara Press, 1985), pp. 105–14.
6. Ibid.
7. John Rossner, *In Search of the Primordial Tradition & the Cosmic Christ* (Saint Paul, MN: Llewellyn Publications, 1989).
8. John S. Spong, *Here I Stand* (San Francisco: HarperSanFrancisco, 1999), p. 441.
9. Norman F. Cantor, *Medieval History*, 2nd ed. (New York: Macmillan, 1969), p. 161; quoted in W. C. Cockerham, *Sociology of Mental Disorder* (Upper Saddle River, NJ: Prentice Hall, 1996), p. 11.
10. Warren Treadgold, *A History of the Byzantine State and Society* (Stanford: Stanford University Press, 1997), p. 849.
11. Vivian Green, *A New History of Christianity* (New York: The Continuum Publishing Co., 1996), p. 67.
12. Max Weber, *The Protestant Ethic and the Spirit of Capitalism* (New York: Scribner, 1958).

16. DOXOLOGY OF PEACE

1. Peter Kivisto, *Key Ideas in Sociology* (Thousand Oaks, CA: Pine Forge Press, 1998), p. 150.
2. Arthur Koestler, *Janus: A Summing Up* (New York: Vintage, 1979).
3. S. H. Gross and O. P. Sherbowitsz, *The Russian Primary Chronicle: Laurentian Text* (Cambridge, MA: The Medieval Academy of America, 1953), p. 111; quoted in Adrian Hastings (ed.), *A World History of Christianity* (Grand Rapids, MI: William B. Eerdmans Publishing Co., 1999).
4. Ware, *The Orthodox Church*, 1964, pp. 82–95.

17. THE MOUNTAIN OF SILENCE

1. See Ware, *The Orthodox Church*, 1964, pp. 70–81.
2. Gregory Palamas, *The Triads* (New York: Paulist Press, 1983); Monk Theoklitos Dionysiades, *O Agios Gregorios O Palamas: O Vios kai E Theologia tou, 1296–1359* [St. Gregory Palamas: His Life and Theology, 1296–1359] (Thessaloniki: Yiannoules-Tsolerides-Dedouses Press, 1984).
3. Abbot Gregory, *O Agios Gregorios O Palamas: Dydaskalos tes Theoseos* [St. Gregory Palamas: Teacher of Theosis] (Mount Athos: Holy Monastery of Gregoriou, 2000), p. 17.
4. Ibid., p. 50.
5. Ken Wilber, *The Marriage of Sense and Soul: Integrating Science and Religion* (New York: Random House, 1998).
6. It is important to note that in spite of the rationalistic orientation which became more dominant in Western Christianity than in the East, the mystical and experiential approach to God was not altogether eradicated in the former. The West has also had its mystic luminaries, from John of the Cross, Hildegard of Bingen, Saint Ignatius Loyola, and Saint Tereza of Avila to contemporaries like the Trappist Thomas Merton and Patre Pio of Italy. However, it seems to me that the tradition of eldership for the systematic transmission of the knowledge of God from one generation to another has survived in a more pronounced and identifiable form in the Eastern part of Christianity, particularly on Mount Athos.
7. Pitirim A. Sorokin, *Social and Cultural Dynamics*, 4 vols. (New York: America Book Co., 1937–41). See also Wilber, *The Marriage of Sense and Soul*; and Richard Tarnas, *The Passion of the Western Mind: Understanding the Ideas that Have Shaped Our World View* (New York: Harmony Books, 1991).
8. Markides, *Riding with the Lion*, pp. 214–332.
9. John Julius Norwich, *A Short History of Byzantium* (New York: Alfred A. Knopf, 1997), p. 239.
10. Ibid., p. 306.
11. Sir Steven Runciman, *The Fall of Constantinople, 1453* (Cambridge: Cambridge University Press, 1965).
12. Edward Gibbon, 1737–94, *The Decline and Fall of the Roman Empire* (London: Penguin Books, 1985).
13. Cantor, *Medieval History*, p. 274.

gLossaRy

AGIASMOS   Ritual of sanctification through the use of holy water.

AGRYPNIA   All-night prayer vigil.

AMARTIA   The state of being cut off from God commonly known as sin. Alienation from God.

ANADOCHÉ   Taking up the spiritual burden of the other. Advanced spiritual elders can take upon themselves a portion of the burdens of their disciples and suffer in their place. The law of *anadoché* can also work in the opposite direction, taking upon oneself the burden of the other in an unconscious way by acting negatively towards the other.

APATHIA   Liberation from destructive passions. When people have emptied themselves of earthly desires.

ARCHONDARIKI   Refectory. The guest room where pilgrims at the monastery are treated to refreshments.

ASKESIS   Method of spiritual exercise such as fasting, ceaseless prayer, all-night vigils, confession, communion, the study of sacred texts and the life and teachings of saints. Life's trials and temptations are considered ongoing forms of *askesis*.

CATHARSIS   Purification of the heart and mind from egotistical passions and addictions. The first stage in the development of the soul towards God.

CENOBITIC   Communal form of monasticism.

CHARISMA   Divine gift. A charismatic is someone considered to be endowed with gifts of the spirit such as prophecy, healing, clairvoyance, and other psychic abilities. Such gifts are natural to the self and emerge when the self is cleansed of egotistical passions.

DIAKONIA   Assignment in the monastery for a particular task. It also means providentially assigned life's task.

ECCLESIA   The sum total of the practices, methods, sacred texts, and testimony of saints and their teachings on how to know God. It includes the organizational structure of the Church. The *Ecclesia* is seen as a spiritual hospital for the cure of the maladies of the heart that obstruct our vision of God.

EFCHE   The Jesus Prayer, "Lord Jesus Christ, Son of God, have mercy on me."

ELDER OR ELDRESS   Spiritual guide.

ELEIMON   Characteristic of God as charitable, compassionate, and nonjudgmental.

EROS MANIAKOS   A term used by Saint Maximos the Confessor expressing the "maniacal eros" of the lover of God. State of ecstatic love of God.

FOTISIS   The enlightenment of the soul. The gift of the Holy Spirit after the soul has undergone its purification. The soul becomes endowed with Divine charisma. See *charisma.*

GERONTIKON   Compilation of biographical short stories about the lives of holy elders.

GNOSIS THEOU   Knowledge of God.

HESYCHASM   Quietude. The silent and ceaseless form of prayer meditation and the hallmark of Athonite spirituality.

HESYCHAST   Practitioner of quietude.

HIEROMONK   A monk who is ordained as a priest. A hieromonk can perform the sacraments such as confession and communion.

ICONOSTASI   The icon screen separating the sanctuary from the rest of the church.

KOMBOSCHINI   Prayer robe usually made of wool in the form of knots used during the recital of the Jesus Prayer. See *Efche.*

LOGISMOS (LOGISMOI)   Thought form(s). Negative *logismoi* obstruct our vision of God. *Catharsis* involves cleansing our hearts and minds of such *logismoi.*

METANOIA   The fundamental transformation of one's mind and heart in the form of deep repentance. The beginning of the process, and a necessary stage, for the soul's reunification with God.

MNEME THANATOU   Remembrance of Death.

NOUS   The heart and mind of a human being. The center and totality of the mental and psychic powers of the individual.

PANAGIA   The Most Holy One (Mother of God). The name of the monastery under study.

PANTOKRATOR   Christ as the Ruler of the Universe.

PARAKLESIS   Prayer invocation to the Holy Virgin or Christ for healing. A set of prayers for such purposes.

PEIRASMOS   Temptation. The Greek word *peirasmos* is broader in scope than the English *temptation*. In Greek it also means trial or test. It could be a trial or test sent to us by God in order to help us progress on our spiritual path. It may also be a suggestion from the devil.

PLANI   Deception, delusion. Error in perception and cognition of spiritual matters. The product of human imperfection.

PNEUMATIKOS   Spiritual guide, confessor.

PROTOS   First. A one-year rotating administrative post managing the domestic affairs of the Holy Mountain.

SKETE   A hermitage attached to a monastery for more intense spiritual work. In a *skete* may live a single hermit or a few monks with their spiritual elder.

STARETS   Russian word meaning "elder." See *Elder*.

THEODOKOS   Mother of God. One of the names of the *Panagia*, the Most Holy One.

THEORIA   The vision of God in a state of ecstasy after the purification of the heart from egotism.

THEOSIS   Union with God. The final destination and ultimate home of the human soul.

THREEFOLD WAY   The stages that a soul must go through in order to reach God. See *Catharsis, Fotisis, Theosis*.

TROPARION   Hymn.

UNCREATED LIGHT   God's divine light. Mystical illumination.

BIBLIOGRAPHY

Amis, Robin. 1995. *A Different Christianity: Early Christian Esotericism and Modern Thought*. Albany: State University of New York Press.

Anonymous. 1974. *The Way of the Pilgrim and the Pilgrim Continues His Way*. New York: Ballantine Books.

Anonymous. 1991. *A Night in the Desert of the Holy Mountain*. Crestwood, NY: St. Vladimir's Press.

Bangor Daily News. Associated Press. January 19, 1996.

Burke, Abbot George. 1994. *An Eagle's Flight*. Geneva, NV: Saint George Press.

Cahill, Thomas. 1995. *How the Irish Saved Civilization: The Untold Story of Ireland's Heroic Role from the Fall of Rome to the Rise of Medieval Europe*. New York: Doubleday.

Cantor, Norman F. 1963. *Medieval History: The Life and Death of a Civilization*. New York: The Macmillan Company.

————1969. *Medieval History*. 2nd ed. New York: Macmillan.

Cherubim, Archimandrite. 1992. *Contemporary Ascetics of Mount Athos*. Vol. 1 & 2. Platina, CA: St. Herman of Alaska Brotherhood Press.

Christensen, Monk Damascene. 1993. *Not of This World: The Life and Teaching of Father Seraphim Rose, Pathfinder to the Heart of Ancient Christianity*. Forestville, CA: Father Seraphim Rose Foundation.

Christou, Panayiotes. 1989. *Ellenike Patrologia* [*Greek Patrology*]. Vol. 4. Thessaloniki: Kyromanos Publishers.

Clement, Olivier. 1996. *La Verite vous rendra libre*. Paris: Editions Jean-Claude Lattes.

Trans. in Greek as *E Alethia Eleutherosi Ymas* [*The Truth Shall Set You Free: Conversations with the Ecumenical Patriarch Bartholomew I*]. 1997. Athens: Akritas.

Cockerham, W. C. 1996. *Sociology of Mental Disorder*. Upper Saddle River, NJ: Prentice Hall.

Damascene, Hieromonk. 1999. *Christ the Eternal Tao*. Platina, CA: Valaam Books.

Dionysiades, Theoklitos Monk. 1984. *O Agios Gregorios O Palamas: O Vios kai E Theologia tou, 1296–1359* [*St. Gregory Palamas: His Life and Theology, 1296–1359*]. Thessaloniki: Yiannoules-Tsolerides-Dedouses Press, 1984.

Dorotheos, Abba. 1981. *Erga Asketika* [*Ascetical Works*]. Athens: Etimasia Publishers.

Dossey, Larry. 1993. *Healing Words: The Power of Prayer and the Practice of Medicine*. New York: HarperCollins.

Father Arseny. 2000. Crestwood, NY: St. Vladimir's Press.

Feuerstein, Georg. 1997. *Lucid Waking. Mindfulness and the Spiritual Potential of Humanity*. Rochester, VT: Inner Traditions International.

France, Peter. 1996. *Hermits: The Insights of Solitude*. New York: St. Martin's Press.

Frankl, Viktor. 1985. *Man's Search for Meaning*. New York: Pocket Books.

Funk, Robert W. 1996. *Honest to Jesus*. San Francisco: HarperSanFrancisco.

Gabrielia, Nun. 1997. *E. Asketike tes Agapes: Gerontissa Gabrielia, 1897–1992* [*The Ascetics of Love: Eldress Gabrielia, 1897–1992*]. Athens: Eptalofos Abee.

Gabrilia, Nun. 1999. *Mother Gabrilia: The Ascetic of Love*. Thessaloniki: Series Talanton.

Gibbon, Edward. 1737–94. 1985. *The Decline and Fall of the Roman Empire*. London: Penguin Books.

Glynn, Patrick. 1997. *God: The Evidence. The Reconciliation of Faith and Reason in a Postsecular World*. Rocklin, CA: Forum.

Green, Vivian. 1996. *A New History of Christianity*. New York: The Continuum Publishing Company.

Gregory, Abbot. 2000. *O Agios Gregorios O Palamas: Dydaskalos tes Theoseos* [*Saint Gregory Palamas. Teacher of Theosis*]. Mount Athos: Holy Monastery of Gregoriou

Grof, Stanislav, and Christina Grof (eds.). 1989. *Spiritual Emergency: When Personal Transformation Becomes a Crisis*. Los Angeles: Tarcher Putnam.

Gross, S. H., and O. P Sherbowitsz. 1953. *The Russian Primary Chronicle: Laurentian Text*. Cambridge, MA: The Medieval Academy of America.

Harner, Michael. 1982. *The Way of the Shaman*. New York: Bantam.

Hastings, Adrian (ed). 1999. *A World History of Christianity*. Grand Rapids, MI: William B. Eerdmans Publishing Company.

Hellenic Chronicle, The. August 12, 1993.

Holy Transfiguration Monastery. 1984 *The Ascetical Homilies of Saint Isaac the Syrian*. Trans. from the Greek by the monks of the Holy Transfiguration Monastery. Boston, MA: The Holy Transfiguration Monastery Press.

Joseph, Monk. 1984. *Geron Iosef Oh Hesychastes* [*Elder Joseph the Hesychast*]. Daphne, Mount Athos.

Kivisto, Peter. 1998. *Key Ideas in Sociology*. Thousand Oaks, CA: Pine Forge Press.

Koestler, Arthur. 1979. *Janus: A Summing Up*. New York: Vintage.

Kontzevitch, I. M. 1996. *The Acquisition of the Holy Spirit*. Platina, CA: St. Herman of Alaska Brotherhood.

Makarios, Hieromonk of Simonos Petra. 1999. *The Synaxarion: The Lives of the Saints of the Orthodox Church*. English text trans. from the French by Christopher Hookway. Ormylia, Greece: Holy Convent of the Annunciation of Our Lady Press.

BIBLIOGRAPHY 255

Markides, Kyriacos C. 1977. *The Rise and Fall of the Cyprus Republic*. New Haven: Yale University Press.
———. 1985. *The Magus of Strovolos: The Extraordinary World of a Spiritual Healer*. New York: Penguin Arkana.
———1987. *Homage to the Sun: The Wisdom of the Magus of Strovolos*. New York: Penguin Arkana.
———. 1991. *Fire in the Heart: Healers, Sages, and Mystics*. New York: Penguin Arkana.
———. 1996. *Riding with the Lion: In Search of Mystical Christianity*. New York: Penguin Arkana, 1996.
Murphy, Michael. 1993. *The Future of the Body: Explorations into the Further Evolution of Human Nature*. New York: Jeremy P. Tarcher.
New Skete, The Monks of. 1999. *In the Spirit of Happiness*. New York: Little, Brown and Company, 1999.
New York Times. October 22, 1998. "Candlesticks Fly, So French Call Exorcist."
Norwich, John Julius. 1997. *A Short History of Byzantium*. New York: Alfred A. Knopf.
Nouwen, Henri J. M. 1987. *Behold the Beauty of the Lord: Praying with Icons*. Notre Dame, IN: Ave Maria Press.
O Megas Synaxaristis tes Orthodoxou Ecclesias. 1989 [*The Great Synaxaristis of the Orthodox Church*]. Vol. 5. Athens: E. M. Langi Publishers [compiled during the nineteenth century by Saint Nikodemos of Mount Athos].
Obolensky, Dimitri. 1971. *The Byzantine Commonwealth*. New York: Praeger.
Paisios, Elder. 1994. *Epistoles* [*Epistles*]. Thessaloniki: Sourote Monastery Press.
———. 1998. *Me Pono kai Agape yia ton Synchrono Anthropo* [*With Sorrow and Love for the Modern Individual*]. Thessaloniki: Sourote Monastery Press.
———. 1999. *Pneumatike Afypnise* [*Spiritual Awakening*]. Thessaloniki. Sourote Monastery Press.
Palamas, Gregory. 1983. *The Triads*. New York: Paulist Press.
Parakletou, Holy Monastery of. 1998. *O Pater Arsenios* [trans. from Russian, *Father Arsenios*]. Oropos, Greece: Holy Monastery of Parakletou Press.
Rossner, John. 1989. *In Search of the Primordial Tradition & The Cosmic Christ*. St. Paul, MN: Llewellyn Publications.
Runciman, Sir Steven. 1965. *The Fall of Constantinople, 1453*. Cambridge: Cambridge University Press.
Smith, Huston. 1991. *The World's Religions*. San Francisco: HarperSanFrancisco.
Smith, Page. 1994. *Rediscovering Christianity: A Search for the Roots of Modern Democracy*. New York: St. Martin's Press.
Sophrony (Sakharov), Archimandrite. 1975. *The Monk of Mount Athos: Staretz Silouan: 1866–1938*. Crestwood, NY: St. Vladimir's Press.
———. 1988. *We Shall See Him As He Is*. Essex, England: Stavropegic Monastery of St. John the Baptist.
———. 1998. *On Prayer*. Crestwood, NY: St. Vladimir's Press.
———. 1996. *Askesis kai Theoria* [*Ascetics and Theory*. Trans. from Russian]. Essex, England: Stavropegic Monastery of St. John the Baptist Press.
Sorokin, Pitirim A. 1937–41. *Social and Cultural Dynamics*. 4 vols. New York: America Book Company.
Spong, John S. 1999. *Here I Stand*. San Francisco: HarperSanFrancisco.
St. Nikodimos of the Holy Mountain and St. Makarios of Corinth. 1990. *The Philokalia*. Translated from the Greek and edited by G. E. H. Palmer, Philip Sherrard, Kallistos Ware. Vol. 1. London: Faber and Faber.

Tarnas, Richard. 1991. *The Passion of the Western Mind: Understanding the Ideas that Have Shaped Our World View.* New York: Harmony Books.

Tatses, Dionysios. 1998. *O Asketes Tes Panagoudas [The Ascetic of Panagouda]* Konitsa, Greece: Melissa Press.

Temple, Richard. 1992. *Icons and the Mystical Origins of Christianity.* Rockport, MA: Element.

Thurman, Robert. 1998. *Inner Revolution: Life, Liberty, and the Pursuit of Real Happiness.* New York: Riverhead Books.

Tolstoy, Leo. 1987. "The Three Hermits." In Ann Charters, ed. *The Story and Its Writer: An Introduction to Short Fiction.* New York: St. Martin's Press.

Treadgold, Warren. 1997. *A History of the Byzantine State and Society.* Stanford: Stanford University Press.

Tsames, Demetrios. 1985. *Ayiologia [Agiology,* the study of sainthood]. Thessaloniki: Pournara Press.

Ware, Kallistos. 1979. *The Orthodox Way.* London and Oxford: Mowbray.

———. 1997. *E Endos Emon Vasilia [The Kingdom Within Us].* Athens: Akritas Press.

———. 1998. "Dare we hope for the salvation of all? Origen, Gregory of Nyssa, Isaac of Nineveh." *Theology Digest* (Winter): 303–17.

Ware, Timothy. 1993. *The Orthodox Church.* New York: Penguin.

———. 1964. *The Orthodox Church.* New York: Penguin.

Weber, Max. 1958. *The Protestant Ethic and the Spirit of Capitalism.* New York: Scribner.

Wilber, Ken. 1983. *Eye to Eye: The Quest for the New Paradigm.* Garden City, NY: Anchor.

———. 1998. *The Marriage of Sense and Soul: Integrating Science and Religion.* New York: Random House.

Yiannitsiotes, Constantinos. 1995. *Konta Sto Geronta Porfyrio [Near Elder Porphyrios].* Athens: The Women's Monastery of the Transfiguration of the Savior Press.

ALSO BY KYRIACOS MARKIDES

AVAILABLE MARCH 2012

THE INNER RIVER

$15.00 PAPER (CANADA: $17.00)

ISBN: 978-0-307-88587-6

In *Inner River*, Eastern Orthodox mysticism once again meets Western Christianity as Kyriacos Markides — scholar, researcher, author, and pilgrim — takes readers on a thrilling quest into the heart of Christian spirituality and mankind's desire for a transcendent experience of God.

A mind-expanding, soul-deepening journey, *Inner River* bridges ancient spiritual practices and modern sensibilities of the soul, posing questions about life, death, and consciousness beyond the grave, and chronicles the struggles of walking a spiritual path in the world of the material.